KATE CHASE
FOR
THE DEFENSE

KATE CHASE
FOR
THE DEFENSE

Alice Hunt Sokoloff

ILLUSTRATED WITH PHOTOGRAPHS

DODD, MEAD & COMPANY

NEW YORK

ISBN 0-396-06330-6
Library of Congress Catalog Card Number: 71-147134

Printed in the United States of America
by The Cornwall Press, Inc., Cornwall, N. Y.

ACKNOWLEDGMENTS

I should like to extend grateful acknowledgment to the many who have aided in the preparation of this book and for the patience and courtesy accorded all my requests for information and material. Special thanks go to Mrs. Christine D. Hathaway, Special Collections Librarian, and Mrs. Mary Russo at Brown University Library, Mr. John McDonough, Manuscript Historian, Library of Congress, and Mr. John D. Kilbourne, Curator of The Historical Society of Pennsylvania.

Valuable information and assistance have also been given by the Rhode Island Historical Society, the Cincinnati Historical Society, the Columbus Public Library, the Ohio Historical Society, the Washington, D.C., Public Library, the Utica Public Library, the New York Public Library, the New York Historical Society, the Media-Upper Providence (Pa.) Public Library, the University of Michigan Library, the Rhode Island University Library, the Mercantile Library in New York City, the Providence Journal, and the library staff at Florida Southern College.

I am most grateful too for background and suggestions from Donald Barr Chidsey, biographer of Senator Conkling, Bill Arter of Columbus, Ohio, Winifred J. W. Kissouth, and Hazelruth Cavnor of Narragansett, Rhode Island.

FOREWORD

Previous biographies of Kate Chase have been invaluable sources of material for this book, notably those of Thomas Graham Belden and Marva Robins Belden, Ishbel Ross, and Mary Merwin Phelps.

Since these books were written, however, a wealth of new material consisting of diaries, letter books and many letters written both by and to Kate Chase, has become available at the Special Collections, Brown University Library.

This hitherto untapped material suggests that the image of Kate Chase as presented by previous biographers should be considerably altered if not changed altogether. To this day Kate Chase remains a much maligned woman, for although all have admitted to her brilliance and beauty, her character was said to be flawed by ruthless ambition and pride. The picture of Kate Chase that has come down to us is that of a cold and imperious woman whose burning desire to make her father President led her to sacrifice everything, including love, on the altar of her vaulting ambition. The purpose of this book is to bring the real Kate Chase finally to light—a warm, passionate woman whose tragedy was not ambition, but love.

ILLUSTRATIONS

Following page 128

INTRODUCTION

The driveway was thickly overgrown with grass and on either side in the scraggy fields was a confusion of briars, trees with broken and drooping branches, vine-covered, tumbled-down fences. Scarcely visible through the brush was an old brick house on the hilltop overlooking the land and in the distance the great shining dome of the Capitol and the Potomac River beyond. On the broad front porch the impression of poverty and neglect increased. The woodwork around the windows was rotting, and spiders had spun their webs across the panes. Silk curtains inside were faded and torn, and dust lay thick everywhere. An old collie thumped his tail lazily on the splintered boards, while a small terrier yapped shrilly.

The wide entrance hall was vacant, with only a few faded photographs in cheap frames on the walls. On the right the large library, surrounded on three sides with bookshelves, was nearly empty. A few shabby chairs and a table by the window were the only furnishings.

In the spacious dining room a large mirror, the gilt of its handsome frame dull with age, reflected only desolation and decay—tattered curtains, a dingy chandelier, and seedy remnants of furniture. Once it had held images of greatness: smiling James Garfield; the flaming hair and beard of Senator Conkling; wreathing smoke from the cigar of General Grant; the grim face of Andrew Johnson; the bright eyes of financier Jay Cooke; autocratic Senator

Sumner; and always the slim, graceful form of a woman whose imperious pose of head bespoke the universal admiration accorded her.

Like its mistress, Edgewood had seen great days, but time had treated both shabbily and there were only memories of grandeur and power now. The woman who through her beauty and brilliance had wielded a power and influence in Washington as no other had before was alone and forgotten, and the chill air of solitude was peopled only by dim ghosts of the past.

She lay upstairs, broken finally by poverty, hard work and grief, her once quick, slim body bloated by illness. The luminous, dark-fringed eyes that had charmed statesmen and soldiers and diplomats were red-rimmed and heavy with fatigue, and the glorious, burnished hair, gray and lifeless.

She sent for the doctor only ten days before the end. Her daughters came to be with her at the last and to look out for little Kitty, her gentle child whose mind had remained locked in some faraway mist. Simple people from the neighborhood were the only ones besides her children who came to her funeral, people who had responded to her need and had left little gifts of food from time to time, or coal in the winter. Pallbearers were former Negro servants. The little cortege moved slowly down the hot dusty drive to nearby Glenwood cemetery, where she would rest until the special railroad car ordered by President McKinley would carry her back to Cincinnati where she had been born. There she would be buried near the mother she had known for only a few brief years and the distinguished father whom she had adored.

Her daughters packed up the few belongings. New homes several miles away were found for the dogs. Edgewood was bleak and empty, a silent witness to the hurtling pendulum that had led from triumph to neglect, from wealth to penury, from enchantment to tragedy.

July 31, 1899—Kate Chase was dead. For a few days her career was recalled and her name was once again featured in the press. "The most brilliant woman of her day. None outshone her," wrote the *Washington Star*. *The New York Times* recalled that "the homage of the most eminent men in the country was hers." The

Providence Journal noted that in many respects she was "one of the most remarkable women ever known to Washington Society." The publisher of the *New York Tribune* had known her well and observed nostalgically: "No name could possibly be spoken in this city among the older residents that would evoke the reminiscences always started by the mention of Kate Chase. No woman so young ever held here the prominent and controlling position as leader that came to her as mistress of her father's household, nor has the most critical observer failed in according to her an exceptional personal brilliance . . . When thus brought so prominently before the world Miss Chase was only sixteen years of age, and but a few years older when her father, taking the Treasury portfolio under President Lincoln, again needed her help as mistress of his Washington home . . . Miss Chase held a court of her own and her reputation spread far and wide as the most brilliant woman of her day. The popular verdict declared her to be at the same time one of the most beautiful."

The *Cincinnati Enquirer* from the city of her birth declared that: "No Queen has ever reigned under the Stars and Stripes, but this remarkable woman came closer to being Queen than any American woman has."

Many men had tried to capture her elusive fascination. "Her figure is extremely graceful and elegant," a correspondent for the *Boston Herald* had once described. "Her face is a study, an enchanting and dangerous study to most men, who are pretty certain to fall in love with it. It has been compared with that of the famous portrait of Mona Lisa . . . [and] has something of the strangeness which has been said to belong invariably to beauty of the highest order."

A few papers referred to the decline in her fortunes: "All that she sought, all that she accepted, all that she gained became ashes on her lips, and the proud woman was thrust down from the pinnacle on which she stood to endure not only the pangs of poverty and neglect but of calumny while she lived," commented the *Philadelphia Times.* The *Providence Telegram* suggested a "pause in pity for the troubles that came early and late and no doubt hastened her exit from this world in which she was once so conspicuous, high-spirited, brilliant, wealthy and happy."

The light shone only briefly on Kate Chase again after her death, and then hurried on to other events and people. A new century was about to begin. Kate Chase's day was long since done.

CHAPTER

~~~ I ~~~

RARELY HAVE the lives of father and daughter been so closely bound together as those of Kate Chase and her father. Each played a major role in the life of the other.

Salmon Portland Chase detested what he sometimes called his "fishy" name. Indeed, when he was a young man he toyed with the idea of changing it. Spencer De Cheyce, or Spencer Payne Cheyce were alternatives that he considered, names that would "disconnect us from the world a little more than we are." [1] We may smile at the pretentious fancy but we can be sure that he did not, even in later years, for Salmon P. Chase took everything seriously, himself most of all.

"More than anyone else he looked the great man," Carl Schurz described him glowingly. "Tall, broad-shouldered, and proudly erect, his features strong and regular and his forehead broad, high and clear, he was a picture of intelligence, strength, courage and dignity. He looked as you would wish a statesman to look." [2] Chase's public image was that of a cold and haughty man and he was dignified to the point of being statuesque. And yet, in that early inclination to those high-flown changes of name we see not only his worldly tendencies but foolish and romantic ones. Beyond his majestic façade, Salmon Chase was a highly complex and contradictory individual. Inordinately ambitious for position and power, he was often almost incredibly naive. He craved political and social influence at the same time that he toted and quoted his Bible, continuously reminding himself of the ephemeral values of this life. He was a righteous man who came dangerously close a few times to the precept that the end, his end, justifies the means.

In his early twenties Salmon Chase made the following resolution: "I will try to excel in all things, yet if I am excelled without fault of mine, I will not be mortified. I will not withhold from any one the praise which I think is his due, nor will I allow myself to envy another's praise, or to feel jealousy when I hear him praised. May God help me to keep it!" [3] Salmon Chase needed all the help he could get. His political goal was the highest—the Presidency. Nothing less would satisfy him. Nothing less did satisfy him.

He came from strong New England stock, the seventh of ten surviving children born to Ithamar and Jeanette Chase. Lawyers, physicians, senators, clergymen were numbered in his family. In later years Chase wrote pridefully of the yellow house in Cornish, New Hampshire, where he was born, January 13, 1808: "The yellow house was more famous than the White House for brains. Indeed, the neighboring folk used to say that in that yellow house more brains were born than in any other house in New England." [4] His father, Ithamar, however, was a farmer and had only the common school education that was given to farmers' boys at that time. Moving to Keene, New Hampshire, he became for a while a tavern-keeper and it was there that the boy Salmon encountered his first shocking experience with drunkeness that may have influenced him in his lifelong hatred of intemperance. One cold autumn morning he came upon the body of a man lying face down in the shallow water of a roadside ditch. Many years later he recalled that no "sermon could rival in eloquence that awful spectacle of the dead drunkard—helplessly perishing where the slightest remnant of sense or strength would have sufficed to save!" [5]

Ithamar later became Justice of the Peace and his son recalled wistfully that he had been "much talked of for Governor," [6] although he was never a candidate. Ithamar's sudden death when Salmon was only nine years of age left his family in straightened financial circumstances. He had never been a good businessman and his affairs had fallen into considerable disorder before he died. When Uncle Philander Chase, Bishop of Ohio, offered to take charge of his nephew's education, the proposal was accepted with alacrity.

Twelve-year-old Salmon "tried to find out where I was going and got some queer information." [7] He knew only vaguely about "The Ohio," as it was then called, and the trip by stage, boat, and horseback was a great adventure for the boy, a last fling of freedom before entering under the stern discipline of his domineering uncle at Worthington, Ohio.

Philander Chase aroused ambivalent feelings in his young nephew. "Usually exceedingly kind and a delightful companion to young and old, he was often very harsh and severe, not because he liked to be, but because he was determined to have everything just as he thought it ought to be." [8] From the relatively casual religious atmosphere of his home, Salmon Chase moved into the strait-laced rigidity of his pious bishop uncle, who saw life as a trial between good and evil, all for the betterment of man's soul. There were many similarities between Philander and Salmon Chase. They were perhaps too much alike to get along well. "My memories of Worthington," Chase wrote in later years, "are not pleasant. . . . I used to count the days and wish I could get home." [9]

School took up only part of the day. The rest was spent doing farm chores. On one occasion having been ordered to kill and dress a pig, young Salmon ran into difficulties in trying to remove the bristles. As failure in a given task was something Uncle Philander did not accept, "I bethought me of my cousin's razors . . . No sooner imagined than done. I got the razors and shaved the pig from toe to snout," [10] Chase recalled. The boy did not always escape punishment so adroitly and often had to submit to extra tasks with a heart full of rebellion. Finally one day, having been ordered by way of punishment to carry into the house before daybreak a huge pile of wood, he said of his uncle that he was "a darned old tyrant." The story was repeated to the Bishop who promptly put the boy in Coventry; no one was allowed to speak to him nor could he address anyone. Several days passed before Salmon could bring himself to confess that he had been wrong, but finally he gave in. Many years later the memory of his humiliation still rankled and he could write, "Even now I almost wish I had not." [11]

Salmon was nearly fifteen when Bishop Chase was appointed head of Cincinnati College, and the boy moved there too. He may have hoped that life would ease somewhat in the new city, but the authoritarian uncle proved to be as rigid as ever. One can imagine that Salmon was delighted when, after a year in Cincinnati, the Bishop resigned the presidency of the college and the entire family headed east.

The next three years were spent in alternate teaching at local schools and study at Dartmouth, where Chase succeeded in entering into the Junior class, having been able by assiduous study to make up the inadequacies of scholastic background. His mother was sorely put to it to find the means to educate her younger children but she was determined to "try hard," as she wrote Salmon, "that being all that your dear father ever expressed a desire for his children," and she declared that "I would be willing to wash or scour" to accomplish this.[12]

Chase was eighteen when he graduated, Phi Beta Kappa, from Dartmouth. He was tall and gangly, an awkward adolescent, with little of the dignity and presence that marked his mature years. Uncle Philander had hoped to persuade him to enter the Church, but Salmon had great doubts whether he was suited to such a life. He did not really know what he wanted to do. School teaching seemed as good a way as any to earn a living while he tried to decide what profession to pursue. And so, armed with a few letters of introduction and a small sum of money, Salmon Chase, "with a mother's blessing, and a sad yet hopeful heart, left home for the world." [13]

Things did not go easily at first. Heading south, Chase stopped at Philadelphia, Swedesboro, Baltimore, Frederick City, all to no avail. His hope was to open his own school, but none of these cities had need of his services. So the young man continued on to Washington. There he advertised for students for his projected school, but after weeks of anxiety, only a single pupil had appeared. Money was running low, was almost all gone, in fact. What to do?

Salmon bethought himself of his Uncle Dudley, United States senator and friend of the administration. Certainly the good uncle could procure a place as government clerk for his nephew. The young man called upon his uncle, explained his predicament and the project of a clerkship. "Salmon," Uncle Dudley told him, "I once obtained an office for a nephew of mine, and he was ruined by it. I then determined never to ask one for another. I will give you fifty cents to buy a spade with, but I will not help to get you a clerkship." [14]

Fortunately fate, in the form of Mr. Plumley, intervened. This lucky gentleman had not only one but two schools and he engaged Chase to take over one of them. Through this appointment the young graduate was provided not only with a livelihood, but an introduction into the social and political life of Washington, for the school was a fashionable one attended by sons of such important men as Attorney General Wirt, Henry Clay, General Bernard, and others. Chase was to remain in charge of this school for nearly three years.

During his first months in Washington he was shy and diffident, too proud to ask for recognition and, by his own admittance, "too much inclined to spend what little time I could command in the society of one or another small circle of young lady friends." [15]

These small circles turned the young schoolmaster's head and sometimes his heart as well. He was especially drawn to the family of William Wirt, the Attorney General, whose bevy of beautiful daughters completely charmed him. This was one of the happiest and most carefree periods of his life.

Under the influence, or the example, of William Wirt he at last decided on a career. He would become a lawyer. Chase later admitted that at that time he read his law books "superficially" more with the object to read a certain number of them than to acquire legal knowledge.[16] He was not quite twenty-two when he was admitted to the bar. "I have a profession," he wrote grandly. "Let me not dishonor it." [17]

The busy Washington years had come to an end, and Chase turned his mind toward his future with a good deal of the grim earnestness which was so much a part of his character. "How pre-

cious a treasure is time, and how have I lavishly squandered it!"
he had lamented on his twenty-first birthday.

It was a solemn and purposeful young man who set out in 1830,
at the age of twenty-two, to carve a career for himself. He chose
Cincinnati, a city of homes, factories, churches, river docks, vigorous energy, and growth. Here Salmon Chase felt he had more opportunity to make his mark than in the older cities of the eastern
seaboard.

He threw himself with a will into establishing his reputation
and position in Cincinnati both socially and in his profession. But
it was not easy. His first month in practice he earned fifteen dollars
which he thought "perhaps shall be paid." [18] But time and perseverance eventually brought him more clients and he began to make
a name for himself. He wrote articles, gave lectures, edited a book
on Ohio statutes, helped found a lyceum, and argued cases in court
whenever he could.

Various members of his family followed him to Cincinnati: his
married sister, Abigail Chase Colby, with her husband and children, the youngest of whom was to prove a sore trial to Chase; his
two unmarried sisters, Helen and Alice, whom he had to assist
financially, and eventually a nephew and two nieces whose education he supervised. In spite of all his activities and responsibilities,
however, and his stern attitude toward frivolity, he still found time
for a good many social pleasures. He was especially happy to be
received by the first families of Cincinnati, for social prominence
was always to impress him in spite of his endless preachings against
the vanities of life. He flirted with a good many young ladies but
not for four years after his arrival in Cincinnati was he ready to
contemplate marriage.

His choice fell on Catherine Jane Garniss. She had been born in
New York, had traveled widely, and was considered to be one of
the most beautiful and brilliant women of the West. Chase was
not impressed with her at first meeting, but her spell grew on him
and he fell deeply in love with her. She must have loved him too,
for she accepted his proposal of marriage in spite of initial hesitation. "He is so uncouth, and has such an unmanageable mouth!"

she is quoted as saying to a friend. "Wait until I polish him up a little—then I'll bring him to you and show him off!" [19]

At the time of his marriage to Catherine Garniss in 1834, Salmon Chase had obviously still not gained the imposing presence that he was to acquire later. As a speaker he relied more on clarity of argument than oratorical effects. He had an explosive temper which he had managed to bring under reasonable control, although there were still times when he could not restrain himself.

Catherine Garniss's gaiety and wit and affectionate nature did much to leaven the puritanical, strait-laced tendencies of her young husband. She could laugh with him and even tease this strangely humorless man. On New Year's Day she hid his present in his boot and never let on even when he admitted to feeling hurt that there had been presents for everyone but himself. She simply smiled to herself and waited for him to find it when he put on his boots before going out.

Chase was poignantly to recall this and other incidents of his all too brief life with Catherine, for she lived less than two years after their marriage. Her death, in November, 1835, soon after the birth of their daughter, was a blow from which it took him a long time to recover, if indeed, he ever did fully. He had left Catherine to go on a business trip, fully confident that all was well and that she and the new baby were in good health. She died a few days before his return. He blamed the doctors for their treatment of her, which consisted mainly in massive bleeding of the patient.

Chase visited her grave every day and for months his diary was filled with the anguish of his loss. He tormented himself that he had not remained with her and especially he agonized about her salvation. "What grieves me most," he wrote, "is, that I was not, while my dear wife lived, so faithful with her on the subject of religion as I should have been; and I have now no certain assurance that she died in the faith." [20]

After his wife's death, Chase threw himself ever more energetically into his work. For a time he lived with the Garniss family, but later two of his sisters, Helen and Alice, kept house for him and looked after the baby daughter whom he had named after her mother, Catherine Jane. This child was to live only a scant five years, but her name was to be given later to another daughter who would make it famous.

As soon as he was in a position to do so, Chase bought a place in the country on the Lower Road outside Cincinnati, and it was to this Clifton Farm that he brought his second wife, Eliza Ann Smith, four years after the death of Catherine. She was not yet eighteen, a shy modest girl very different from the brilliant Catherine. She was devoted to her small stepdaughter and shared deeply her husband's piety. There was a quiet atmosphere of contentment and harmony, if none of the overwhelming joy of the first marriage. But even that modest happiness was soon shaken by the death, from scarlet fever, of four-year-old Kitty.

Salmon and Eliza Chase grieved over their loss but found sustenance in their faith. "What sorrow, and yet blessed be God! what consolation," Chase was able to exclaim. "My most cherished hope blasted! but she safe forever." [21] They talked often of the child and her extraordinary goodness and religious feeling and they recalled that she had several times been found praying that God would take her to her mother in heaven. She never fretted or cried when anything was denied her, saying always, "Pa knows what is best for his little daughter." [22] Little Kitty had been the most amenable and gentle of children.

Three months after her death another and very different baby girl was born. Salmon Chase took no chances at the arrival of his second child. A doctor, a nurse, his wife's mother, and a friend were called in attendance. He himself took over the matter of prayer for the preservation of mother and child and especially that they both be saved from sin.

Like many a father, his first view of the baby who was to become one of the most noted beauties of her time proved disappointing. "The babe is pronounced pretty," he remarked, but added stubbornly, "I think it quite otherwise." And then he recorded: "Catherine Jane Chase, second daughter of S.P.C. and E.A.C., born August 13, 1840." [23]

One may wonder what the gentle Eliza thought about the name chosen for her baby; another child named for the beloved first wife. It is certain that she did not dispute it. Eliza Ann was far too docile for that and her kind heart was undoubtedly large enough to include Catherine Garniss Chase without any jealousy. Besides, it was very difficult if not impossible not to do as Salmon Chase wanted anymore. Like his Uncle Philander, "he was determined to have everything just as he thought it ought to be."

CHAPTER

✤ II ✤

LIFE WAS carefully ordered in the Chase household. Morning
started bright and early with private devotions, family prayers, and Bible readings; the day was devoted to work; more Bible
reading and family prayers followed in the evening, after which
any spare time was usually spent on improving or uplifting reading. It was a pleasant and productive life from Chase's point of
view. His law practice was expanding and he was becoming more
and more interested and active in politics.

In spite of Chase's growing success, money was in short supply
and the Christmas after Kate's birth, thrifty Eliza made the presents for everyone herself. After prayers, husband and wife attended
church and then went for Christmas dinner to a friend's house. "A
small but not very interesting party," Chase complained. "Might
have made it more interesting and profitable had I taken the
proper course." On their way home the couple stopped at the house
of Eliza's mother to pick up baby Kate, "who has now grown finely
and is very healthy," Chase remarked.[1] From there they went on to
pay a call on the Garniss family. Eliza had caught cold and went
early to bed.

Kate was too young to remember that first Christmas, but the
pall of illness that had descended on Eliza was not to be lifted
again, so that Kate's earliest years would be filled with darkened

rooms, consultations with doctors, vain trips to various health re-
sorts. The pattern was altered only twice.

Shortly before Kate's second birthday another baby arrived,
named this time for her mother. She survived a brief three months.
Exactly twelve months later a third daughter was born to Eliza.
This little girl seemed to be stronger and to do better and Eliza
rejoiced to celebrate the baby's first birthday. Less than two months
later this child too was dead. Eliza needed all her courage and her
faith to accept the loss of her two little girls and to sustain her in
her own vain fight against consumption.

Kate was five years old when her mother died. Her short life had
so far been filled with illness and death. Although Chase did not
go into the same paroxysms of grief over the loss of his second wife
as had affected him after Catherine's death, his mood was grim
and he sought solace in his Bible. It is not surprising that he himself should turn to the Book of Job, but that he should choose it to
read to Kate gives an indication of his views on the psychology of
children. Chase dwelt on the trials of Job with little Kate although
he was not sure that she understood much more than the solemn
rhythm when he read aloud to her. But he prayed with her and
talked to her and listened to her read from the Bible too. He was
determined to teach her to be pious, humble, and disciplined, and
he surely set her the example of angelic little Kitty who, in the
tender image his sorrow had kept alive, had never been naughty or
disobeyed or disputed anything she had been told to do. Kate,
however, was not the paragon her older sister had been. She had
fire and temperament and a temper, too, which she inherited from
her father.

Chase's sisters had once again taken over his household and the
care of little Kate. He was freed of all domestic responsibilities and
he knew that his sisters would carry out his wishes in regard to
Kate's education. His increased activity in politics and the antislavery cause had brought his name to the attention of prominent
abolitionists throughout the country. Salmon P. Chase began to be
known as a man to keep your eye on.

He had defended John Vanzandt, on whom the character of John
Van Trompe in *Uncle Tom's Cabin* was later based, and Chase

himself in the book would be the "Attorney General for Runaway Slaves." The Vanzandt case went all the way to the United States Supreme Court and although the case was lost, it brought Chase into national prominence. In 1845, Chase received a silver pitcher inscribed to him: "A testimonial of Gratitude to Salmon P. Chase from the colored people of Cincinnati, for his Various Public Services in Behalf of the Oppressed . . ." [2] In accepting the gift Chase stated the beliefs from which he was never to waver. "True democracy makes no inquiry about the color of the skin, or the places of nativity, or any other similar circumstances of condition. Wherever it sees a man, it recognizes a being endowed by his Creator with original inalienable rights . . . I regard, therefore, the exclusion of the colored people from the election franchise as incompatible with true democratic principles." [3]

Chase was prominent in the formation of the Liberty party, the purposes of which he outlined in a speech at one of the conventions. "It founds itself upon the great cardinal principle of true Democracy and of true Christianity, the brotherhood of the Human Family. It avows its purpose to wage war against slaveholding as the direst form of oppression, and then against every other species of tyranny and injustice." [4]

With his expanding activities and obligations Chase had little time for his small daughter in the year after her mother's death. He had even less time for her the next year. Thirteen months after he buried Eliza, Salmon Chase brought home a new wife.

Sara Bella Dunlop Ludlow was the granddaughter of one of the founders of Cincinnati. She was a handsome, confident, and intelligent young lady of twenty-six. It helped, too, that she inherited some money, for Chase had again allowed himself to get deeply into debt. Belle Chase, as she was called, was a fitting partner for the rising politician. She could assist her husband in his career as the gentle, pious Eliza could never have done. She was in sympathy with her husband's political ambitions and looked forward to a brilliant future for him.

It was not easy for Kate to see this new wife take over her mother's place. Belle Chase moved with assurance in her new home and filled it with her friends and relatives. Little Kate had been bewildered and saddened by the long train of tragedy that she had witnessed during the first five years of her life. She was even more confused by this high-spirited young woman who took charge of everything and occupied so much of her father's attention. "Funny Kate! She desires love," a friend had written to Kate's mother when the child was three and a half years old.[5] Any child, but especially one of Kate's intense emotional nature, would have needed special assurances of security and love with a mother whose strength was slowly wasting away, who grieved for her two lost babies, and a father preoccupied with his career whose constant exhortations to her were concerned with sin, death and salvation.

The new mother was hardly the person to give Kate the affection she needed. Belle did not have Eliza's gentle patience with the child, and tension soon built up between them. Chase had to intervene: "This evening little Kate disobeyed her stepmother and made untrue representation; admonished her and promised to punish her if I could not otherwise induce her to amend." [6] It is not difficult to imagine how grimly Chase viewed this recalcitrance on the part of his confused little daughter and how sternly he admonished her. Her father, with his Jovian stature and attitudes, was everything to Kate: security, stability, and the font of all wisdom. He spared no effort to impress upon her the duties and obligations she owed him. Kate tried hard to please him but it was not easy to live up to his rigid demands or to the image of the idealized Kitty.

On September 19, 1847, Bella's first child, and Chase's fifth, was born. It was another girl and this infant was to survive. She was named Jeanette Ralston, after Chase's mother, and was known affectionately as Nettie.

As an outstanding leader of the Liberty party, Chase had been active at the various state and national conventions. He also took part in the Free Soil movement and presided at their national convention at Buffalo in 1848. With all his political activity he had so far not held public office, but that was to come now, and in February 1849 he was elected to the United States Senate by a combination of Democrats and Free Soilers. There were those who felt that an unsavory deal had been made in order to insure his election and that he had betrayed his party to further his own ambition. This accusation was to pursue him for years, and even after his death his friends in their eulogies would defend him. Party lines were shifting and party principles changing during that emotional period. Others besides Chase were seeking a platform on which they could not only stand for their antislavery principles but work actively and effectively for them. Chase felt that party interests were subordinate to the main issue. "Convinced now that the question of slavery was the paramount one, and satisfied that the great principle of equal rights was correct, I began to test opinions by this standard." [7] Abiding by his principles, Chase saw nothing wrong in gaining position to fight the battle he felt was vital. What he believed in was important. What he wanted to do and was sure he could do for the cause was what counted.

Entering upon a senatorial term of six years, Chase decided that it was time to alter the family living arrangements. Belle was expecting another baby in July of that year, but he planned that as soon as she was able she would join him in Washington with Nettie and the new baby. Belle's uncle, John McLean, was an associate justice of the Supreme Court. She knew that his family would guide and help her in the new city and she looked forward to the stimulating life at the capital. Her health, however, had been giving increasing cause for concern and after the birth of the new baby, Josephine, she did not regain her strength as rapidly or completely as she had hoped. It was for this reason perhaps, among others, that it was decided that Kate would not move with the rest of the family to Washington but would be sent to boarding school instead.

Kate was nine years old and younger than most of the girls at Miss Haines's fashionable school for young ladies in New York City.[8] The older girls would sometimes be attentive to Kate, who was already showing signs of beauty, but more often than not they undoubtedly found her a nuisance and infinitely preferred talking and giggling among themselves and passing secrets which they did not want the child to hear.

The school regime was inflexible. For Kate, who was used to her father's strict habits, the six o'clock rising bell was not hard to respond to. Prayers and breakfast followed and then a walk for one hour until nine o'clock, when classes began. Lessons continued until two when there was another hour-long walk. These walks were highly decorous, the girls marching two by two in a long file with a teacher bringing up the rear. No skipping or laughing was allowed. From three to four the girls were actually allowed to do as they pleased, within strict limits of decorum, then an hour of study, after which came dinner. From six thirty until nine was study hall, or if they chose, the girls could listen to Miss Haines read aloud. The study hour, according to one student, "was pretty severe, for we could hardly breathe without . . . permission." This young lady also commented: "I never either in Europe or America saw classes so well drilled; but mercy, we have to have our wits about us." [9]

Miss Haines was a tall, impressive figure always dressed in black, holding herself ramrod straight. Although the girls whispered about a rumored tragic romance in her youth and decided that she must have been at one time extremely pretty, even the older girls were awed by her. Kate, being so young, was under Miss Haines's special care. She shared a room with Mlle de Janon, the French teacher; but it was Miss Haines who dispensed justice and with a very firm hand. Chase had explained to her in emphatic detail his ideas for Kate's training and education, most importantly the moral development he expected of her.

It was a difficult winter for Chase. Almost as soon as Belle had arrived in Washington she had been taken gravely ill. Christmas was spent in anxious worry while she received treatment at a health resort near Philadelphia, and for weeks her condition fluctuated alarmingly. When summer came she went to Northampton for more treatment and Kate joined her and the two younger girls there for a short visit. Little Nettie was overjoyed to see her big sister Kate and the baby Josephine seemed to be getting along well, growing stronger and almost able to sit up alone. But by the end of July, Kate, already back with Miss Haines, received the news that the baby had died. Kate felt isolated from her family and wrote asking Belle to tell her about Josephine's death, as she knew nothing except the bare fact. When winter came Belle went to Texas to stay with her brother in the hope that the warm climate might relieve her illness. Belle wrote Kate that she and Nettie think how pleasant it will be "when I am well and you come home from school. Nett gets quite beyond herself when I talk to her of you, and she jumps about, clapping her little hands, saying Oh, Katey, Oh, Katey's coming home!" [10] But Katey did not come home, although Belle and Nettie returned to Clifton Farm. Belle's health continued to deteriorate in spite of everything that was done, and Kate stayed on at school.

Chase was in deep despair. Nevertheless, he flung himself into the battle for the new territories between slave states and free that was rousing passions in the Senate. In contrast to the flaming oratory and drama of some of the titans on the Senate floor—Webster, Calhoun, Clay, Douglas—Salmon Chase was an ineffectual speaker. His speeches were appeals to reason rather than to passion. "Light without heat," one of his colleagues said of him. "Mind without passion." [11]

When Charles Sumner entered the Senate, he and Chase formed an immediate friendship. Both over six feet in height, they were called the two handsomest men in the Senate. They made an effective team and a dangerous one, as Stephen Douglas was to find out when they attacked his Kansas-Nebraska bill. It was a hard-fought battle and although they lost it, they won a mass of ardent followers for their cause. Sumner and Chase had drawn up a manifesto which had been published in three New York newspapers on the day that Douglas was to present his bill for discussion. The violent attack on the document and its authors by the famous Senator from Illinois brought it "prominently before the country," as Chase declared. "It will now reach thousands and tens of thousands who would not read it but for the discussion that has taken place today." [12]

It is doubtful whether Kate knew much if anything about her father's political activities in her early years at boarding school. Miss Haines surely had the girls instructed in "Current Events" and they were sometimes taken to hear important lectures. Both these activities, however, were reserved for the older girls and were not allowed to children of Kate's tender years.

Certainly Chase himself wrote nothing to Kate about politics. His letters to her were concerned with quite other matters. He wrote often affectionately, but always with admonishments for self-improvement. And in nearly every letter he wrote about death. Not surprisingly, he was obsessed with the idea of death as Belle's condition grew ever more hopeless. "What a vale of misery this world is," Chase wrote to Charles Sumner not long before Belle's death in January, 1852. "To me it has been emphatically so. Death has pursued me incessantly ever since I was 25 . . . Sometimes I feel as if I could give up—as if I *must* give up. And then after all I rise and press on." [13] The thrice-widowed man buried three wives and four infant daughters in the space of eighteen years. It is not surprising that his letters to Kate were hardly cheerful ones, but they kept the pall of sorrow with which she had lived from infancy ever over her.

"Remember, my dear child, that the eye of a Holy God is upon you all the time," he wrote her when she was barely eleven years old. ". . . Remember too, that you may die soon, and cannot, in any event, live very many years." [14]

Chase was naturally anxious about Kate's health and he stressed to her that she was not as strong and well as most girls and with her inheritance had to be especially cautious in everything she did. "You must not drink coffee or tea, or allow yourself in anything which will derange your nerves," he told her. "You are naturally delicate, and what would not greatly harm another might be fatal to you." [15]

Most of his admonitions, however, were moral and Chase dwelt constantly on sin and salvation with Kate. "Remember, my darling, that you have a naturally evil heart and that it is through God's grace alone, that you can overcome sinful inclinations." [16] He did not spare the child his own inner conflicts and frankly revealed his own feeling of sin to her. "Sin is very bitter and very hateful. It may seem pleasant, but it will bite like as an adder," he impressed on her. "I who write you—your dear father—am a sinner—Oh, that I might be free from sin. God helping me I mean to strive and pray for deliverance." [17]

Chase obviously had little or no thought as to the effect that such letters might have on a sensitive, lonely child of eleven. To tell her that she had a naturally evil heart; to stress, as he constantly did, that death, her death, lurked right around the corner, was a forbidding dampener to any joy in life. To write with an almost exultant self-accusation of his own sense of sin may have given him relief, but it could not help but inflict a burden on Kate's youthful spirit.

Chase constantly criticized Kate for her lack of freedom of expression. In her letters, he wanted more than "mere dry bones." He told her to "express freely your thoughts in the confidence of a beloved child to a beloved father." [18] By now, however, Kate had little habit of spontaneous expression. She had learned to control her thoughts and feelings. The redoubtable Miss Haines read all her letters before they could be sent and every letter was criticized not only for content but for form, handwriting, spelling, and expression, both by her father and Miss Haines. And still she was expected to "write freely!"

Kate saw very little of her father once she was sent to boarding school. Miss Haines was prepared to keep several of her charges over any of the vacations and Chase availed himself of this service often for Kate. The summer before her twelfth birthday was unusual in that, as Miss Haines did not "make her accustomed arrangements for retaining a number of her pupils with her during this vacation," [19] Chase had to find another solution for Kate's summer. Grandmother Smith had long begged for a visit from Kate and Chase agreed to let her go to Clifton under the care of her aunts. The visit was not an unadulterated success, however, and we find Chase writing to Kate in August: "I am sorry you feel so lonely . . . But the best remedy against loneliness is busying yourself with duties and, so far as circumstances admit, with amusements. I wish I could feel it safe to allow you to visit more freely, but your conversations with Miss Haines have made known to you the reasons why I think it safest for you not to do so at present." [20]

The contradictions in Chase's nature seem more apparent than ever in his dealings with Kate. As a handsome widower, he lived a very active social life in Washington and had many friends there.

Although his attitude toward drinking or gambling was as rigid as ever, Chase, as always, derived considerable pleasure from his social pursuits. With Kate, however, he did not see any need for indulgences until and unless she met absolutely the severe standards that he and Miss Haines required of her. In his punishments of Kate he sometimes took the attitude, so confusing to a child, that it hurt him more than it did her, nor did he always avoid hiding behind the skirts of Miss Haines when he could.

"I am very, very sorry that Miss Haines thinks you had better not come to Washington at this time," he wrote Kate four days before Christmas, and he goes on to tell her that Miss Haines had just written him that in her judgment, "it will be much better for Kate not to go to Washington, both on account of her health and other considerations, indeed I do not feel that she deserves this pleasure at present and would much prefer that she should remain in New York." He feels that it is his duty to acquiesce in Miss Haines's view as to what is best for Kate since she has shown "too deep and too earnest a solicitude for your welfare to permit any doubt that she seeks, in all her decisions and requirements, your truest happiness." [21]

What a bitter disappointment the withdrawal of permission for this trip must have been to Kate! The previous Christmas Chase had been too concerned with his ailing wife even to send Kate a present, and she must have stored up a whole heart full of joy and excitement over the projected holiday with her father. For once she had had something to look forward to and to boast about to the other girls. No wonder she was hurt and that her letters to her father did not go off so regularly for a while. Chase was quick to admonish her about this: "You are allowing yourself a habitual disregard of your father's wishes (to write once a week), and are permitting the growth of a habit, which will cause you a great deal of misery," he wrote her.[22] In fact, he told her severely, he had decided not to write to her any more that winter since she took so little pains to obey his wishes. By February, however, his wrath had diminished and things returned to normal.

Chase saw his younger daughter, Nettie, sometimes more often than he did Kate, for although his duties kept him in Washington a great deal of the time, he did return to Ohio several times each year, occasionally for fairly lengthy stays between sessions. Nettie was living at Hillsboro with her mother's cousin, Mrs. Collins, and Chase visited her whenever he could.

Nettie had a less complex nature than Kate and she was never subjected to the stern disciplines that Kate received. As so often happens to the "baby" of the family, far less was demanded of her than of her sister and she retained a delightful simplicity and spontaneity all her life. Chase's letters to Kate speak often of "darling Nettie," and praise her charm, her loving nature, her winning ways. On occasions his references to Nettie are rather pointed. "A very lovely child, everybody thinks her," he gushed to Kate. "Artless, guileless, truthful, affectionate, and winning, she gains all hearts. It is by loving others that she makes others love her. There is a lesson in this, dear Kate. Can't you tell what it is?" [23] One would think that invidious comparisons such as these would do little to strengthen Kate's affection for her younger sister, but Kate seemed really to love Nettie and always to feel protective and close to her.

Chase's visits to New York were rare and often he would see Kate only twice during a year. Her summers were spent mostly in New England with some of the many relatives that seemed to abound in the Chase family. One year she stayed with the Garniss family near New York for a short summer holiday. Another summer it was with Cousin Eliza in Concord. Kate's visits to Washington were few and brief though she did go there once in a great while during her school years. On one occasion she met her father's friend, the imposing Senator Sumner, who enjoyed Kate and pronounced her "very intelligent."

Chase was eager to prepare Kate to be a credit to him and, when she would be old enough, to be a companion and help. The lessons of the Washington drawing rooms and the influence that he saw women exert there on behalf of their menfolk was not lost on him. He could already see what Kate, with the proper training, could do for him. "In a few years you will necessarily go into Society," he wrote her in her thirteenth year. "I desire that you may be qualified to ornament any society in our own country or elsewhere into which I may have occasion to take you. It is for this reason that I care more for your improvement in your studies, the cultivation of your manner, and the establishment of your moral and religious principles, than for anything else in respect to you." [24]

By the time Kate entered her 'teens, Chase's letters to her contained far less of the morbid preoccupation with sin and death that had so marked his thoughts and feelings earlier. Also as she moved into the higher grades at Miss Haines's school, her life there became less confined and she was allowed to participate in a broader range of activities and interests. Miss Haines and Chase gradually raised the restrictions on visits and Kate began to be allowed not only to receive visitors at the school but occasionally to go for weekends with relatives and friends. A very important part of the education of a young lady consisted of the social graces, and Miss Haines was admirably fitted to teach her young pupils the proper manners and decorum for the world of society. In spite of this added freedom, Kate nevertheless remained in great awe of Miss Haines, and it must have represented a real victory for her when she was finally able to persuade her father to let her out for good from under the sharp eye of Miss Haines. Undoubtedly she made good use of her "fear" of the headmistress and the censorship of her letters which even her father now admitted was hardly conducive to a free and affectionate exchange.

In the autumn shortly after her fourteenth birthday, Kate moved to a school outside Philadelphia at Aston Ridge. Miss Maria Eastman was in charge of the new school and Chase was thoroughly shocked when he took Kate to her home to find that she set all her guests to playing games of chance. He wrote Kate afterward that he was opposed on any account to let her learn to play cards, and preferred that she abstain altogether from all such games.[25]

At first Kate was happy in the new school, but by spring she was fretting and Chase wrote her that: "It gives me some pain to find you growing discontented. You complain of Miss Eastman . . . You must make a great deal of allowance for one who has so many cares upon her." [26] And he told her about his own lapses of control when he was a teacher in spite of all his good resolutions.

Kate was growing up rapidly that year and had even acquired

an admirer. A tiny letter, probably slipped secretly to her from a boy named Joe, addressed to Miss Kate Chase, Esq. Next door to the window, Schoolroom Aston Ridge, begged: "Will you do me the very very great favor to sit by me next Sunday evening? I shall be *very very* much obliged to you if you will." [27] Kate Chase had obviously made a conquest, but in spite of such extracurricular amusements she had had enough of boarding school. Kate felt she was a grown-up young lady now, at nearly fifteen, and her father began to treat her less and less as a child. After her visit to Washington in June of 1855, he began sending her copies of various speeches in the Senate, including one of her old friend Senator Sumner, and to see that she was supplied with newspapers. He started taking her into his confidence too and discussing his plans and prospects with her. His term as senator expired that year and by the end of May he had his eye on the office of governor of Ohio. As he was always to do, he appeared at first somewhat diffident. "It is very uncertain whether I shall be Governor," he wrote Kate, "or even a Candidate, but some of the papers begin to abuse me a little which is a good sign." [28] By the end of June he found "the prospect now is that I shall be nominated for Governor." [29] If that happened, he added, he would not be able to spend much time in New Hampshire, where Kate was visiting relatives as usual.

By August, Kate was back at Hillsboro with Nettie and her aunts and Chase was campaigning actively. He was scarcely ever at home, as he traveled widely throughout the state even into what he called the comparatively new part of Ohio where the means of travel were uncertain and difficult.

The big news for Kate, however, was that before she returned to Ohio she had extracted a promise from her father that she would not have to go back to school either to Miss Haines or Miss Eastman and that she could finish her education at home. She had stopped in New York and outfitted herself in fine style for her entrance into the "Society" about which Chase had been talking for so long. Confident that he would be elected governor, she had chosen a trousseau which would befit her father's position. Chase may have been somewhat staggered at the hundred items amounting to more than three hundred dollars that she acquired, and he probably remembered his mother's early strictures about his own extravagances. But with his desire that Kate grace his home and be a young lady whom he would be proud to show off, it is certain that he did not complain much.

Kate's six years away from home had come to an end at last. Besides her intellectual and social training, she had had to learn hard lessons of independence and self-sufficiency at an early age. There had been many times in those years when she could pour out her thoughts and feelings only to her diary and, long afterward, she would recall how she used to turn to it "for relief . . . when I was alone and trouble overtook me." [30] The years of separation from her father, and from any kind of family life, far from alienating her affections had served only to increase her need and attachment. Intensely emotional, Kate's heart had been kept in check along with her conduct and there was a whole surging wellspring of feeling that had not been permitted free expression or outlet. Now she was to go home again, to be in a house of her own, not as a boarder or as a guest, to be with her father who was involved in such exciting things, and to share in his life and interests.

CHAPTER

III

AT THE AGE of fifteen, Kate Chase was part elegant young lady
and part hoyden. She was tall and slender with burnished
golden-brown hair drawn smoothly back from her face. Her eyes
had a wonderful luminous quality, and seemed often to change
color with her mood from deepest brown to almost gold. A tip-
tilted nose added an element of puckishness to her face, still soft
with the roundness of childhood.

When Salmon Chase was elected Governor of Ohio in 1855,
there was no governor's mansion and he moved with his family
into a rented house in Columbus. It was an imposing house with
a pseudo-Gothic exterior, large and spacious as befitted a governor
and one which would provide ample room for his two daughters,
his sister Alice, and the many other relatives who came and went,
staying often for long visits.

Her first year in Columbus, Kate attended, as a day pupil, the
Esther Institute, where Nettie had been a student for some time.
It was an excellent school academically and was housed in a fine,
large building. Twenty-foot ceilings and elegant furnishings made
a perfect setting for the monthly reception and ball at which one
can imagine the governor's daughter was among the most popular.
A daring innovation was a gymnasium in which the young ladies disported themselves, undoubtedly swathed in ankle-length
bloomers.[1]

The boys at the high school, which was located near the Chase house, found a delightful occupation in teasing Kate. She did not burst into tears, as did so many of the other girls to their disgust. Kate was a spitfire and gave as good as she got. Sticks and stones, and strong words, flew back and forth over the fence. "She was always on hand with missiles and words ready for use—the words were most deadly," a former opponent recalled many years later.[2] Kate had learned long before how to take care of herself and woe betide any young snip, as the young ladies at Miss Haines's School termed boys, who tangled with her.

Kate was released at last from the supervision of stern boarding-school headmistresses, under which her free and wild spirit had been thwarted relentlessly during her school years. She had learned to meet the austere requirements and to control herself, but her essential nature remained as eager and emotional as ever. The pressure of his duties took a great deal of her father's time, and guileless Aunt Alice was hardly one who could mete out discipline to a girl who had matched wits with the doughty Miss Haines. Kate was left to her own devices far too much and she made many mistakes for which she was to pay heavily.

Kate was growing up and young men soon stopped looking upon her as fair game for shouted insults and stick throwing. Not only did her position as the Governor's daughter fix attention on her, but Kate herself drew the spotlight. She had that rare quality of charisma, an indefinable appeal which makes certain individuals stand out above the crowd and engages intense interest in everything they do. Not all of this interest is approving, for this quality can arouse bitter negative feelings too, and Kate was to make enemies as well as draw admirers about her. Notoriety and gossip were to pursue Kate all her life and became evident already the first summer that Chase was governor. He must have heard some rumors from Hillsboro, where Kate and Nettie were visiting, for he wrote Kate severely: *"Go nowhere* and *with nobody* and *do nothing* of the least importance with[out] consulting freely your Aunt Charlotte. You are at a time of life when all your acts will be observed."[3]

Although Chase reacted at once in this reproof to her for whatever indiscretion Kate was supposed to have committed, one early observer felt that in general he never recognized the harm that envy and malicious slander could do to his daughter: "With his benign belief in the universal goodness of mankind, Chase was singularly deficient in that knowledge of human nature which should have enabled him to throw about her that sort of aggressive protection which she peculiarly required." [4]

As time went on Chase entrusted more and more of the management of the house to Kate, but Chase was not a man to let anyone have a free hand with anything. He once sent her to Cincinnati to purchase furnishings and his daily letters to her are burdened with minute directions of exactly what she is to buy, and where, and what she is to pay for it. As always, he was worried about his finances, and with reason. His salary as governor was only $1,800 a year, and his expenses were running way above that. Nevertheless, everything must be done in style. Kate agreed, but it was not easy to satisfy every part of his detailed demands.

During her second year at Columbus, Kate took lessons in music and painting and continued with her study of French, at which she was already expert. With her flair for the dramatic she was fond of amateur theatricals and organized a group of players in which she participated as actress, director, and sometimes even playwright. She was devoted to little Nettie, whom she began at last really to know, and acted toward her half as mother, half as sister. She would sometimes correct Nettie and instruct her, but often she would intercede with her father for indulgences toward her.

The demands of the household, however, and the role she began increasingly to play as her father's hostess occupied most of her time. Chase began to depend on her more in every way, not only to run his house and entertain the stream of friends and acquaintances he was constantly inviting, but as companion and confidante. It was the first time in many years that he had a real home life. His long time dream had been to train Kate to take her place at his side, and he was constantly instructing her in the minutiae of the strict etiquette of those times, on whom to call and so on. He found Kate a quick and apt pupil. She was equally adept in her grasp of politics and government affairs for she had an extraordinary memory and the ability to penetrate to the essentials of a subject. Chase began discussing his problems with Kate primarily to clarify his own thinking, but he soon saw that she not only was able to follow and understand what he was talking about but had ideas and opinions of her own which he found helpful.

In her position as the Governor's daughter and his official hostess, Kate was called on to serve on various committees. In view of her youth one can imagine that the other ladies merely tolerated her presence and expected that she would be more seen than heard at their meetings. But on at least one occasion Kate surprised them and they did not forgive her for it. A doctor, who had often attended members of the committee, but who had offended some of them, was made the object of lengthy and senseless abuse. As Kate listened to the vicious attack, her wrath grew and finally, seeing that no one else had the courage to rise to the doctor's defense, she appealed to the chair to put a stop to the whole affair. Although some of the ladies may have been pleased by what this sixteen-year-old girl did, there were several who were furious and "she won on the spot an ill-will that followed her long after those who cherished it had forgotten its original cause." [5]

Chase undoubtedly applauded Kate's action in spite of the animosity he knew it would arouse. He had too often in his own life risked a great deal to attack what he considered an injustice not to be proud when his daughter took the same course, and he undoubtedly did not reprove her for her rash conduct.

On one occasion, however, during his second two-year term as governor, Chase was reported as having taken drastic action. There was a young man, recently married into a prominent Columbus family, who began to pay attention to Kate, first in little ways, then more flirtatiously and finally by taking her for drives openly through the city. Growing bolder, the young man even came to visit her at home and was reported to have boasted of his familiarity with her. As soon as Chase heard of this he is supposed to have forbidden him the house. But that was not the end of it, for, the story goes, the young man and Kate still saw each other and went driving. The climax occurred one day when the young

Lothario, thinking the Governor was away, came to the house to pick Kate up for a drive. Chase returned unexpectedly and the errant husband, thoroughly frightened, hid under a sofa from which he was pulled out by the irate father and horsewhipped with a whip from his own buggy. It was such a whipping that the young man was unable to appear in public for several days. With Chase's famous temper one can imagine that there may have been some truth in the story. Not long afterward, however, Chase let Kate go East by herself for a long visit, which he never would have done had he believed her to be guilty of anything really serious.

The tale was undoubtedly dramatized and colored in the telling and it made marvelous grist for the mills of Columbus gossips. Arguments were heated pro and con as to whether there had been more in the incident, as several of the girls insisted, than a careless indiscretion on Kate's part of accepting attentions from a married man. Although it was supposedly hushed up, the story was to follow Kate for many years and to be repeated with various embellishments, none of which were to the advantage of her reputation.

Many years later, when it had all once again been raked up, an older woman who had known Kate well during her Columbus days, came publicly to Kate's defense: "I am satisfied that the evil things said about . . . [Kate Chase] during her residence here were simply the work of a coterie of envious young women who were jealous of the lady's beauty, talent and social position. Why, Miss Kate, as she was then, had a dozen beaus where her associates had one, and that alone was enough to make the other girls jealous. I knew Kate Chase well and I always looked upon her as a magnificent girl, a little too independent to care what the world said about her to make her cautious. She was not as diplomatic in her youth as she has since become, but was outspoken and at times almost defiant if anyone attempted to turn her from a cherished purpose." [6]

Kate's success was always to be more with men than with women and she had an intelligence which was essentially more masculine than feminine. Men enjoyed talking to her, for she knew how to draw them out and was able to hold her own with them in any kind of discussion. Had she been what they used to call a blue-stocking, an earnest, grim, and usually unattractive female, the other girls would have felt sorry for her and not minded her a bit. But when they saw not only an unusual intellect but a remarkable femininity and charm plus beauty, it is not surprising that Kate was the recipient of a great deal of envy and jealousy from the Columbus girls, and that they whispered and gossiped about her with delicate venom.

Chase, however, felt that the best way to meet personal attacks was to ignore them. He himself had always followed that course and he undoubtedly suggested to Kate that she do so also.

Kate was especially attached to her Grandmother Smith and seemed to feel a real obligation toward her. Although Chase was not overly fond of his second wife's mother, he did praise Kate for her attentions. "It was very right in you to pay so much attention to your grandmother. The old lady has very few to care for her, and her peculiarities make it difficult to be agreeable to her. I love to have you attentive and kind to her." [7] Kate was always to show great loyalty toward her Grandmother Smith, and later would even persuade her father to allow the matriarch to live with them.

Chase took the greatest pride in Kate and enjoyed the good impression she made on people, and he missed her sorely whenever they were separated.

It was a very different relationship that had now developed between father and daughter than in the old boarding-school days. Chase was a demanding man, intensely so, and he required full attention and devotion. His interests and occupations were all absorbing to him and he drew everyone around him into the magnetic circle of his powerful personality. He wanted Kate to have no secrets from him, nothing in which he did not share. Especially, her life was to center on him. Although he remained a strict and domineering parent who was ready to censure any breach of manners or conduct that came to his attention, he began increasingly to treat young Kate as an equal and there grew to be something in his attitude toward her not only of dependency but of possessiveness. When she was away he would grow almost petulant if she did not write him as often as he thought she should: "We must not when absent from each other be so uncommunicative. My conscience reproaches me with having allowed three whole days to elapse without writing, and if I, who have so much to do and so much to think of, ought to have written sooner . . . what ought your conscience to say to you." [8]

Kate responded wholeheartedly to her father's demands and gave him in full measure the attention and devotion he required. When his sister Alice died suddenly in early 1859, Kate was left in complete charge of the household. Although at times one feels a certain restiveness in her, a desire for more of a personal life of her own, she had been deprived too long of any close family relationship and was far too devoted to her father not to be happy and gratified by the bond of love and dependency he was developing toward her.

The warmth and affection that Chase showed for his family were a great surprise to the men who knew him only as a public figure. The observant Carl Schurz had always felt that Chase's public bearing gave the appearance of a "somewhat cold, haughty and distant man. Without the least affectation or desire to pose, he was apt to be superbly statuesque . . . His dignity of deportment never left him, even in his unbending moods, for it was perfectly natural and unconscious. It really belonged to him like the majestic figure that nature had given him." But when Schurz on a visit to Columbus had the opportunity to talk with Chase in his own home, he decided that Chase's reticence was the result more of an innate shyness than of haughty superiority and found that "there was something very captivating in the grand simplicity of his character as it revealed itself in his confidences when he imparted them with that almost childlike lisp in his deep voice." [9]

Chase had invited Schurz, who was on a lecture tour, to stay at his house. The visitor was rather embarrassed to arrive early in the morning and was surprised that the Governor himself was up to greet him. Chase took him to the breakfast room, saying that his daughter would be down presently. "Soon she came," Schurz described his first meeting with Kate, "saluted me very kindly, and then let herself down upon her chair with the graceful lightness of a bird that, folding its wings, perches upon the branches of a tree. She was then about eighteen years old, tall and slender, and exceedingly well formed. Her features were not at all regularly beautiful according to the classic rule. Her little nose, somewhat audaciously tipped up, would perhaps not have passed muster with a severe critic, but it fitted pleasingly into her face with its large, languid, but at the same time vivacious, hazel eyes, shaded by long dark lashes, and arched over by proud eyebrows. The fine forehead was framed in waving gold-brown hair. She had something imperial in the pose of the head, and all her movements possessed an exquisite natural charm. No wonder that she came to be admired as a great beauty and broke many hearts. After the usual polite commonplaces, the conversation at the breakfast table, in which Miss Kate took a lively and remarkably intelligent part, soon turned upon politics, and that conversation was continued during a large part of the forenoon in the Governor's library." [10]

As the national elections of 1860 approached, Chase began to view his chances for the Republican presidential nomination from what he felt was a commanding position. He had been active in the Republican party since its inception; he had four years of executive experience behind him in the highest state office; he was a staunch antislavery man. As governor he had continued to do all he could within the framework of the state constitution to defend the rights of fugitive blacks. He was irrevocably opposed to the principle of slavery and to any extension of it outside the slave states. Chase wanted the Republican nomination desperately and he was intensely interested in what Carl Schurz thought about his prospects.

It was Schurz's first meeting with a man who had the "Presidential fever" and he was fascinated to see a "public man who was in the largest sense of the term, possessed by the desire to be President, even to the extent of honestly believing that he owed it to the country and that the country owed it to him that he should be President." [11]

When Chase asked bluntly about his chances for the nomination, Schurz replied with equal bluntness: "If the Republican Convention at Chicago have courage enough to nominate an antislavery man, they will nominate Seward; if not they will not nominate you." [12] Schurz admitted that it would have given him the greatest happiness to have been able to encourage Chase's aspirations. He sincerely felt that Chase's abilities warranted his ambition and he was also strongly drawn to him personally. If Schurz, who was only a casual acquaintance, felt this way about Chase's dreams of the highest office, how much more strongly must Kate have felt.

Chase talked freely with Kate about his plans and his hopes, and she entered into them wholeheartedly. By now she was an experienced hostess who was able to handle everything from huge state banquets to intimate dinners with skill and aplomb. Her influence was subtle. She knew how to create the kind of atmosphere which was conducive to good talk and persuasion and she continued to charm her father's friends and colleagues.

Although Chase was reelected to his former seat in the United States Senate when his second term as Governor ended, what he waited eagerly for was the Republican National Convention which assembled in May 1860 in Chicago. Chase still hoped for the Presidential nomination in spite of those who told him frankly that his chances were nil. He was so sure that he could steer the country out of its tragic impasse that he could not understand why everyone else did not recognize this fact too. But he was never even in the running. The most he received were 49 votes out of more than 670 and even these dwindled rapidly. When Lincoln was nominated on the third ballot, Carl Schurz could not help thinking of the man waiting anxiously in Columbus for news. "No doubt he had hoped, and hoped and hoped against hope . . . and now came this disastrous, crushing, humiliating defeat. I saw that magnificent man before me, writhing with the agony of disappointment, and I sympathized with him most profoundly. I should have pitied him, had I dared to pity such a man." [13]

Kate perhaps did not pity her father either but she felt deeply his hurt. He must have talked and talked again with her, trying to understand why and how he had been rejected. He was not bitter toward Lincoln, though he could not comprehend how such an ungainly man had been selected. He offered Lincoln his congratulations and his full support, but he could not resist, in his congratulatory letter, to mention the defection of members of the Ohio delegation from himself which he felt was a breach of trust.

No blow, however, no disappointment seemed to lessen Chase's confidence in himself. Even after this rejection, which should have shaken him profoundly, he could still write: "Would to heaven that it were in my power to compose the strife which disturbs the peace of our country!" And he declared: "If the executive power of the nation were in my hands, I should know what to do. I would maintain the Union, support the Constitution, and enforce the laws." [14] Chase instilled deeply into Kate this confidence in himself, in his vision, and in his abilities.

Undaunted, Chase planned to resume his place in the Senate, but Lincoln had other ideas for him. Here again, however, the proud man was forced to accept humiliation. Lincoln allowed seven weeks to pass after his election before he wrote Chase asking him to come to Springfield for a conference. Chase may have made the journey with ideas of the top Cabinet office in mind and could not have been pleased when Lincoln told him that he had felt obliged to offer that post to Seward, his closest rival for the nomination. And so Chase was tendered the second spot, Secretary of the Treasury. Except it was not exactly an offer. Lincoln was only sounding him out, and the whole appointment was left up in the air. To make matters worse, Chase knew that he had not even been Lincoln's first choice for the Treasury post and his feelings were not assuaged when the President-elect told him that had Seward refused the position of Secretary of State, he would have offered it to Chase.

Chase was impressed with Lincoln's frankness and sincerity, and once he had recovered from his initial reaction to the "grotesque qualities which so confounded" him when he first saw Lincoln, he felt that the President-elect was "a man to be depended on. He may, as all men may, make mistakes"; he wrote Thaddeus Stevens, "but the cause will be want of sufficient information, not unsoundness of judgement or devotion to principle." [15]

In spite of his encouraging impression of Lincoln, the meeting at Springfield was hardly a satisfying one from Chase's point of view, and he must have felt deeply offended. Left dangling for even the second Cabinet post, he did not really know where he stood and as time went on and he heard nothing further from Lincoln he gave up all thoughts of any occupation outside the Senate. It was not until after the inauguration, and Chase had already taken his seat in the Senate, that Lincoln, without informing Chase in advance, sent his name for confirmation to the Senate as Secretary of the Treasury. Chase happened to be absent from the Senate floor at the time and his name received immediate confirmation.

When Chase learned that he had been nominated and confirmed for the Cabinet office, he went at once to the President to state his disinclination to accept the position. Lincoln persuaded him to think the matter over and pressure was brought on Chase from other sources to accept. "I finally yielded to this," he wrote, "and surrendered a position in every way more desirable to take charge of the disordered finances of the country under circumstances most unpropitious and forbiding." [16]

Kate's Columbus days had come to an end and she was never again to return to Ohio for more than short visits. A whole new world was ahead of her, one in which she was to reach dazzling heights.

CHAPTER

IV

WASHINGTON in 1861 was a combination of grandeur, simplicity, extravagance and privation. "As in 1800 and 1850, so in 1860 the same rude colony was camped in the same forest, with the same unfinished Greek temples for workrooms and sloughs for roads," wrote Henry Adams.[1] The Capitol loomed over everything with its new, unfinished, truncated dome bristling with derricks that stood up like giant sprouts of hair. It was flanked by marble wings, opulently finished within but standing bare and undecorated without. Materials, workmen's sheds, tools, blocks of marble were strewn about the grounds. Down broad Pennsylvania Avenue was every kind and shape of building: fine restaurants and hotels, shops, shoddy wooden houses, markets. It was the only paved street in the city and even it was filled with holes and ruts, dusty in dry weather and treacherous with muddy slime in wet. The White House grounds included barns and sheds, vegetable and flower gardens, all giving the impression of a prosperous country estate. Paths within the grounds led to various department buildings, War, Navy, State, and the impressive but uncompleted marble mass of the Treasury. The general public walked freely across the north side of the White House grounds, undoubtedly finding it a pleasanter route than along Pennsylvania Avenue. The old city canal was still used for dumping refuse and it often spilled over into the marsh that formed the south boundary of the Executive Mansion grounds. Throughout the city, outhouses abounded, gutters were often used as refuse dumps, and the water supply came from wells of extremely dubious hygienic quality. Mosquitoes bred luxuriantly in the low-lying swamps, and although malaria was not uncommon, it is a miracle that a vast epidemic did not sweep through the city. There were digestive upsets occasionally but after the Republican victory in 1860 they were laughingly blamed on disgruntled Democrats.

Washington was a city of 61,000 inhabitants, 10,000 of which were Negroes. In contrast to the opulent marble government buildings, there were areas of frightful poverty which bred crime and disease. Gangs roamed the streets and people hardly dared venture out alone at night. The police were scant and poorly organized, with extremely low morale. Fire brigades clanged out several times each night with not much effect in putting out fires, as the water supply was low and their methods disordered.

As with every new administration, office seekers swarmed to the capital. Large, rambling Willard's Hotel was the centre of activity. William Howard Russell, correspondent for the *London Times*, described the scene he found there on his arrival in March of 1861. "It is a quadrangular mass of rooms, six stories high, and some hundred yards square; and it probably contains at this moment more scheming, plotting, planning heads than any building the same size ever held in the world . . . Up and down the long passages doors were opening and shutting for men with papers bulging out of their pockets, who hurried as if for their lives in and out, and the building almost shook with the tread of the candidature." Meals for not less than twenty-five hundred people were served in the public rooms every day, and Russell told of a breakfast he heard being ordered: "Black tea and toast, scrambled eggs, fresh spring shad, wild pigeon, pigs' feet, two robins on toast, oysters." All in all he found that the "tumult, the miscellaneous nature of the company . . . the heated muggy rooms, not to speak of the great abominableness of the passages and halls, despite a most liberal provision of spittoons, conduce to render these institutions by no means agreeable to a European." [2]

Holding itself completely aloof from the depressed and sordid aspects of the city was Washington society. It held sway in elaborate mansions surrounded by gardens within the city, and at great estates in the sourrounding countryside; in the dignified brick houses of Georgetown and at receptions at the Executive Mansion. Washington ladies vied with each other for the inventiveness, the splendor and size of their entertainments. Levees, dinners, balls, parties, and entertainments of all kinds so crowded the week that a hostess was hard put to it to find a free evening for her party. All was done on an extravagant scale. President Buchanan had drawn on his own purse to supplement his salary. One senator was reputed as spending $75,000 a year to live in style in Washington, and more than one member of the Buchanan Cabinet had lived on a similar scale. Mr. Corcoran, whose art gallery was in the process of being built, lived almost regally, and at dozens of other homes lavish entertainments were considered commonplace. The comings and goings, the activities and costumes of the ladies were avidly noted and discussed. And wagging tongues were ready to criticize any error of dress or decorum. Miss Harriet Lane, niece of President Buchanan and his hostess at the White House, had been much admired for her lovely appearance, and for the skill and formality with which she had discharged her social duties. Mrs. Stephen Douglas was another who charmed everyone by her beauty, her tact, and the modesty with which she accepted the adulation that came to her.

The ladies of Washington played an active role not only on the social but on the political scene. They filled the galleries at the Capitol, they arranged intimate entertainments where politics could be discussed far from the heat of the day. They knew how to soothe ruffled tempers, how to charm and persuade. These ladies of the political scene were more than merely decorative hostesses. They interested themselves passionately in political questions and participated energetically in all that was going on. Unlike the privileged wives of New York tycoons, who too often lived in a hothouse world of unreality, many of these ladies played important roles in the careers of their husbands. Salmon Chase had known what he was about in his education of Kate and he had trained her well to take her place in this spirited and demanding society.

Everyone was intensely curious about the new President. Powerful Senator Sumner had never even seen him and this Boston aristocrat admitted that he was "amazed and puzzled" when he first met Lincoln. Utterly without sense of humor himself, he not only missed the point of Lincoln's stories but saw no reason or excuse for them. To Sumner, the office of President required a stately, majestic personage, someone of great dignity and presence. Someone perhaps like his good friend Salmon Chase.

Washington society too was dubious about the new Lincoln Administration. The ladies found it difficult to make up their minds about Mrs. Lincoln. Was she the fashion or not? "They miss their Southern friends," Russell noted, "and constantly draw comparisons between them and the vulgar Yankee women and men who are now in power." [3]

The Lincolns' first levee was termed a "monster gathering" by *Harper's Weekly*. "The oldest frequenters of the Executive mansion," it went on, "declare that they do not recollect ever to have seen so many people pass through the House at any previous levee. An hour before the doors of the house were opened, the great driveway was blocked with carriages and the sidewalks and approaches to the White House were thronged with ladies and gentlemen . . . By half past eight the crowd inside was so intense that—it being impossible to pass out of the door, owing to the large numbers outside waiting for admission—it was found necessary to pass the ladies and gentlemen who desired to retire out through the windows." [4]

Many stories circulated through Washington about the new President and especially about the First Lady. Tart Mr. Russell, who found little if anything to admire in what he viewed as the crass young country's social life, was "agreeably disappointed" in Mrs. Lincoln, as he had looked forward to verifying the many anecdotes he had heard from secessionist ladies about her gaucheries, stories which, he had to admit, "could scarcely have been founded on fact." Among the wives and daughters of the Cabinet ministers, there was only one whom he found worthy of mention:

"Miss Chase, who is very attractive, agreeable, and sprightly." Salmon Chase too passed muster with this critical Englishman, who found him to be "one of the most intelligent and distinguished persons in the whole assemblage." Russell even ventured so far as to suggest that on the whole Chase "is one who would not pass quite unnoticed in a European crowd of the same description." [5]

Kate was twenty when she arrived in Washington to take her place as the third lady of the land. Mrs. Seward, wife of the Secretary of State, was in poor health and took almost no part in the Washington social scene. Mrs. Lincoln, plump and middle-aged, overdressed, tense and anxious about her new position, was hardly a match for the young girl. Kate was tall and regal looking. She dressed with artful simplicity, needing no artifice to emphasize her beauty. Her mind was quick. She was fascinated by government and politics and thoroughly knowledgeable about them. Young as she was, she not only was an accomplished hostess but an intelligent conversationalist. Most of all, she had a verve, a freshness, a delight that was contagious. Washington was exciting and new for her and she brought a sparkle and animation to the anxious and tired men in power. Mrs. Lincoln grew more and more jealous of Kate, but then Mrs. Lincoln was jealous of all women who came near her husband.

A story has been handed down about Kate's first state dinner at the White House. At the close of the evening, Mrs. Lincoln said to Kate: "I shall be glad to see you anytime, Miss Chase." Whereupon Kate, drawing herself up to her full height, replied: "Mrs. Lincoln, I shall be glad to have you call on me at any time." Apocryphal or not, this story was reported many years later by Mrs. Charles Walker, a friend and admirer of Kate. Mrs. Walker lived for some years in the Chase household and knew Kate intimately. Her comment on the story was that Kate could be arrogant when she chose, "and was frequently so towards women whom she never loved, and whom, after her dark experience at Columbus, where she was cruelly maligned, she hated. She felt that they had persecuted her, and she bore them no good will." [6] The protocol of calling in those days was a complex affair and carried a good deal of weight. Mrs. Walker reported that Mrs. Lincoln "of course, resented" Kate's answer, and undoubtedly showed it. A more socially adept woman would have turned the tables on the impertinent young lady.

Chase rented a house, a three-story brick affair, on the corner of Sixth and E streets Northwest for eighteen hundred dollars a year. Kate set about furnishing it and engaging servants to staff it. Her father's salary was only eight thousand a year and he had left Columbus followed by his usual debts. Chase felt sorry for himself. He had dedicated his life to public service and he did not see why he should be in financial straits. "It does seem a little hard that we who have so much important work to do as I have had during the last twelve years should all the time have had to pay so large a part of [our] own expenses," he wrote Kate.[7] Yet Chase, in Washington, felt he had a position to maintain and although he counseled Kate to economy from time to time, and worried about his finances, he continued to live beyond his means. He was forced to borrow from his friend and appointee, Hiram Barney, Collector of the Port of New York. Soon he was to profit from the advice and help of Jay Cooke, the Philadelphia investment banker, brother of his old friend from Ohio. Cooke was not loath to cement his connection with the Secretary of the Treasury. Jay Cooke & Co. would handle, and with considerable skill, vast amounts of Government bonds during Chase's tenure.

March was quiet in the capital, ominously quiet. But events moved rapidly after the attack on Fort Sumter. On April 15 Lincoln issued a proclamation calling out seventy-five thousand militia. Sixteen states responded immediately. Massachusetts telegraphed: "The quota of troops required of Massachusetts is ready. How will you have them proceed?" Part of the New York troops were already on their way to the capital. Ohio responded: "Your dispatch calling on Ohio for thirteen regiments is just received, and will be promptly responded to." [8] Virginia joined the secession; the border states gave outraged replies to Lincoln's call. Maryland was seething. First of all to act had been the governor of Rhode Island. Even before Lincoln had issued his proclamation,

Governor Sprague had offered twelve hundred troops outfitted at his own expense and headed by himself.

Washington grew uneasy. Communications with the North were cut. Rumors spread rapidly that Rebel troops were planning to attack the city. "The just indignation of an outraged and deeply injured people will teach the Illinois Ape to retrace his journey across the borders of the Free negro states still more rapidly than he came," fulminated the *Richmond Examiner*.[9]

The Capitol was boarded up; the Treasury was fortified. Guards were posted about the city and the militia guarded all public buildings. Tension increased hourly. The promised troops did not arrive. Chase decried Lincoln for having no policy "merely the general notion of drifting, the Micawber policy of waiting for something to turn up." [10] Secessionist sympathizers left the city in droves, leaving their houses boarded up. Hotels and theaters closed. Everything was in a state of anxious suspended animation. Even Lincoln was discouraged and said wryly: "I don't believe there is any North. The Seventh Regiment is a myth. Rhode Island is not known in our geography any longer." [11]

The ice jam broke suddenly and by the end of April troops began to pour into Washington: the handsome Seventh from New York; the Eighth Massachusetts joined their own Sixth, which had been fired upon going through Baltimore. Among the most colorful was the First Rhode Island, led by their dashing young Governor, with Colonel Burnside in command. Dressed in gray uniforms with scarlet blankets slung over their shoulders, they were well drilled and looked in fighting trim.

The Rhode Islanders were quartered in the Patent Office; the Eighth Massachusetts in the Capitol building itself; some of the New Yorkers were at Georgetown College; others were at the Treasury. Every day more troops arrived, marched up Pennsylvania Avenue to the cheers of welcoming crowds. They were sworn in at colorful ceremonies where patriotic hope and feeling ran high.

"The Rhode Island regiment was sworn in in the east Capitol garden by Major McDowell," a newspaper correspondent reported. "The men were inspected by companies, and then formed in a hollow square, the American and Revolutionary flags were brought to the centre, and then, holding up their right hands, the twelve hundred men repeated the oath after General Thomas . . . The scene was very imposing, and the setting sun, lighting up the front of the Capitol . . . made the *tout ensemble* most beautiful. Then, breaking into column, and wearing their red blankets as overcoats, the regiment marched back to quarters, Governor Sprague heading them on horseback." [12]

Kate Chase was surely present at the swearing in of the Rhode Islanders. She had met the Boy Governor, as he was called, the year before when he went to Cleveland to attend the dedication of a monument to Rhode Island–born Oliver Hazard Perry, commemorating the victory over the British at Lake Erie. At the ball that followed, he paid her marked attention. And she commented, "What a charming man Governor Sprague is!" [13]

Men were not always overly impressed with the young Governor, although Lincoln was supposed to be fond of him, but the ladies found him dashing and romantic. Astride his white horse, which he rode with reckless abandon, with his fine uniform and his yellow-plumed hat, he looked the picture of a gallant officer. He was slight of figure, but lean and supple. His dark hair, worn rather long, was brushed back casually from a broad brow, and his deep set gray eyes held a look of sadness which charmed the ladies. But underneath they sensed a taut, nervous energy and more than a hint of wildness. In addition he was one of the wealthiest men in the country.

During the late spring of 1861 Washington was turned into a garrison as more and more troops poured into the capital. Soldiers were everywhere. The grounds of the Smithsonian Institution were used for target practice. Drills were held in every public square and the sound of drum and bugle echoed up and down every street. Sanitary conditions became unbearable and the stench of the city grew overwhelming as time passed and summer heat came on. As the weeks of inactivity stretched the young soldiers grew increasingly restless. There was liquor aplenty to be had and wild young men found release in roisterous drinking bouts, fights, and noisy hilarity. But life in society circles went on as before, and Washington ladies were as active and gay as ever.

Kate was in her element at last. Showered with attention, at the very center of government, busy from morning till night, she bloomed in every way. She was undoubtedly the most popular young lady in Washington. But she was more than that. Lord Lyons, the British Ambassador, found her utterly charming, and it was said that she did much through him to influence the maintenance of a friendly relationship between Britain, where strong sympathies for the Confederacy existed, and the Union. Kate not only graced official functions with her charm but brought subtle influence to bear. In this she was in no way outside the tradition of Washington ladies interesting themselves in the great questions of the day. The only difference was one of degree: Kate did it so much better than most of the others.

Everyone was eager to dance attendance on the beautiful Kate Chase. At dinners, receptions, balls she was the center of attention. She who had so often felt lonely and cut off in her childhood, never lacked for companionship and attention now. She was a magnificent rider and loved to gallop through the countryside around Rock Creek. She visited army camps set up on the outskirts of the city and often appeared at the Rhode Island headquarters, moved now from the Patent Office to a hillside north of the capital.

All this was heady stuff for a young girl, and it would be surprising if it had not had its effect on Kate. She herself described long afterward how she had been "used to command and be obeyed, to wish and to be anticipated." [14] She was cocky and exultant, riding high on a wave of excitement and novelty. She had always had something imperious in the pose of her head and she now carried it higher than ever, and with reason, for she was Kate Chase, "belle of belles" in Washington. To say, as has been often said and believed, that Kate was consumed with the one ambition to see her father as President and herself as First Lady; that all her efforts, all her thoughts were bent to that single purpose; that she calculated and connived and cold-bloodedly concentrated with only that end in view—to take such a view of Kate Chase is to drain from her all fire and blood and warmth and reality. She was, as Jay Cooke described her, a "glorious girl," full-bodied and spirited. Of course she loved her father and wanted for him what he wanted for himself. But what she longed for and dreamed about was her own fulfillment as a woman, to love and be loved. To view her as a one-dimensional creature devoured by envy and ambition is to deny the greatest part of the pulsing, passionate woman that she was.

Mrs. Lincoln was especially hostile toward Kate. In part this was due to her distrust of Salmon Chase who, she was sure, was trying to usurp the President's place; in part it was due also to the natural rivalry toward a successful, far younger woman.

One evening, before a White House party, Lincoln, who well knew his wife's jealousy toward all women, asked her: "Well, Mother, who must I talk with tonight—shall it be Mrs. D[ouglas]?"

"That deceitful woman! No, you shall not listen to her flattery."

"Well, then what do you say to Miss C[hase]? She is too young and handsome to practise deceit."

"Young and handsome you call her! You should not judge beauty for me. No, she is in league with Mrs. D[ouglas], and you shall not talk with her."

"Well, Mother, I must talk with some one. Is there any one that you do not object to?"

"I don't know as it is necessary that you should talk to anybody in particular. You know well enough, Mr. Lincoln, that I do not approve of your flirtations with silly women, just as if you were a beardless boy, fresh from school."

"But, Mother, I insist that I must talk with somebody, I can't stand around like a simpleton and say nothing. If you will not tell me who I may talk with, please tell me whom I may not talk with."

"There is Mrs. D[ouglas] and Miss C[hase] in particular. I detest them both. Mrs. B. will also come around you, but you need not listen to her flattery. These are the ones in particular." [15] In Mrs. Douglas and Kate Chase, Mrs. Lincoln had picked out for her animosity the two most beautiful women in Washington.

Chase, as representative of the antislavery groups in the Cabinet, was also held by Mrs. Lincoln to be part of the growing calumny and criticism from the Radicals that pursued her and that constantly grew in intensity during her years in the White House. Not only was she accused of political meddling and wild extravagance, but of disloyalty and even treachery toward the Union. Small wonder that her temper grew ever more uncontrollable, and that she lashed out at any tangible figure in the faceless hostility that surrounded her.

Soon Mrs. Lincoln would no longer be a social rival for anybody. An extravagant party for five hundred people, exclusively by invitation, contrary to the custom that only state dinners were not open to the general public, aroused more than the usual attacks and criticisms. Nearly two thousand pounds of elaborate meats were served at the supper; delicious confections in all sizes and patriotic shapes graced the tables; wines and liquors flowed in abundance; there was champagne aplenty for everyone. Patient Lincoln paid for it out of his own pocketbook. But Mrs. Lincoln, who looked upon the gala as a gesture of defiance against her calumniators, found little if any satisfaction in the evening. Her son Willie was lying upstairs with high fever. Two weeks later the boy died. It was to be Mrs. Lincoln's last large entertainment, except for unavoidable official functions. Kate Chase would soon become in fact, if not in name, first hostess of Washington.

In spite of the handful of prisoners lodged in Washington jails, the war had not yet become a reality to the people of Washington. The month of June passed. Only minor skirmishes were taking place. Parades on Independence Day increased the people's pride in their regiments marching by the thousands through Washington. The Radicals in the Congress were eager for a chance to punish the South. Chase had urged an attack at Manassas and Alexandria even before Virginia had ratified secession. Seward was convinced that the war would be a short one. Many in the militia regiments had enlisted for only three months, and their term of service would soon expire, greatly reducing the number of troops available. The country demanded action.

General McDowell, who had been in command of the army in Virginia for less than two months, begged for more time. Especially he hoped to influence his old friend Salmon Chase in this.

But the time to move had come and there was no putting it off any longer.

On July 21, the people of Washington poured out of the city in carriages, on horseback, loaded with picnic baskets. "Every carriage, gig, wagon and hack had been engaged by people going out to see the fight," Russell described.[16] Congressmen, senators, Matthew Brady, the fashionable photographer, young boys on horseback, ladies in their carriages with opera glasses in their reticules, all wanted to see the great victory they anticipated. Quiet crowds stood about the public buildings of Washington. Telegrams began coming in to the War Department. Dispatch riders brought more news. All of it seemed good. Federal troops were advancing steadily. As Russell approached Centreville he heard "loud cheers suddenly burst from the spectators as a man dressed in the uniform of a Union officer rode up. 'We've whipped them on all points,' he cried. 'We have taken all their batteries. They are retreating as fast as they can and we are after them.'" Russell, whose sympathies were with the Confederacy, noted supercilliously that the congressmen spectators cried out at this, "Bully for us! Bravo! Didn't I tell you so?"[17]

The truth reached the capital only in the late afternoon. At six o'clock Seward went to see the President. "Tell no one," he said. "The battle is lost . . . McDowell is in full retreat."[18] The Battle of Bull Run had turned into a disaster.

The President and a grim Cabinet met that evening. At home Kate Chase waited anxiously for more news. The Rhode Island regiment had been reported to be in the thick of the fight. Governor Sprague's horse had been shot from under him. Of all the beaux who danced attendance on her, there was only one who had touched her heart, who would ever touch her heart, the dashing Governor of Rhode Island.

CHAPTER

V

"D EAR SISTER," wrote Nettie to Kate. "Is Gov. Sprague back
yet? I wish (if you do not think me impertinent) that you
would marry him. I like him very much. Won't you? But of course
not until I grow up. I shant give my consent before that. Perhaps
though he may get tired of waiting." [1]

Nettie was not alone in her interest about Kate and Governor
William Sprague. They were so often together and so obviously
enjoying it that rumors of their engagement spread everywhere.
The millionaire "Boy Governor" was considered the greatest catch
of the season.

Sprague was ten years older than Kate, although he did not look
it. Born September 13, 1830, son of Amasa and Fanny Morgan
Sprague, William was brought up with the knowledge that he was
heir to a great fortune. It was his grandfather who had laid the
foundations for the family empire, building one of the first cotton
mills in Rhode Island, which he soon expanded into calico print-
ing and dyeing. He passed on to his sons extensive holdings in
stock farms and lumber and a thriving manufacturing concern.
The sons, especially Amasa, were to continue the phenomenal
development of the A. & W. Sprague Company and greatly to
increase the scope and power of their diverse business interests.
Seven children were born to Amasa and Fanny Sprague, four of
whom, two daughters and two sons, were to reach maturity.

When William Sprague was twelve years old a tragedy occurred which was to haunt him for the rest of his life. One bitter cold, snowy afternoon of New Year's Eve, his father did not return home as expected from a visit to one of his farms. Late that afternoon his body was found on a lonely stretch of road between the farm and his house. He had been disabled by a shot and then beaten to death with frightful brutality. Footsteps in the snow, in a direction away from the body, led to the discovery in a nearby swamp of a dismantled gun, covered with blood and hair, and a bloodstained coat. The tracks continued to a pond where they were picked up again on the other side. But there were no marks on the ice to show that anyone had crossed the pond. The tracks were finally lost when they reached a much-traveled road. Not far along the road there were other tracks which led off it to the house and store of Nicholas Gordon and his two brothers, John and William.

The Gordons had planned to sell liquor in their store, but Amasa Sprague had opposed granting them a license and had succeeded in blocking it. Amasa, and especially Fanny Sprague, like Salmon Chase, was strongly against liquor and card playing. Nicholas Gordon was angry that powerful Amasa Sprague had interfered with his plans and was heard to threaten to "be revenged of him." But Nicholas had an alibi, and it was the two younger brothers who were brought to trial for the murder. The whole case was explosive and feeling ran high on all sides. The Gordons were recent Irish immigrants. Amasa Sprague had been one of the most powerful men in the state.

More than a hundred witnesses were called at the trial of John and William Gordon. The evidence for the prosecution was entirely circumstantial but included identification of the bloodstained gun and coat as having once belonged to Nicholas Gordon. William Gordon, like his brother Nicholas, was found to have an alibi. John Gordon was convicted of the murder and executed.[2]

William Sprague never forgot that ghastly New Year's Eve and the tragedy of his father's brutal murder. There was a general dissatisfaction with the results of the trial, and many believed that the wrong man had been executed. Amasa's brother immediately resigned his position as United States senator and returned home to take care of the business of the A. & W. Sprague Company. Nevertheless, nothing was ever to be quite the same for William Sprague. In spite of his mother's hopes for a thorough education for him, after a short period of time at the Irving Institute, in Tarrytown, New York, William, at the age of fifteen, left school and went to work in the family business.

Although his education had been inadequate, young William Sprague showed considerable business acumen and he passed through a strict apprenticeship in the company office. He was twenty-six when his uncle died, at which time he assumed full charge of the vast Sprague interests. His brother, Amasa, was a sportsman who loved fine horses and horse racing and never showed much interest in business, although nominally he was a partner also. What made William Sprague's pulse race was the sound of trumpet and drum and marching feet. He joined the Providence Marine Artillery at the age of sixteen and later, when he became a colonel, he loved nothing better than to ride at the head of his company on one of the magnificent horses that Amasa knew so well how to choose. Handsome, wealthy, successful, William Sprague assumed early prominence in Rhode Island far beyond what could be expected from one of his years.

Fanny Sprague was a devoted mother and did her best to instill in her sons her strict ideas of discipline and virtue. Although she was a delicate and pretty woman, she had a strong will and inflexible beliefs. But her son, William, had been forced into maturity too early and had had to assume responsibility too young to accept her guidance for long. He was a free and independent spirit and lived his life as he pleased and although he attended to the business affairs of the family with skill and attention, there were dark whispers of unsavory entanglements with women and wild drinking bouts.

When he was twenty-nine he took a trip abroad where he indulged his military hobbies, visiting battlefields and studying the arms and equipment of the Continental armies. It was during his absence that several prominent citizens conceived a plan to name him as candidate for governor, and in this they received great encouragement from Fanny Sprague. A delegation met him in New

York on his return from Europe and a triumphal ovation greeted him on his arrival in Providence. Salutes from a hundred guns welcomed the returning traveler, his own Marine Artillery marched behind him through the streets of Providence and he was feted at banquets like a returning hero.

Sprague was surprised at first at the idea of the governorship and more than a little hesitant. He knew nothing of politics and was actually a few months short of the required age of thirty when he was given the nomination for governor. But once the decision was taken, Sprague plunged into the campaign with a will. Large sums of money were expended on both sides, but no one could match the Spragues for money. There were charges of bribery and Sprague was reported as having spent over a hundred thousand dollars to win the election. He was to be reelected as governor twice more, in 1861 and 1862, the last time unopposed. Sprague's dramatic and heroic role in the first months of the war would catch the people's imagination and prove an even more powerful influence than money.

When Sprague arrived in Washington at the head of his Rhode Island regiment during the tense spring of 1861, one of the first people he called on was Kate Chase. He had not forgotten his first meeting with her at Cleveland the year before, and years afterward he could still recall it vividly: "You remember when we first met at Cleveland," he wrote Kate later reminiscently, "when surrounded with all the paraphernalia of war and of young manhood, you cared little for the appreciation and nearly refused to participate in doing honor to the city's great. You did come dressed in that celebrated dress . . . and I can now see you as with Bancroft you became my gaze and the gaze of all observers, and then you left the house taking with you my admiration and my appreciation but more than all my *pulsations*. I remember well how I was possessed that night and the following day. I can recall the sensations better than if it was yesterday. Well, we came to Washington. I well remember the call Goddard and I made upon you. I remember the troubled times that led to the Battle of Bull Run." [3]

It had been love at first sight for Sprague, and Kate too had evidently been stirred, for although they did not meet again for some eight months, they corresponded after the Cleveland meeting and Sprague was to tease her later that even before he had come to Washington to join "the Army of the Potomac, my dear did you know you were then taking a good deal more interest in me, than mere friendship[?]" [4]

The relationship progressed rapidly. Sprague was not a man to stand on ceremony, nor was he a man to flatter and do homage. It was simply not in his nature. He did not enjoy or admire the artificial manners of fashionable society. Often a woman who is accustomed to great and easy success with men, and who expects all sorts of blandishments and honeyed words from them, is challenged by the man who remains outside this flattering circle, and who is bold and direct with her. Sprague courted Kate but not as she had ever been courted before.

How did she come to fall in love with William Sprague? Of the many suitors that she had, why did she lose her heart only to this one? In spite of his wealth and prominence, Kate was considered by everyone to be his superior in every way except one—money. It was Sprague's enormous fortune with which Kate fell in love, people said and still say, not the man himself. They pointed out her intelligence, her social skills, her intellectual and cultural inclinations, her exquisite discrimination and her strong will. Never, they said, could Kate Chase love a man who was not her superior, or at least her equal, in all these areas. Sprague was a man who did not like society, whose manners were often brusque and rude, who was reported to have bought his political position, and who was anything but an intellectual. But they did not understand that under her cool and perfect exterior, Kate was a passionate romantic. She had learned control and discipline under her early training and a part of her responded to the challenge of intellectual and social eminence, of fine minds and high purposes. She could be critical in her judgments and dismiss this suitor or that because he did not come up to her ideals. But what she longed for was a man who could penetrate beneath the fastidious discernments, the critical judgments, who could make her forget them all, someone who would free her from her own inner reserve, a bold, wild, romantic man who would break through her barriers of repression. Sprague was to her this man and when he rode into her life on his white charger with the yellow plume in his hat dancing in the wind he swept her off her feet. Kate gave her heart to William Sprague and he was in her own words, "the first, the only man that had found a lodgement there." [5]

As Kate waited anxiously for news of him after the first reports of the disaster at Bull Run began to come in, she was sure only that he would have been in the thick of the fighting, for she knew that he was eager to test himself in battle, that he "wanted to feel the enemy . . . to see him." [6] He had been under fire for the first time on a reconnaissance mission three days before the actual battle, and although the division was forced to retreat in disorder, he was not wounded. When the big attack came, Sprague and the Rhode Island troops were to attempt a flanking movement on the left. Because of delays, by the time they reached the river the Confederates were there to meet them in full force.

Sprague was in charge of a battery of artillery and he never forgot the savage hours that followed. One of his guns "was the first cannon discharged at the enemy's line of battle of the war," he claimed. "I furnished the first ammunition, bringing cannister and powder from the limbers, and distributing it from a lap-full from on horseback during the first ten minutes of the fight." "I took special charge of the battery," he recalled. "The men, detached and separated, were a little confused; some stood firm." The enemy was only a "half pistol shot distance" away. "Horses were struck down; men laid down and died." Sprague continued to supply ammunition and tried to "give confidence to the line. I kept my horse during the fight; the bullets scratched me and made holes in my loose blouse."

The Union lines were holding, but with difficulty. It seemed like hours, but was only forty minutes, before the First Rhode Island troops came to the rescue of the embattled Artillery. Years later Sprague would recall "the blast of enthusiasm with which those twelve hundred men received me. We were ripe for a charge. I led . . . my horse was then shot. I took off his saddle in front of the line; and the men, without order . . . fell back."

The disorder increased rapidly and when the Confederates were reinforced by General Johnston, who had cleverly avoided the trap that was supposed to keep him occupied elsewhere, the rout was on. Sprague and his regiment "received the full blast of Johnston's reinforcement, not twenty paces off," he recalled. "I saw the men scattered; they were not held to the line."

Confusion reigned everywhere. Wagons moving toward the battle were blocked by ammunition carts going in the opposite direction. Russell of the *London Times* reported: "Every moment the crowd increased; drivers and men cried out with the most vehement gestures, 'Turn back! Turn back! We are whipped.' . . . The crowd from the front continually increased, the heat, the uproar, and the dust were beyond description." He saw men who "were hastily walking or running, their faces streaming with perspiration, and generally without arms," as he worked his way for about a half a mile "against an increasing stream of fugitives, the ground being strewn with coats, blankets, firelocks, cooking tins, caps, belt, bayonets." [7]

Sprague did his best to exhort the men to fresh attack, but without success and the retreat continued. The First Rhode Island Regiment, Sprague's pride and joy, refused to advance, claiming that their three months' enlistment was up and that they wanted to go home. And home they went, not stopping long enough even in Washington to answer the call for help to defend the capital that was tense with apprehension of an attack.

Sprague was furious and bitter and never forgot what he considered the cowardice of these three-month volunteers. He called them the million-dollar men who would not stay to fight.

Sprague had hoped until the end for reinforcements and had even sent Burnside to the General's conference that was called at Centreville to plead that the positions be fortified and that "we should not go back like sheep to Washington; that we should not be further disgraced."

Exhausted by the battle, Sprague himself fell asleep, hoping to be awakened by the fresh troops. Instead, he woke at two in the morning to total stillness. No one had come. No one was left. "I saddled my horse, jumped the fences, and reported to Lincoln;

and begged him to send forward new troops which he had to stop the disorder. My petition was to no avail."

Sprague's position in the army was somewhat anomalous as he did not hold any regular commission. He had suggested earlier that he be commissioned as major general and that he would thus be in a better position to persuade the three-month men to enlist for longer periods of time. He claimed that his state would not accept a lower rank for their Governor and when he was offered a brigadier generalship, he declined, stating that he believed he could be of more service to the cause in his present position. Thus, at the Battle of Bull Run, Sprague, without a commission, was not protected by the laws of war.

He had proved his personal bravery under fire, but even that was never to blot out for him the bitter memory of the defeat. He returned to Rhode Island a hero and it was to be many years before he revealed his violent feelings about the "million dollar men." It would not do for the Governor to express such sentiments during wartime, when he must make every effort to enlist more men for the cause.

Sprague returned to the war in the fall and took part in several skirmishes in Western Virginia, near Harpers Ferry. But in the meantime, he had seen all he could of Kate and their romance flourished. He recalled an evening with her "with greater pleasure than ever," when they "sailed down the Potomac." It was an occasion "fraught with consequences of great importance to my personal relations and to my natural instincts. Do you remember," he asked Kate, "the hesitating kiss I stole and the glowing, blushing face that responded to the touch[?] I well remember it all. The step forward from the Cleveland meeting, and the enhanced poetical sensation. For it was poetry if there is ever such in life." [8]

Chase was growing a little disturbed at Kate's independence. She went off to New York for a visit in September and he wrote her pointedly: "I write at this time not knowing where you may be, as you have not thought it worth while to keep me advised of your movements." All that he had heard through a friend was that she had left New York. "I always feel anxious about you when I do not hear. It would hardly be too great a tax on your time to send me a few lines every day," he added plaintively.[9] It is possible that it was at this time that Kate made a quick trip to Providence and that the undated page of a letter of that period from her father reached her there: "I am sorry that you went to Providence, if, as I suppose, Gov. S—— is nothing to you except a friend. If any other relation is desired by him towards you I ought to know it," he wrote acidly.[10]

Chase had not noticed his daughter's deep interest in the young Governor. Close as they were, Kate was too reticent to confide in him and she had succeeded in keeping her feelings from him. Or perhaps he was simply too engrossed in himself to see what everyone else saw. Nettie was more observant possibly because she may have had a little crush on the handsome young Governor herself. Shortly after the New Year she wrote to Kate: "Dear Sister, I am going to ask you a question, which you may think I have no right, but I do love you so dearly, that all that concerns you *seems* to concern me also. Are you really engaged to Gov. Sprague? If you think it is not my business and I have no right to ask please say so and I will never ask you again." [11]

Nettie, at fourteen, had been sent off to boarding school to Miss Eastman, who had moved her school to Media and named it Brooke Hall. Nettie was extremely homesick and was having a hard time to settle down. She had loved the Christmas holidays at home and had started back to school with great reluctance. On her way back she was taken suddenly ill and Chase's good friends, the Jay Cookes, kept the child at their house in Philadelphia. Kate went at once to her sister. Everyone was concerned, as the illness was diagnosed as scarlet fever. Nettie made a good recovery, however, under the kind ministrations of the Cookes and of Kate, who herself was ill for a time. Chase was extremely anxious about his children and vastly relieved when they were both well again and Kate could return to Washington.

Nettie's letter, shortly after Kate's return to Washington, asking about her engagement to Sprague, may have upset Kate a good deal and perhaps her illness in Philadelphia had been more psychological than physical. For, with no explanation, a sudden stop had come to her relationship with Sprague.

Where and how he heard about it, who it was that told him, or wrote him is not known, but somehow, from somewhere he was informed of the scandalous gossip about Kate's Columbus days. Kate's "Ohio Friends" did not spare her then, nor were they to spare her on later occasions when they filled the mails with anonymous letters about her. No paragon of virtue himself, Sprague nevertheless would not consider paying court to a young lady whose reputation bore any blemish and he at once ceased his attentions to her completely.[12]

Sprague was a man of strange contradictions. In appearance he was of medium stature, slender, dark, mercurial, restless. Although he was impatient of conventionalities either of manners or of dress, he had been drawn to pay court to the daughter of one of the most correct and distinguished men in Washington. He was irritated by restraint or discipline and yet he longed for the firm guiding hand of his father and had terrifying nightmares about his tragic murder. At an early age he had achieved business and political success, yet deep down he was unsure of himself and longed to find assurance in dreams of martial glory, of valor on the battlefield, of a hero's life where doubts and uncertainties would be banished by the sweep of a shining saber. But the dark thoughts would not stay away and he would become wild and restless again, trying to find in drink and women escape from the endless questions of self-doubt that tormented him. He kept his inner conflicts well hidden, masked by a reserved and sometimes brusque manner. But one could sense in him deep, driving, unrevealed forces, violent ones, exciting ones to a woman. For women found him fascinating, as men of that type are always fascinating to them. And dangerous.

There was a girl in Providence who well knew Sprague's fascination and his danger. Her name was Mary Eliza Viall. She was young and impressionable and she fell desperately in love with William Sprague. She felt he resembled Napoleon. "There was the same eccentricity of manner and of dress," she was to recall, "that belief in a destiny, that antagonism for the lawyers; a custom, so to speak, of cloaking himself and his movements in a veil of mystery." [13] Although Mary Eliza came from a fine old Providence family, conservative and strict in background, she was taken up with all sorts of wild and romantic notions—of free love, of the right of a woman to bear a child out of wedlock. She wanted her "Launcelot," as she sometimes thought of Sprague, to be the father. Her infatuation with him was beyond all bounds of reason or control. To her he was perfection and she always remembered him as he rode off to war at the head of the Rhode Island regiment when, in her description, "there was not a man, woman or child, in all that vast crowd assembled along the line of march, who did not gaze with wonder and admiration upon the handsome cavalier, the magnificent patriot, the noble young man going forth from their midst to fight for them—for Liberty and God." [14] Small wonder that Sprague was caught up in an affair with this passionate adorer, but he did not choose to marry her when the baby she wanted was on the way. Her family was distraught. A hasty marriage of convenience was arranged with a young man named Anderson who vanished as soon as the formalities had been observed.

In spite of Sprague's treatment of her, Mary Eliza never ceased to love him and many years later she poured out her still turbulent emotions in a small book in which the whole story is scarcely veiled at all. There she described the tormented feelings of the girl she had been: "To *her,* it was no *part,* nothing to take up and put down, to remember and forget. It was the whole. All else was only waiting, and yet she served; all else but sleeping out the great gap of time her Antony is away . . . It must *needs* a week, to live out the memory of the last look, the last embrace . . . The postman's rap . . . startled her with the wild fancy it *might* be *he* . . . It never was . . . Ten times more in love, than all else, do we value lost treasure." [15] She tried to explain his rejection of her saying that "a man may love a woman too well to marry her . . . What if, in so doing, he must needs sacrifice a human heart, upon the altar of his ambition—*call* it what we may? Will not the true love sacrifice itself for the beloved? Did he not honor her by believing she asked for his glory, though he must win it without *her?* She forgave him." [16]

The whole affair was hushed up, although there were people who said that it had been the reason for Sprague's trip abroad. There were rumors and whispers, of course, but the fact that they were true did not affect Sprague's position or career at all. Nor did it soften his immediate reaction to the gossip he had heard about Kate Chase. When he suddenly stopped even seeing her, it was a rude and bitter shock for Kate, especially as she could not have had the slightest idea as to what had caused the break.

Even the interesting life of Washington must have seemed bleak and hard to her after this blow, and in June she left for Ohio where she visited her grandmother and other relatives and friends. Whoever was responsible for the breakup of her romance with Governor Sprague must have gloated that summer to see Kate without her fine Governor in attendance.

Chase missed her sorely. "You left us on Thursday the 19th," he wrote her "and the house seemed very dull after you were gone." [17] He wrote her often and his letters were filled not only with the minutiae of his everyday life but with news and views on the political and military situation. She was his confidante, the one person he could be absolutely sure of. He wrote her in great detail of McClellan's defeat before Richmond adding: "I write you very freely. Say nothing of what I write unless the news is in the papers. I trust your sense and prudence." [18]

Chase was growing restive and frustrated. As always, he was sure that he understood the problems facing the country more clearly than anyone else. "Everybody is full of speculation concerning the causes of our late disaster. *I know them,*" he wrote Kate confidently.[19] But he thought that his counsels were little heeded and began to feel that it was "more and more doubtful whether I can remain here. The war is at a standstill . . . Heaven save our poor country!" [20]

In spite of his prodigious duties and the burdens of trying to finance the rapidly increasing costs of the war, the summer for Chase, with both his daughters absent, was not all hard work and grim news. There were plenty of charming ladies, only too eager to shower him with attentions. His old friend Miss Susan Walker was nearby in Baltimore serving at the Army hospital there, and Chase invited her to Washington for a visit during the stay of his friends the Cookes. An attractive widow, Mrs. Carlotta Eastman, corresponded regularly with him when she was not in Washington.

Mrs. Eastman came closer than any of the others to intriguing Chase into contemplating a fourth marriage. The lady would have been more than willing, but Chase never considered it with any real seriousness. Although Kate and Mrs. Eastman were not very compatible, Chase was to keep up the gentle, intermittent flirtation with Mrs. Eastman for some years.

In spite of the fact that Chase treated Kate as an equal when it suited him, there were still flashes of the old parental displeasure and autocracy. "A daughter ought in all things to respect a father's feelings," he wrote her severely, "and if wishes conflict and no moral principle is compromised by yielding, she ought to yield gracefully, kindly, cordially. You will easily remember instances in which you have tried me pretty severely by not doing so." [21]

Kate was not happy that summer in Ohio and her father's letters and his affection meant a great deal to her. "Your appreciation of my long letter as a mark of love and confidence and the gratification it gave you are more than ample reward for the time and trouble of writing it," he told her. "My confidence will be entire when you entirely give me yours," he continued, "and when I feel —that is, am made by your acts and words to feel that nothing is held back from me which a father should know of the thoughts, sentiments and acts of a daughter. Cannot this entire confidence be given me? You will, I am sure, be happier and so shall I." [22]

Poor Chase. How little he understood young girls, especially his daughter Kate. He believed that she should confide in him her most secret feelings and thoughts at an age when reticence with parents comes naturally, even with extroverted natures. Nettie was an affectionate, outgoing little girl who bubbled on happily in a delightfully humorous way about her friends, her likes and dislikes among them, her teachers, and all her various little doings. But Kate had always had a natural reserve, greatly increased by her early life. Fond as he was of his younger daughter, it was to Kate that Chase showed his greatest attachment. Nettie was even sometimes jealous and had written to Kate after her illness in January: "I have not received any letter from home since you left and when *you* were here Father wrote every day." [23] Chase enjoyed Nettie enormously—no one could help loving that winsome little creature

—but it was from Kate that he demanded a total sharing of all facets of her life. This she was unable to give him. There would always be corners of her heart that she kept secret from him. Especially during that long summer in Ohio. She could not bring herself to bare the sadness and humiliation she felt concerning her interrupted relationship with William Sprague.

Kate took out some of her frustration in care and solicitude for her Grandmother Smith and finally prevailed on her father reluctantly to invite her to stay with them in Washington. "I enclose the note to your grandmother which you suggested, and shall be glad to join you in making her as contented here, if she comes, as possible," he wrote Kate without much enthusiasm. "One of the things in you which I love best is your thoughtfulness of her." 24

Nettie joined Kate in Ohio when school ended for the summer and later the two girls journeyed east together, stopping on the way to visit the wife of General McDowell in upper New York State. Nettie enjoyed her visit, but Kate found it dull and soon managed to get off for a few days to Saratoga with friends. She had had a dreary enough summer as it was.

Sprague, in the meantime, had been dividing his time between his official duties in Providence and service with the army. He acted as advance scout and was commended in several dispatches. After McClellan's defeat at Richmond, Sprague was as discouraged as everyone else and evolved a plan which he proposed in a letter to Lincoln. What he suggested was that the Army of the West, under General Halleck, sweep north and relieve the pressure on McClellan. Lincoln agreed to let him visit Halleck in Corinth on the Mississippi-Tennessee border and consult him about such a plan if it did not endanger the operations in the Southwest. After Sprague's arrival, Halleck wrote the President and the end result was not the projected sweep, but Halleck's appointment as commander of all the Union armies.

Kate undoubtedly read of Sprague's exploits and his mission to Halleck, but she did not see him when she and Nettie returned to Washington in the autumn. Nettie soon went off again to school, this time to Mrs. Macauley's school in New York, an interesting choice and one in which Kate may have participated, for Mrs.

Macaulay was Miss Haines's chief rival in that city. The house in Washington was full, as always, of visiting friends and family, and a wounded officer stayed for a long convalescence. Although some six years later a lady columnist wrote about Kate that she "shrinks from the hard and lowly task of visiting the wretched hut, the sick, and the afflicted," [25] a letter from Nettie reports that she had heard from a friend "saying that she had read of you in one of the Chicago papers as an 'angel of mercy tending to the sick soldiers.' " And she commented, "Quite romantic." [26]

Whatever her activities in regard to the sick and wounded were, one thing is certain—Kate had not forgotten William Sprague. He had been reelected Governor for the third time but resigned shortly in order to assume, in March of 1863, the office of United States Senator. His fighting days were over. He would soon come permanently to Washington to assume his new post.

Sprague, too, had not forgotten Kate. Almost a year had passed since he had seen her, but she was never long out of his thoughts. One day he met a gentleman from Columbus and asked him about the charges against Kate. When he was assured that, although she might have been a little indiscreet, she was always considered to be a respectable young lady, Sprague could not control his impetuosity and went to call on Kate the same evening.[27]

Years later when Sprague recalled the poetry of his first stolen kiss he also remembered: "Then came the blank. Wherever there is day there must be night . . . So with us it came. We will cover that with a veil, but the shadow past [sic]. We did again join hands, and again our fortunes." [28]

The trial that their relationship had been through during the past year had done nothing to diminish the strength of their feelings for one another. Kate had been deeply hurt and Sprague assured her that, "I will now make up to you for all you have imagined from my past want of consideration and justice to you." [29] The ugly anonymous letters from Ohio were soon to start up again, but now Sprague would pay no attention to them.

Many young ladies were disappointed by Kate's evident success with the young Governor. On one occasion when a new warship was being tried out off New York, Kate, her father, Sprague, and a distinguished company, which included the daughters of several wealthy New York families, were on board; one of these girls returned home that evening in a sulky humor. "Kate Chase and Senator Sprague were on board," she grumbled, "and Kate got the Senator on one corner of the ship and kept him entirely to herself." And she added acidly, "I cannot see what there is to admire in that girl." [30] Kate had walked off with the biggest catch of the times, and the other girls were green with envy.

The one remaining problem was how to break the news to Chase and how he would react to the thought that his beloved Katie wanted to marry. A trip to New England was arranged, which included a visit to Providence where Chase was received with a pomp and acclaim that put him in an excellent humor. Sprague set himself out to please and impress the man who he hoped would accept him as son-in-law, but he left the first steps of the delicate affair to Kate, who undoubtedly convinced him that this was the best way. In spite of the fact that even he must by now have begun to understand the state of affairs between Kate and Sprague, Chase was evidently as demanding as ever with her, judging from a letter Sprague wrote her immediately after the Providence visit: "You are forgiven before you asked me . . . I not only forgive you, if you want me to, but cannot see how you could avoid doing your father's bidding, as he has a way of having things about as he thinks best; even his daughters." Sprague admired Chase and knowing Kate's devotion to her father made sure to impress her with this fact: "I like him for his talents, the dignity and influence of his presence, his successes, his perseverance, *himself.*" And he added cautiously: "I shall be glad to hear from you when you reach home all about our hopes and fears." [31]

Chase accepted the news with equanimity and gave a guarded consent to the engagement. Although Sprague would have liked to be married at once, no definite date for the wedding was set.

Chase sincerely liked his prospective son-in-law and admired his business and political successes. What he hoped for Kate, as he had once written her, was to see her united "to a really worthy and good man—a gentleman—and a Christian gentleman who would be to you the affectionate protector you need." [32] Did Chase really believe that Sprague was such a man? Quite certainly he did. Intelligent and experienced as Chase was, nevertheless he was almost incredibly naive about people and his judgments of them were often shallow and mistaken. Too often he saw in people only a reflection of what he hoped to see.

CHAPTER

VI

ALTHOUGH Chase had agreed to the engagement, he predictably felt that the young pair should pass through a trial period which would test the strength and reality of their feelings and that the greater part of this time should be spent apart. He did not seem to appreciate the fact that they had already passed such a test in the year-long break in their relationship. And so in early June, after a brief visit to Washington, Sprague returned alone to Providence to look after his business affairs. His feelings were mixed. On the one hand, he missed Kate dreadfully, but he also knew that he must bow to her father's wishes.

Sprague, with his inner insecurities, was drawn strongly to Chase's solid self-confidence and he looked to the older man as the embodiment of the father-image he had been so cruelly deprived of. "To get the esteem of one like your father is a great satisfaction to me," he wrote Kate soon after they parted, "and now to have excited in him anything like affection is second only to my hope in yours." But all this does not make the separation easier. "As a drowning man seizing at anything to sustain him so I grasped your looked for note. You do not, cannot know how strong a hold you have upon me." [1]

Chase, as always wanting to be wholly within Kate's confidence, read the letters which Sprague wrote to her. Fortunately for the young pair he was favorably impressed by them and promptly wrote Sprague approvingly: "Katie showed me yesterday your letters to her and I cannot refrain from telling you how much they delighted me. The manly affection expressed in them satisfied me that I had not given my daughter to one [who] did not fully appreciate her, or to whom she could not give the full wealth of her affections. It is said that there are fathers who wish to retain the love and duty of daughters even in larger measure [than] that [which] they shall give to their husbands. If there are I am sure I cannot be one of them. I want to have Kate honor and love you with the honor and love far exceeding any due to me and I shall feel happiest when she makes your happiness most complete." [2]

It looked as though Sprague was beginning to pass muster with his highly critical prospective father-in-law and he wrote Kate at once delightedly: "I was not mistaken in my confidence when I placed it all with him," he told her. "We must be guided by his better judgement and his affectionate interest. You must fortify yourself to bear the separation from daily contact with a father's restraint and affection for the watchful care of one who will try to make his place less vacant." But he adds a little plaintively, "I don't know about my letters being exposed to the inspection of other eyes than one who will look over the faults and see only improvement in the future, but as the last experience was so pleasant I will not complain." [3]

Although he wrote smugly to Sprague that he was not the kind of father who wished to retain a larger share than her husband of the love and duty of a daughter, the thought of losing Kate was evidently painful to him. They had been such good companions for so long. It is not hard to imagine that Chase was not only a little bewildered but hardly pleased to see his Kate so much in love, so occupied with her fiancé, writing and receiving daily letters, even hinting hopefully at a September wedding date. He was sincere, as he always was, in his protestations that he wanted Kate's first loyalty to be toward her future husband, but it was difficult to break his habit of supremacy and he could not help feeling a little sorry for himself. Knowing Chase's demand for attention and affection, his petulance when he felt neglected, he must sometimes have sighed and made allusions to his impending loneliness.

If Kate felt responsible and protective toward her Grandmother Smith, how much more did she feel so now to her father, and as she observed Sprague's growing affection for Chase and his desire to be under his influence and guidance, she suggested that her father might make his home with them. Such an arrangement was hardly the rare thing then that it is now and there had always been relatives living in the Chase household.

Chase at first expressed some hesitation about the plan. As he was always to want to appear as a reluctant political candidate who would serve only if he were sought out, in this instance too he wanted to be persuaded. Kate found a ready ally in Sprague. "I hold to the old opinion that it would be better for me to have a guide in my new career," he wrote her. "I am a child and feel like one. Whether it would be as well for you I cannot tell. Your father has his doubts. It is this which makes him hesitate. That it would be agreeable to you none doubts. That it is admirable in you to feel a father's interests and pleasures so keenly all will admit. I might fear that the contrast between myself and your father would tell against me in *your* eyes, but of that I must take the risk. It will make little difference whether it is exhibited under the same roof or not." [4]

Sprague was still somewhat in awe of Chase and preferred not to write directly to him about all this but to send messages through Kate. Nevertheless he had no anxiety that Kate would love him less because of her devotion to her father. Quite the contrary.

In spite of this high-minded devotion of the young couple to Chase and Kate's eagerness to include him in her new life, he was not always easy to get along with that summer. He fussed at Kate about all sorts of little things and she sometimes complained to her fiancé about these misunderstandings. "My darling," Sprague assured her, "you will find no such companion in me. I will take and share the responsibility with you." And Kate's problems with her father raised questions in his mind for the first time about sharing a household with someone as accustomed to wield complete authority in his home as Chase. He was determined to make clear that he would not have Kate subjected to any interference with her prerogatives once they were married. "I could never consent to occupy any house with a divided authority. Where I live the house which is to cover us must have no power in it but yours. We may visit. We may journey. We may do anything which we think it expedient to do, but our permanent home must be that which we command without the first vestige of conflicting authority." [5]

Part of Sprague's reactions were occasioned by Kate's confidences to him about some of her problems with her father. But he was already beginning himself to feel frustrated at the continuing delay in Chase's permission for any firm plans, either for the summer or for a wedding date. He was worried about Kate's health and could not understand why at the very least Chase did not allow her to leave the unhealthy climate of Washington. Besides, he longed to see her. Kate finally prevailed on her father to allow them to meet for a short trip up the Hudson, heavily chaperoned, and a visit with Mrs. McDowell. Sprague wrote Chase happily that "the fresh air, the scenery . . . and the novelty of the excursion has worked very favorably to Kate's health, which was almost broken after her arrival." [6] The brief pleasant interlude did little to assuage Sprague's frustration, however, and he grew increasingly impatient at Chase's attitude.

"I have written your father, I think *three* letters," he grumbled, "[in] one of which I requested an answer, the other two referring to our various trips and have received no reply. Perhaps I am the *Jonah*. Perhaps he has repented of his consent to give me his daughter and does not care to listen to any arrangements. You may be the sufferer for my faults." Evidently the scandal mongers had been busy again not only against Kate but against Sprague too, for he continues: "His ears may have been open to similar attacks as your own has been and he is looking for something 'to turn up' to protect his darling from the evil communion of one he has consented to confide her to." And he tells her with some bitterness that someone said that "the length of time taken to consummate our marriage might end in no consummation. Small minds resort to small and despicable measures." But his primary frustration is with Chase. "Your father, troubled and embarrassed by the multitude and conflicting duties which are thrust upon him, may find no thought for that which he dreads to have [take] place. He may view with reluctance any innovations upon his own arranged plans. At any rate, time will determine and events will give us a place whether with or without the consent or plans of those we look to for them." [7]

Kate must have been distressed by this letter and more than a little worried. Caught between her father's self-engrossment and obstinacy and her fiancé's impatience, she saw that she must try to persuade her father that things could not continue in this way and make him realize that Sprague could not be treated in such a cavalier fashion, even if she herself could be. She was evidently successful in this for a few days later Sprague wrote her, "I have had three letters from your father. I am afraid it rather chokes him to write but am none the less gratified . . . I hope now before the summer is entirely gone your father will decide that you may have a little more invigorating air. Let him limit my indulgence of your society as he deems best. I am an encumbrance but I must not stand in the way of a proper attention to health, etc." [8]

In spite of his impatience with Chase's dilatory behavior and his clear understanding of the older man's possessive attitude toward his daughter, Sprague rather strangely sometimes acted as his advocate when Kate complained of some decision she found harsh, and he tried to find a reasonable explanation for her father's actions toward her.

In August Chase relented and allowed Kate to join her fiancé, along with Nettie and some friends for a few weeks holiday. Sprague was a great believer in the air of "old ocean" and he took her for the first time for a week's visit to Narragansett, where she was to spend so many later years. There was a pleasant cruise along the coast and the party was a gay one.

Kate's father was not the only jealous one in the family, however. Fanny Sprague found it hard to accept the new element in her son's life. "My mother is *still jealous* (a little only) of my darling," Sprague told Kate.[9] And his sister, too. "Mother says my sister Almyra a day or two since, began to feel that she was alone in the world. Nobody to love her. Nobody cared for her and everything dark and gloomy. I love her more for feeling so, as it rests with me to show her to the contrary . . . You my darling will help me will you not?" [10]

Sprague was a little anxious about Kate's first meeting as his fiancée with his family. He had assured her before she came: "I will see that my family are put in the right way and," he cautioned, "you must then exercise your own good judgement to represent yourself as you really are." Kate was full of good resolutions and some apprehensions herself, for Sprague added: "My dear as to being 'worthy of me' I will hear no more of it. That distinction can not be permitted a moment as it is not so in reality. Don't be modest in that respect to please even one you love best." [11]

With all her good resolutions, however, the meeting was not a success, and Kate evidently did not behave very well. Although Sprague was understanding with her about it, he did not let her off what he expected of her toward his family. "I am glad you wrote Mother. I made no explanation of your STRANGE conduct in fact I have made none at all. Write please to Mrs. Amasa Sprague. She expected you, is sensitive very. So is Mr. Amasa. Tell her you will hereafter & so forth & so on. You send it to me and I will see if it is all right." Then, he goes on forgivingly: "Now let me tell you that I am delighted with your note. I don't know how to be separated from you, but we must make the best of it. I am as one lost." [12]

Kate and Fanny Sprague eventually became good friends, though it took time, but Kate was never to get on well with Sprague's brother, Amasa, whom she found crude and negligent in his manners. Everyone had evidently been tense at this first meeting and Kate most of all.

Part of her "strange conduct," however, was undoubtedly due to the fact that she and Sprague had for the first time each met head on the fiery temper of the other, and it was a shattering experience for both. "I trust we may never undergo another such crisis of great discomfort and discouragement," Sprague wrote her after her return to Washington. "We must set, each of us, a guard upon ourselves and be careful of each other's temper. We must not be such cowards as to allow it to control us." [13] The quarrel was soon forgotten, however, and they seemed closer even than before.

One of the things that Sprague had been busy about on his occasional trips to New York was the choice of a suitable wedding present for Kate. He had been very much put off at first by the publicity which attended their every movement and was almost tempted to have something made in Europe instead of trying to purchase it in this country. His choice, however, finally fell on a handsome diamond-and-pearl tiara and bracelet from Tiffany. Sprague consulted with Kate's friends, General and Mrs. McDowell, who went to Tiffany's and made suggestions about how it could be designed so that parts of the tiara could be worn separately as a necklace and brooch. "The original agreement was $5000 for the two pieces," Sprague confided to Kate. "Gen'l McDowell's additions run it up to 5500 and I included ear rings which still advances it to 6000 to 6500$." [14] As he wanted it to suit her in every way, he urged her to have no delicacy about going to Tiffany's to see it, which she later did. Kate was enchanted with the lovely gift but evidently wrote him with some concern about the cost, for he answered her: "I am not sorry I named to you the price. It is not extravagant in the general sense. It is merely bending to the scheme of my own devotions." And he begs her to "let me indulge only once. You know I am but gratifying my own desires when I contribute to your pleasure. I have earned the right to do this." [15]

Newspapers later reported on the beautiful gift and *Harper's Weekly* among others gave a full description of it, accompanied by a large sketch. The cost of it became more and more inflated in the public mind until it was generally said and believed that Sprague had spent $50,000 on his gift to his bride.[16]

Exaggerated newspaper reports were not all the young pair had to contend with, however. It was the old story of anonymous letters again. "I rec'd yesterday one of *those* notes which I did not for a moment hold in my hands but consigned to oblivion." And Sprague warns Kate, "You may have others. So do with them likewise." [17] The notes continued through the whole summer and Sprague reported their arrival with repugnance. "I am again a little annoyed by an unsigned note," Sprague complained. "Your Ohio friends are getting desperate. I wonder if you are attacked in a like manner. What cowardly sneaking wretches they are." [18]

Chase had finally been prevailed upon to allow them to set a wedding date in November and as the time began at last to draw near Kate's letters were full of plans and of all the fine things she was buying for her trousseau. "I wish I could buy you all the pretty things you name," Sprague responded. "It will be some comfort hereafter in doing so." [19] Kate was in a flurry of activity making arrangements for the wedding and the reception afterward, and one of the bills found its way by accident into a letter to her fiancé. "I return you a bill which I presume you enclosed by mistake." And he asks: "May I send you the money for these bills and you pay them[?] I am anxious that some course should be adopted concerning them, as I wish to save you from any inconvenience." [20]

It would be easy to suppose that Kate had purposely enclosed the bill for Sprague to see, hoping that he would react exactly as he did. But Kate's reply was sharp and Sprague hastened to smooth her ruffled feelings: "I asked for the bills to relieve you; forgive me if I have been too blunt about it. I would not be so. Please do as you think best and when *you know* just what you prefer me to do let me know." [21]

Like most girls, Kate was excited and pleased with all the fuss and fanfare, with the presents and the trousseau and all the trappings of a big wedding. Sprague was hardly of a similar temperament, but he wanted to indulge her as much as he could. He describes a handsome set of silver goblets and pitcher from Providence friends and adds, "Amasa is upon horses and is hunting up the country for the best pair that can be found . . . his wife shall do something very uncommon. Mother will carry out your idea as talked over with you by Mrs. McDowell. For my own part, my birdy, I would rather these things were not to come, but I presume you are rather worldly yet and find pleasure in all the fine 'things' that the great Father has permitted us to enjoy. I think that my old-fashioned ways will bye and bye find favor with you but I can hardly expect it now from my elegant and accomplished partner. With me all the 'appearances' of life have little attraction, except

[if] the mind, the appreciation and the correct knowledge of them can go with it. You, my darling, will I trust know how to appreciate the gloss from the reality." [22]

Chase too may have been somewhat overwhelmed with all this female flutter and flurry and perhaps began almost to look forward to having another man in the house. The living arrangements had finally been agreed upon. Sprague was arranging to purchase, for $32,000, the house at Sixth and E streets which Chase had been renting, for he had no desire to make his home in a house he did not own. Chase would pay a share of the household expenses. Chase had been in a very bad humor when Kate returned from her holiday trip. Sprague well understood the reason for this and did his best to comfort her. "I am sorry you are in trouble but never mind. . . . I did write a short note to your father, but I did so to in some respects lessen his manner towards you as I had begun to think that I might be more the cause of his displeasure than yourself. I am the cause of your neglect of him. I kept you away and I caused you trouble. I am, my dear, loving you more as others put discomforts upon you. You may lose one way, but you will gain another." [23]

As the wedding date approached, however, Chase became more reconciled to the prospect of Kate's divided allegiance and he sent Sprague what amounted to a formal renunciation: "Katie is very dear to me, and I commit the solitary care of her and for her which I have used for so many years over to you, without emotion. As she has gained in experience in life, she has certainly become more thoughtful, more affectionate, more loving and at this hour is aware of their use." Sprague quotes this to Kate and his comment is that "she is at this hour aware *to me* [of] their use. I shall treasure his letter and try to be worthy of his confidence." [24] And he responded with a long, revealing letter in which he assured Chase that "I think I realize the delicate link which has so long united father and daughter . . . and that I know something of the great soul of the one, and its counterpart in the other . . . and [I] shall never be happier than when contributing to continue the same relation . . . If resolves are anything. If a single mind and heart absorbed in the happiness of another can be any guarantee of a bright and happy future for Katie, I think I can faithfully and truly promise it to her." And then in a burst of confidence he tells at length of his dissatisfaction with his past life and his hopes for the future.[25]

Sprague had resolved to curb his habits of drinking and smoking. He recognized his weakness for drink and the harm it had done him and although Chase had learned to unbend in the question of alcohol a little, even allowing wine to be served at his table, Sprague well knew what were the older man's feelings, and undoubtedly Kate's to some extent too, toward liquor. Typically, he put off the reform until almost the last moment and it was only three weeks before the wedding that he warned Kate: "I shall I fear be very cross for a few days as I have stopped the use of the weed which stills but does not satisfy." [26] Tobacco was a danger, he felt, because after it "follows brandies and whiskies. Then dispepsia and an unhappy life. Look out for this won't you my love," he begs Kate. "You won't have tobacco smoke about, or whisky or brandy and then we will have no war." [27]

Sprague's impatience at the months of waiting had not diminished as the wedding approached. His restlessness and the reversals in the war had even tempted him at one point to take up "again the sword . . . but alas I am not my own master and you are making me less so daily." [28] Three weeks before the wedding he wrote her, "You cannot imagine (I don't believe you can) how utterly lonely I am." [29] His mood would soar quickly at a "Splendid letter" from Kate. ". . . to get *such a letter*. Well! *I don't know what I shall do*." [30] But he could not stand much more. His nervous temperament had been strained almost to the breaking point and when he received a telegram from Kate, at the last moment, telling him to hold the cards of invitation for the wedding until he received her letter, the full force of his pent-up feelings exploded: "[I] am impatient to know the reason why I may not issue the cards. Must I wait for your explanation[?] What explanation must I expect? Are you to put of[f] the time[?] Are you to continue the torture[?] Must I be forced to forgo that which absorbs all my thoughts and unfits me to live or breath[e?] You don't know my darling how much I suffer. Mrs. Frieze says she would like so much to see one of my letters to you. Shall I send her this[?]" And he tells her what Mrs. Frieze said to him: " 'You who never expressed a sentiment in your life, a consummate old bachelor, now to talk on of being engaged or of loving anyone. I should have thought as much of an untamed horse. No I cannot believe it.' Thus my dear was I commented upon. Had you married me at once, offhand, all this would have been passed, not thought of, much less said. Have you never relented[?] You have much to thank me for. If I had known what I was to undergo, you would not have found me so willing and plastic in your hands. I shall be careful in future." He goes on to tell her that a white marble mantle that had arrived broken could be repaired. *"We can mend the marble,* but when human stays are broken, when the pillars which sustain and carry on God's handiwork are severed; we cannot bring them thus easily together. I see you tonight so clearly. I so want you in my arms. I am so lonely. I am so heartsick. I will get over this. I strive and strive. I shall soon become desperate and will then I hope have an antidote for that which is consuming me. Darling good night. Say something to help me, or do something to change the current of my thoughts. Is this the reserved, cold uncommunicative man which you have tied yourself to[?] Forgive the childishness of it all and I will be different bye and bye, as if I feel I need not make my feelings overpowering, strengthening by repetition. My darling birdy good night. Angels guard you." [31]

Here, in this strange, wild letter are revealed the dangers facing these two passionate, strong-willed people. Sprague had deep reaches in his nature of violence and despair. Accustomed to having his own way, unused to self-discipline, he reacted explosively to frustration or restraint. With his lack of self-confidence, any disappointment or obstacle could send him plummeting into the depths of gloom and then he grew wild and uncontrollable.

Kate felt that Sprague was "reserved, cold, uncommunicative" in spite of the obvious love and dependency that so often filled his letters. "Funny Kate! She desires love." It was as true of her now as when she had been a small child. She was a woman of power, both in intellect and femininity, and her whole being sought a "pervading, tender devoted love" [32] to which she could give herself completely. Sprague's feelings for her were equally strong, but he was like an "untamed horse" which must have its head, free to do as he pleased. Had there been less passion in the attachment of these two who were basically so unsuited to each other much of their future unhappiness could have been avoided.

CHAPTER
❧❧❧ VII ❧❧❧

W ASHINGTON SOCIETY was making merry with a vengeance, two and three parties a night, dinners, balls, receptions, matinees crowded the days and lengthened the nights until almost dawn. One of the most important events that introduced the new season was the marriage of Kate Chase and William Sprague, at half past eight in the evening of November 12, 1863. Kate looked ravishing "in a gorgeous white velvet dress, with an extended train, and upon her head wore a rich lace veil. But little or no other ornament was perceived upon her person. The Senator was clad in a suit of rich black cloth, with the usual addition of a white satin vest." [1] The ceremony was performed by Bishop Clark of Rhode Island in the presence of some fifty close friends and relatives in the parlor of the house on Sixth and E streets. Some five hundred guests attended the reception which followed immediately afterward.

President Lincoln "came in his private carriage, without escort and alone." Mrs. Lincoln was still in mourning for her son Willie. Other guests included members of the Cabinet, foreign ministers, and distinguished military figures. The Marine Band furnished music for dancing and a wedding march composed for the occasion and dedicated to the bride.

Lines of carriages filled the street outside the house, where a large crowd had gathered to see the dignitaries. "They were very good-natured, as large crowds generally are . . . As one [carriage] after the other discharged their inmates, some spicy and good-natured remarks were passed by the eager crowd in attendance."

Among the five hundred guests at the reception were many who had come to see Kate sacrifice herself, as they thought, on the altar of her father's ambition, and her own, convinced as they were that she was throwing herself away on a man she did not love for the sake of his money and what it could do to advance her father's career. Kate knew the ugly whispers about her marriage, the continuing stream of anonymous letters would have accomplished that if nothing else. She scorned, as she had always done, any sort of reply or reaction and only those most intimate and close to her, and they were very few, had the slightest idea of her real feelings. Kate was proud and confident and she felt secure in her future. Long afterward she told a friend, "You, at least, have never made the mistake that I made. I never cared for the opinion or goodwill of people. I ran my head against a stone wall. It did not hurt the wall but it has hurt the head." [2] Only once in her life would she try to explain herself and her actions and it led to even greater attacks on her, for by then the hard image was fixed in the public mind and she could no longer change it. But when she married, the dark clouds of the future had not yet formed and Kate had no need to justify herself or parade her private feelings. Five years afterward in her diary she was to describe herself as she had been on the eve of her wedding, in words which reveal a very different Kate Chase than the one which has endured for more than a century, that of an ambitious woman, hard and cold as a diamond, incapable of feeling for anyone beyond herself except for an almost unnatural love for her father, which fixed on him more as a means for fulfilling her own obsessive ambition than a tender object of a daughter's affection.

"Life was so real to me," she wrote, "my heart so warm and keen with sympathy, hope so confident, ambition high, and holy things so sacred. That night I spent in one long prayer, that in my new relation, I might fill each office to completeness, that to my waiting husband, I might be the messenger of every joy, and holding him above all, the dearest and the best, I might become his companion, friend, and advocate—that he might be, in a word—a husband satisfied. All there is of love and beauty, nobleness and gentleness, were woven in this fair dream, and I believed *no* future brighter than that our united lives spread before us—And the next night—when I was folded in that husband's loving arms, oh, the sense of ineffable rest, joy, and completeness. It was like a glimpse of Heaven for purity and peace. All strife ended, all regret silenced, in those strong arms I was a child, in security and trust. A lover won, a protector found, a husband to be cherished. Every thought, every desire, every feeling merged with the one longing to make him happy. Not a reserve in my heart, not a hidden corner he might not scan, the first, the only man that had found lodgement there!" [3]

The honeymoon started off in a gay continuation of the wedding festivities. After a brief stopover in New York, the young couple, accompanied by Fanny and Almyra Sprague, Nettie, and several members of the wedding party, went on to Providence where a royal welcome had been prepared for them. Alice Skinner, Kate's cousin and one of the bridesmaids, wrote Chase about the preposterous way the house had been decorated for their arrival—flags, red, white, and blue streamers, a huge arch with *Welcome* in gold letters. One of the guests was reminded of a horse fair, not too far-fetched a comparison in view of Amasa Sprague's interest in horses. The contrast between the discriminating taste of the elegant bride and that of her in-laws was striking and probably uncomfortable for both sides, for the "overwhelming" decorations were quickly removed after Kate's arrival.

There was a large reception of several hundred for the newlyweds which "passed off quite brilliantly," Sprague informed his father-in-law. Kate seemed "a little fatigued at the commencement but as progress was made she was herself again. She is very well indeed this morning and I think quite happy. Nettie chatters happy and gay and enjoyed herself hugely," he added.[4]

The last part of the wedding trip was to Ohio where Kate showed off her new husband and her handsome trousseau. They dropped Nettie at school in New York where she had a hard time settling down after the fun and excitement of the wedding parties, which she had enjoyed enormously.

Sprague took over most of the letter-writing duties with Chase during the honeymoon, dutifully informing him about their doings and reassuring him about how they were getting along. "I am delighted that you see a brighter future for us as I have known that you trembled a little for that which was yet a solution of that which was to come. We are happy. We feel we base it upon a foundation which will not give way. With God on our side, and the ever watchful eye and council of one so dearly loved, we share with you in feeling that misfortune can never come though trials may. I am glad you speak so of Katie's anxiety for your future and I am amply glad to have you speak of your connection with Mr. Lincoln." [5]

Coming into an election year, Chase's blood had begun again to heat up with active Presidential fever. His position in the Cabinet was becoming increasingly precarious and his friction with Seward had forced him once already to tender his resignation. He knew of the opposition to Lincoln, especially from the radical elements of the party, and he dreamed mightily that his time had come.

Lincoln was completely aware not only of Chase's aspirations for the Presidency, but of his active efforts to gain the Republican nomination, and told his secretary, John Hay, in the fall of 1863, that "it was very bad taste, but he had determined to shut his eyes to all these performances; that Chase made a good Secretary, and that he would keep him where he is: if he became President. All right! I hope we may never have a worse man. I have all along seen clearly his plan of strengthening himself . . . I am entirely indifferent to his success or failure in these schemes, so long as he does his duty as the head of the Treasury Department." [6] Hay also reported that Lincoln seemed "much amused at Chase's mad hunt for the Presidency."

Not all of Chase's supporters had their sights on the Presidency for him, however. Aged, doddering Chief Justice Taney could not be expected to live very much longer and there was some talk among Chase's friends of the possibility that this office would be offered him. Sprague had visited with Hiram Barney in New York a month before the wedding and wrote Kate what Barney had said about Chase's prospects. "Mr. Barney's conversation is upon the proposition of the Gov. acceptance of the Judge's position. He urges with much force [that] the bringing him forward as a candidate [for the Presidency] at this early day, brings upon him the opposition of the present powers who look themselves forward for an endorsement of their doings. He cites many instances of almost inevitable failure to reach the position by combinations, as they produce counter irritation. He urges the high position of the one proposed, the necessity to make the decisions here work with the acts of Congress, and the acts of the Administration upon them, the lifelong period and the greater dignity of it."

In spite of Sprague's disordered style, one thing is clear: Barney was dubious about Chase's chances for the Presidency and seemed instead to favor his appointment as Chief Justice. One other point is also clear: the political career of Salmon Chase was not a subject which absorbed a great deal of the attention of the two young people, for Sprague adds, "I don't know as this will be interesting to you. I don't know as I should write you about it at all, but let it go my darling for all it is worth." [7] After their marriage the newlyweds were even more absorbed with each other and their own affairs.

Shortly after their return to Washington, Sprague left for Providence to look after his business interests. Kate was desolate. "Shall I tell you," she wrote him, *"how I miss* you and how the sunshine has all gone from our beautiful house. Paradise is no paradise without a God and my Eden is indeed deserted. I absolutely felt afraid of the dark last night in my loneliness but, my own darling, I prayed God very earnestly before going to rest for your protection and safe return. The fire in your Sanctum burns cheerfully and bright—and there are letters lying for you unopened upon the table and I feel every now and then that you will come in with your accustomed smile and I shall have the joy of welcoming my husband home again. Oh darling, I hope these separations will not come *very* often. They are so hard to bear. She tells him what she has been doing—"the entire morning spent in talking over the *house* matters with Father and in making out *lists* with Auntie. I keep busy to be happy, as happy as possible without what embodies all that happiness consists in for me." Kate had a large household to take care of and in ordering some supplies from New York asks for "a sufficient quantity to last for *four (4) months* for a family of *16*." [8]

The purchase of the house at Sixth and E streets had not yet been completed and Kate explained that, "Father is unwilling to sign the Agreement for you until the question of furniture is disposed of. He tells me you agreed with him that you had better *own* everything from the start. I am not at all disposed to have you buy the dilapidated and worn out articles which Mr. V[arnum] leaves in the house and objected to that arrangement, Mr. V[arnum] himself telling me last evening that this question would just as well be detailed later. If I reject now what articles we should never wish to own it would leave a good portion of the house unfurnished. I don't know what to do. Father throws the responsibility of a decision upon me and when I make my decision objects to it." Chase was evidently up to his old habit of giving Kate freedom to decide things on her own with one hand, and taking it away by criticizing her decisions with the other. He was evidently having difficulty in breaking his habit of directing her, but Kate was determined that Sprague should be the one to wield authority, for she adds, "If you telegraph me dear as soon as this reaches you perhaps it will not be too late to help me out of the difficulty, for to you, darling, and to you only, do I turn now for help in all trouble and sympathy in all joy." [9]

Kate found this separation so soon after their marriage very hard to bear and she wrote with a warmth and freedom quite different than her usual reserved expression. "Oh my darling can you not shorten the long, weary hours of absence or does the constant occupation of your mind and attention shorten them for you. I hope it does my dear husband. I don't want you to feel as I do; my pillow grows more lonely and my rest less peaceful. Today it is dark and drizzling, not enough however to keep *me* indoors . . . I trust dearest William you have found your business and all else in *Providence* (I am jealous of the term *"at home"*) just as you have wished it and you will leave it in such good order that it will not require your personal supervision for a *long while.*" And then she chides him a little for neglect of her. "You have not sent me the Dispatch you promised nor have I this morning the letter I hoped for from New York. Forgotten so soon! Oh darling how could you serve me so?" [10]

Sprague, however, now that his strong sexual desire for her was no longer frustrated, was not as obsessed with the thought of Kate as he had been, nor did she represent the totality of things to him as he did to her. Although he had been three times Governor of Rhode Island and was now its Senator, he did not really like the political scene nor did he feel at home in it. In the Senate, he felt quite out of his depth among the famous men he saw there. In the world of business, however, he was a great deal more secure and sure of himself and was proud of his success and power. A widely printed newspaper article must have exacerbated these feelings and is indicative of the kind of publicity he and Kate were faced with: "Personally, Mr. Sprague is not attractive; pecuniarily, he is—several millions." Although admitting that he is "one of the best informed manufacturers in the country," it states that he is "wholly innocent of even an appropriate understanding of the arts or sciences, polite or vulgar literature." And it concludes that in the Senate "he will make no speeches, for he neither writes nor talks; he will not contribute to the dignity of the Senate, for he is small, thin and unprepossessing in appearance; he will vote regularly, and just as papa Chase tells him, and he will always regret that he forsook his congenial factory, where he made his mark and could hold his own with the best of them, for the marble halls of legislators, whom he can neither influence or comprehend." [11] Small wonder that he wrote Kate as he did after his return to Providence a few days after the appearance of this article: "I have been around today and am gratified with the faithfulness with which all my plans have been carried out. In my modest unobtrusive way at Washington, one would suppose I had no business or no interests, but they are the largest of their kind in the *world,*" he boasted. "I take pride in them, not so much for the money that is made out of them (for that is many times small) as for the great system that it has, and the power it controls." [12]

If Kate hoped that this first separation would not be repeated for a long while, she was soon disappointed, for Sprague came back for only a few days to Washington before returning once again to Providence two days before Christmas. "I am lonely but that you know," she wrote him the day after his second departure. "Nettie has just come in and taken us all by surprise and requires a good deal of attention. I must however take time enough to say good morning to the absent one." [13] Although the usual large household was swelled with extra visitors for the holiday, Kate wrote her husband every day at least once and sometimes twice. The vagaries of the post, however, caused some delay in her letters reaching him and he evidently reproached her for neglecting him. She was hurt and quick to answer: "I received your *brief* note written 'Sunday' this morning just as I was leaving home, and was a good deal grieved by the imputed reproach of 'forgetfulness' it contained. Of one thing always rest assured, if a promise I have made does not *appear* to have been kept, the fault is not mine. The day after you left home—Thursday—I wrote you *twice,* a hasty note in the morning when posting some official communications as you directed, and a longer letter in the evening. Since, I have written *every day* and in the *morning* until now, in order as I thought, to have my letters get off in the noon mails. I can only regret the delay that has prevented your receiving them darling for they were sent in such good faith." Kate's quick temper was ready to flare at any criticism, especially when it was not justified and she could not resist retaliating in kind: "I confess I thought it hard that five days should elapse before I heard a word from you. First came your telegram, then on the 27th an envelope was handed me with the loved superscription. Imagine my disappointment upon opening it to find nothing but two sheets of autographs. I hardly knew what to think. Later in the same day, the evening brought me your note of the 26th and a letter to Father saying you would not return for New Year's Day. That it was a bitter disappointment to me you well know. New Year's Day with us this year promises to be a great failure." But as she wrote her pique seemed to evaporate and she ended her letter: "Good night darling. May Angels guard you for your own wife." [14]

New Year's Day in Washington was by long custom a day for "at homes" with open house kept by all the high government officials and hostesses competing with each other for the number of callers who would drop in. The home of the Secretary of the Treasury had always been high on the list and would be so this year especially in view of the interest in Kate's recent marriage. She had hoped to have her husband beside her at her first official reception since her wedding, but Sprague had been free to follow his own whims and fancies too long to settle easily into double harness.

Early in their engagement, Sprague had once congratulated Kate "upon your success in reducing my turbulant [sic] subject to quiet submission and to glory in the chains which bind him." [15] But that was before they were married. Now he was not at all pleased by Kate's rather mild reproach and decided to make his position forcefully clear to her at once. "That your January festival will prove a failure I very much regret. I would that you would make it a success in consequence of my inability to be with you. And you would lighten my burden this much by exhibiting a willingness to deny yourself for that purpose. I am every moment engaged in large and numerous duties and engagements trying to do my best in every way, and I have a right to ask both your aid and sympathy. You my love are not I hope to prove an additional burden to me, as you certainly will do if my acts especially when devoted to duty, are the cause of any unhappiness, or want of success in any of your undertakings." [16]

Even before receiving this letter, however, Kate had repented her reproaches and had written a more encouraging letter which cheered Sprague greatly.

Fanny Sprague was happy to have her son at home and told Kate of his schedule which entailed spending the mornings in the counting room and then going in the afternoon to Cranston, where the mills were, and not returning home until nine or ten o'clock in the evening. "I am quite happy now," she tells Kate, "and shall be willing he should return to his duties again hoping he will be of use to his country." And then she adds a revealing remark: "If men could realize the sacrifice woman makes when she marries this world would be filled with happiness untold." [17]

When Sprague wrote Kate before their marriage that she would not "have tobacco smoke about or whiskey or brandy" he undoubtedly sincerely intended to give them up for good. He recognized that intemperance had been his great fault in the past and had led him into actions he regretted. In one of his confiding moods of self-deprecation he had written Chase, "I deem nearly all our defects occasioned by this practise; and I know that in my own life whatever of improprieties I may be charged with, is from this cause." [18] But at thirty-two, with deeply ingrained habits, a man who combined Sprague's moodiness and his weakness would hardly be able to change easily. How long he restrained himself is a question, but doubtless not for long and very probably he fell back into his old habits as soon as he returned to Providence, certainly no later than the unhappy anniversary of his father's death. The moodiness and excitability of his New Year's Eve letter, and the progressive illegibility of it, would so indicate.

Kate and Sprague were alike in several respects: each was highly sensitive, proud, quick to take offense and very much in love; each demanded a great deal of attention and devotion from the other, an overpowering amount; each was easily hurt by what was felt to be the least slight or lack of understanding on the part of the other. In many ways they differed. Undoubtedly Sprague's drinking was a source of conflict and certainly his indolent manner and eccentric behavior were. He did not like "society." Kate adored it. Politics did not really interest him. For Kate it was fascinating and absorbing. Both Kate and her father were confident and vocal in the expression of their ideas. Sprague was not. Nor did he have the cultural and intellectual interests which Kate enjoyed. Adding to the normal tensions and adjustments of the first year of marriage was the acute crisis that developed in Chase's political fortunes.

Chase's relationship with the President during the first weeks of 1864 were more strained than ever, due in part to Chase's defense of his friend, Hiram Barney, Collector of the Port of New York. Barney's management of his post had come under attack and Lincoln wanted to replace him. Chase, however, was adamant in his support of Barney and threatened once more to resign if Barney were replaced. Lincoln "backed down again" but the incident increased the tension between him and his Secretary of the Treasury.

In February, however, something occurred which was not so easily managed and which played a climactic role in Chase's hopes for the highest office. Senator Pomeroy, who was one of the leaders of a committee which had been formed to promote Chase's candidacy, decided that the time for action had come, and a circular was prepared, for confidential distribution. This Pomeroy circular was to prove explosive. Ostensibly secret and private, it of course fell into the hands not only of Lincoln supporters but of the press and was very soon made public. It was a clear and vicious attack on the President. It declared that not only was it "practically impossible" for him to be reelected, but if that should occur, "his manifest tendency towards compromises and temporary expedients of policy will become stronger during a second term . . . and the cause of human liberty, and the dignity of the nation, suffer proportionately"; that the "one-term" principle was "absolutely essential to the certain safety of our republican institutions" because of the power and the patronage of the Government. Chase, on the other hand, the circular went on to state, united "more of the qualities needed as President during the next four years than are combined in any other candidate; his record is clear and unimpeachable, showing him to be a statesman of rare ability and an administrator of the very highest order, while his private character furnishes the surest available guarantee of economy and purity in the management of public affairs." It ends by stating that a "central organization has been effected which already has its connections in all the States, and the object of which is to enable his friends everywhere most effectually to promote his elevation to the Presidency." [19]

The publication of the Pomeroy circular drew from Chase an immediate letter to Lincoln disclaiming any connection with it. "I had no knowledge of the existence of this letter before I saw it in the *Union*," he wrote. He described his meetings with "several gentlemen who called on me" expressing their desire that he allow his name to be submitted for consideration in the coming election, but went on to say that he had not been consulted in the organization of the committee or in its actions. If there was anything now in his action or position prejudicial to the public interest he begs Lincoln to tell him. "I do not wish to administer the Treasury Department one day without your entire confidence." And then he adds a note of sentiment. "For yourself I cherish sincere respect and esteem; and, permit me to add, affection. Differences of opinion as to administrative action have not changed these sentiments." [20]

Except for a brief note acknowledging the receipt of this letter, Lincoln waited a full week before answering it. He admitted knowledge of the Pomeroy circular several days before its publication, but added, "I have not yet read it, and I think I shall not." As for Chase's remaining in his present position it "is a question which I do not allow myself to consider from any standpoint other than my judgment of the public service; and, in that view, I do not perceive occasion for a change." [21]

In spite of their differences and the sore trial Chase often was to the President, Lincoln had real admiration for his abilities. "Chase is about one and a half times bigger than any other man that I ever knew," he once said.[22] He recognized that Chase was "a little insane" on the subject of the Presidency but he continued to hope that in spite of this Chase's abilities could be used to good effect.

In effect the Pomeroy circular and the extremely unpleasant impression it made destroyed any hope Chase might have had for the nomination, for in spite of his denial of any complicity in it, no one wholly believed him. Many even insisted that Kate had had a hand in writing it.[23] Not long afterward, Chase himself denied that she was in any way politically active and wrote a friend: "I am sure Katie would not be pleased if made aware of what use has been made of her name, so far as that has any political import. Her own good sense teaches her, and it is my earnest wish, that she should keep entirely aloof from everything connected with politics." [24] Certainly the days that Chase waited for the President's reaction to his explanation about the Pomeroy circular and for the repercussions of the whole ugly incident to die down, were anxious ones for him and he was well aware that not only was his position in the Cabinet hanging in the balance but even his whole political future. There is no indication that Kate was involved in any way—quite the contrary, for had she been politically active in all this, as she was accused of being, she would have been hard at work in Washington mending fences and using her influence in her father's behalf. Instead, she went blithely off to New York to visit Nettie, with one of the McDowell girls and Sprague's young cousin, Susie Hoyt.

Sprague accompanied them but continued on to Providence and Kate was glad that a mix-up in their baggage made it necessary for her to write him immediately "altho' you can not be more than 3 hours journey from me." She found Nettie "very bright and well and of course overjoyed to see me. She accepted your 'love' gratefully but says she thinks it rather hard she is never to see you." And then she confides: "Will you believe me, I am already homesick, and wish myself by your side. Don't neglect me, dear, as you did before, for a day without some tidings of you seems so very long." She asks him not to forget the calico cloth for Nettie, but mentions not one word about her father and his difficulties.[25]

After Sprague reached Providence his brother Amasa's wife fell seriously ill and he hoped that Kate would come and join him if he had to stay the week. But Kate was reluctant to go. It was not the dramatic events that were developing in her father's political fortunes that kept her away from her husband. She did not like Providence and felt suffocated by the "pinched, prejudiced narrow atmosphere" there. She did not feel at home with the people except, perhaps, for Fanny Sprague with whom she was on friendly, even if not very close, terms. Her relationship with her brother-in-law was strained, to say the least, and she found his conduct toward her lacking in all consideration or politeness. She was later to blame her husband for this, complaining to her diary that "William had seen his brother repeatedly offer me every rudeness short of positive insult without a thought of checking *him*, or protecting *me*, when a word or a look would have done it. And in these ways, he has made my place among his friends and family as difficult as possible." [26] Sprague was evidently aware of her feelings as in his letter suggesting that she join him he assured her: "No one would imagine you was here and you would be free from all but your own disposition—I have no wish to gratify except to see you and to be with you." But Kate was not to be persuaded. Two weeks later Amasa's wife died and Sprague remained until after the funeral.

There was more, however, than merely difficult social or family relationships that spoiled Providence for Kate. She had looked forward to sharing her husband's business interests and activities. "How happy and proud he might have made me in it," she confided later to her diary. "Instead, I have his letter, complaining (early in our relation) weakly to his *man of business* of his wife's different ideas and ways of life from his own. How my blood boiled in indignation when I read it, at the indelicacy of a husband retailing his annoyances to an employee or even a confidential friend." And then she asks: "Why should that letter have come to me[?] Whose is [the] hand, that has so persistently dropped poison into our cup." [27]

Who indeed? Evidently it was not only Kate's "Ohio friends" who tried to destroy her marriage. Someone had made sure that she would read this letter which she could only have found distressing. Incidents such as this were hardly conducive to a tranquil relationship and on at least one occasion Kate appealed to her father after a quarrel with her husband. But Sprague hastened to set her right on this point. "I go to New York tonight to be absent Wednesday. I have concluded as a special favor to forgive you all the unkindness you have put upon me believing it is more a fault of judgement than heart. I hope you will as a better guarantee of our continued happiness that you will not hereafter refer any of our differences to your father, as that can only bring on a difference which can not be healed." [28]

These two had an unusual power to hurt themselves and each other. Violent explosions of anger occurred often, but as with many people of fiery temperament, furious outbursts cleared the air and were followed by calm and happiness in a way that it is difficult for people of more placid disposition to understand. "Kate seems very happy," Chase observed. "She and her husband seem to love each other dearly. He is a noble fellow and I love him almost as much as she does." [29]

Kate's health, which had always been somewhat precarious, took a turn for the worse in the spring and everyone was very concerned about her for a while. "Katie is almost herself again after her illness, which frightened me not a little," Chase wrote Nettie in May. "Her husband was all devotion, and to be so petted it was almost worth while to be sick." And then, as so often before, he added plaintively "I wish I were out of official harness. It certainly grows more irksome. I have toiled hard and patiently, and it is painful to find my labors made the occasion of calumny and reviling. I am thankful, however, that no calumny or reviling can destroy any good I have accomplished.[30]

This latest outburst of discouragement was occasioned by a virulent attack against him in the Congress made by Frank Blair, a brother of one of Lincoln's Cabinet officers. The saying ran that when the Blairs went in for a fight they went in for a funeral, and when Blair finished he had accused Chase of practically every crime in the book: of corruption, of using patronage to further his ambitions, and public money for his own political ends.

Chase flew into one of his towering rages when he learned of it, and he wrote his old friend Jay Cooke: "I hope my wrathiness was not excessive. Indeed it was vexation in thinking that all my labors to serve our country had found recompense, so far as Mr. Lincoln's special friends were concerned, and with his apparent (but, as I hope and believe, merely apparent) indorsement, only in outrageous calumny . . . On Monday I learned that the Ohio delegation had called on the President, who disavowed in the most explicit terms all connection with, or responsibility for, Blair's assault, and expressed his decided disapproval of it." [31]

By this time Chase's sensitive nerves were raw and even patient Lincoln found the strained relationship with his Secretary increasingly difficult to bear. It was inevitable that things could not continue much longer and that the next incident of friction would be decisive. It was bound to come and come it did toward the end of June. The issue once again concerned an appointment, and although any final decision was postponed when the incumbent agreed to stay on for a few months longer, Chase felt obliged once more to tender his resignation.

This time Lincoln did not hesitate to accept it and replied:

"Your resignation of the office of Secretary of the Treasury, sent me yesterday, is accepted. Of all I have said in commendation of your ability and fidelity, I have nothing to unsay; and yet you and I have reached a point of mutual embarrassment in our official relations which, it seems to me, cannot be overcome or longer sustained consistently with the public service." [32]

During all this, Kate was in Narragansett, where Sprague had purchased a farm and several hundred acres overlooking the ocean. He had persuaded her to go on ahead with Nettie while he and Chase stayed on together in Washington. The girls received the news of Chase's resignation with some distress, especially as Sprague had evidently written Kate that he thought her father had been badly treated, but Chase advised her: "If you think me wronged or not appreciated let nobody *think* you *think* so. People never sympathize with such feelings." [33]

Nevertheless his return to private life came as a shock to him, and he admitted in his diary "that it would be uncandid not to say that I felt wronged and hurt by the circumstances which preceded and attended my resignation." [34]

A great deal has been made of Chase's aspirations for the Presidency, but his achievements as Secretary of the Treasury were massive. It was a post of tremendous responsibility. The demands on the Treasury for the war were unprecedented, and Chase had to find unprecedented means to finance it. And he succeeded. His most important contribution, however, was probably the establishment of the national banking system. In spite of the obvious opportunities for personal gain of such an office, Chase left the Treasury poorer than when he entered upon it.

After the unceasing activity of the preceding three years, it is small wonder that Chase was restless after leaving office. He toyed with the idea of running for Congress, but in the back of his mind was the possibility of the appointment as Chief Justice about which Hiram Barney had spoken so persuasively more than a year earlier. But Chief Justice Taney, aged and ill, lingered on and on giving rise to all sorts of stories. Ben Wade is reputed to have said: "No man ever prayed as I did that Taney might outlive James Buchanan's term, and now I am afraid that I have overdone it." [35] Lincoln had dropped hints to friends of Chase that he would have the appointment, but when Taney finally died in mid-October, Lincoln let Chase dangle for several weeks. There were other candidates for the position, powerful ones, but Lincoln had long since determined on Chase although he recognized Chase's restless ambition and the danger that even the Chief Justiceship might not satisfy him permanently.

Chase was on his way to Washington when Lincoln finally sent in the appointment, which was confirmed immediately by the Senate without referral to committee. It had been a long and anxious period of uncertainty for Chase since his resignation from the Cabinet and he wrote Lincoln the same evening: "Before I sleep I must thank you for this mark of your confidence, and especially for the manner in which the nomination was made. I will never forget either, and trust you will never regret either. Be assured that I prize your confidence and good-will more than nomination to office." [36]

There are two quite different versions of Kate's reaction to the appointment. The first was given, some ten years after the event, by Senator Sumner to one of Chase's biographers, Robert Warden, with whom Kate was having a royal feud. According to Warden, Sumner said that when he arrived to tell Chase of his confirmation as Chief Justice he met Kate, who shook her right forefinger at him and said: "And you too, Mr. Sumner? You, too, in this this business of shelving Papa? But never mind! I will defeat you all!" [37]

A quite different impression is given by Nicolay and Hay, Lincoln's young secretaries, who were close friends of Kate, and by others. They related that Kate met her father at the door when he reached home in Washington the night of his appointment and was the first to salute him with his new title of Chief Justice.[38] "And they were very happy together about it." [39]

CHAPTER

❧❧ VIII ❧❧

THAT Kate exploded to Senator Sumner about the appointment of her father as Chief Justice makes a dramatic story but it seems hardly credible. Chase wanted the appointment, he wanted it very much indeed and he was delighted that his friends were so active in pushing his candidacy. Senator Sumner himself was well aware of this, for when he informed Chase that he had written the President urging "anew the considerations to which he yielded last spring, in favor of your nomination as Chief Justice," Chase responded: "Your action is like you, generous, earnest, and prompt . . . As yet I have heard nothing from Washington of a definite character . . . but what I do hear leads me to think that the President is of the same mind expressed to you last spring . . . It is perhaps not *en regle* to say what a man will do in regard to an appointment not tendered to him; but it is certainly not wrong to say to you that I should accept. I feel that I can do more for our cause and country in that place than in any other." [1] Chase had been on tenterhooks ever since his resignation from the Cabinet, restless and discontented at being out of things, and fearfully anxious that he might be passed over for this office, the dignity of which could do so much to assuage his hurt and confused feelings. It would have been completely out of character for Kate to have so misunderstood her father and his situation as not to have been vastly relieved and delighted at the honor given him.

In addition, Kate, at the end of her first year of marriage, was still completely absorbed by her new relationship and was wholly in the grip of a tremendous emotional attachment, one that was unusually demanding in view of the violent fluctuations of tension and release that were a part of it. Kate was not occupied with her father's political fortunes that year; she was too caught up in her own turbulent love affair with her husband.

By the summer of 1864 Kate's health had still not improved very much. She was coughing a good deal and Chase remembered anxiously her mother's long illness and death from consumption, for he had always worried that Kate might have inherited a tendency toward the same disease. Sprague was a great believer in the healing power of sea air; Chase had greater faith in mountain air, and hoped Kate might join him for a visit to the White Mountains. But Narragansett won out. They were beginning to make changes in the farmhouse, which later would assume vast proportions, and Chase urged Kate as part of her treatment to "Go out among the workmen; see what is being done and why. Occasionally take a row, but do not exercise too violently. Open air; interest in common obligation; cheerfulness and an active life are the best medicines." [2]

He was happy to see that Kate looked a little better when he came at the end of August for a visit to Narragansett and enjoyed himself thoroughly with the house full of family and friends. He was, however, upset at witnessing one of the violent quarrels between Kate and her husband, although he knew the strong bond that existed between them. With his own towering temper he recognized that explosions such as he had witnessed between them are not representative of the whole truth of a relationship. He had struggled too long against his own temper not to understand it in others.

The degree of the torment that both Kate and her husband were passing through at the end of their first year of marriage is poignantly shown in Sprague's letter to his wife on Thanksgiving Day. He was again in Providence and had just returned from Thanksgiving dinner at his mother's house. "I carried there, and have brought away with me, sad impressions of the contents of your note of the 22nd which I received this morning, sorrowfull and sad that you must write it, that you must feel as you write.

"I always have thought that we are oppressed with care and sorrow for more wise purposes of our creation. Perhaps to teach us our weakness that we may be the stronger. Perhaps to purify our passions and to correct them. Perhaps for other reasons. I am not satisfied yet that these have application to us, to the great suffering already upon us, and that which is in store, God knows.

"Can we not place ourselves in His hand with the spirits of little children, forgiving and forebearing and then hope for a brighter future[?]

"Shall we not forgive wrongs real or imaginary, to us all real as one greater, higher and holier than any other did towards those who reviled and persecuted Him[?]

"Consider these things in the spirit of the evening by ourselves at our own little home. You brightened my heart and contributed to my restoration to health, by the simple promise. You felt it then, when I worn down, sad and almost helpless you cared for my physical being and administered to my affections, so simply, so effectually . . . If all the disagreements and all the sufferings we bring upon ourselves cannot fade away before the strength of our mutual affections, God help us. Darling I believe they will. Let us meet them fearlessly and dispassionately, sensibly and we shall have a happy and usefull future." [3]

Beyond the strong mutual physical attraction that existed between them, and the image of the dashing cavalier on a white horse who had captured Kate's imagination, ran a deeper current of tender affection and concern. The quiet grief at their differences that Sprague shows in this letter, rare as such a controlled manifestation must have been, reveals the warm and sympathetic understanding of which he was capable and which Kate so passionately wanted from him in a greater degree than he was able to give her. Kate knew that she was sentimental, even childish, about little attentions and once admitted so to her father in speaking of a birthday greeting she had received from Nettie: "I was so pleased that she remembered to think of me on that day. I fear I am a good deal of a child about such things yet, though the yearning for love is hardly one of the childish things one would wish to put away." [4]

Sprague's unhappy letter was undoubtedly in answer to one from her reproaching him with having forgotten their first wedding anniversary.

In her later diary she remarks sorrowfully about his omissions in this regard: "Each year the day has rolled by and been forgotten by him, and when reminded, it was through such a melancholy show of interest, that I was left to regret that I had recalled it." [5] This year she was expecting their first child. She had not been well and evidently the first months of her pregnancy had not been easy. In her letter she had apparently given vent to grievances and miseries in a bitter summing up brought on by what she felt was yet another example of his neglect. But once again the storm blew over and Kate must have been happy at the note she found from her husband, with a fine gift of money, in her Christmas stocking: "I place in your stocking tonight this token—Let it stand in the place of a reminder . . . of power for happiness and of usefullness . . . yet not powerful enough or rich enough in resources to purchase from you the smallest particle of my affection or to represent, with all its power a millionth part of the strength and fondness of my love to my wife." [6]

Hope came with the New Year for everyone, especially hope at last that the end of the war was in sight. Kate was present when her father, as Chief Justice, administered the oath of office to Lincoln on the occasion of his second inaugural and she was wakened too during the "night of horror" that followed so soon, when Chase was informed by messenger that the President had been shot. He recalled that: "My first impulse was to rise immediately and go to the President, whom I could not yet believe to have been fatally wounded; but, reflecting that I could not possibly be of any service, and should probably be in the way of them who could, I resolved to wait for morning and further intelligence. In a little while the guard came—for it was supposed that I was one of the destined victims—and their heavy tramp, tramp was under my window all night." [7] Early the next morning he went to Ford's Theatre and learned at the house across the way that the President was already dead. He then visited Seward, who had been attacked and nearly killed too, and Vice-President Johnson, whom he found "calm apparently, but very grave." Arrangements for administering the oath of office were made for ten o'clock that same morning. Kate and Nettie were among the few women who attended the funeral services for President Lincoln in the East Room at the White House.

Not long afterward, Chase left for a tour of the South, taking Nettie with him for company. Nettie was now a young lady approaching her eighteenth year. She and Kate were the best of friends and complemented each other in style and appearance. Nettie was blond, with a tendency to plumpness, and a great fund of gaiety and good humor. She had a gift for drawing, which she had inherited from her mother, and undoubtedly her sense of humor and fun came from that side of the family, as the Chases were not notable for those qualities. Kate assumed most of the responsibility for her and Chase was as indulgent as ever with his younger daughter. On one occasion, when even Kate apparently found adolescent Nettie a little trying, Chase admonished her: "Be *very* kind to her and very considerate for her. Let your *thought* supply her thoughtlessness." [8]

Chase missed Kate sorely in spite of Nettie's company on their long trip South. No one could take Kate's place with him. As he traveled up the Mississippi River on the last part of his journey, Chase was anxious about Kate's confinement, which was imminent. When he finally received word from Sprague announcing the birth of a son, on June 16, he was vastly relieved. "I received your telegram on the river," he wrote. "It was a great relief for I was very anxious about you." And a letter from Kate, received a few days later, "did me a deal of good. I was delighted to hear that you were well and engaged in improvement of the place. It gives you a healthful employment and will be useful in every way. Still more delighted was I to read what you say of your excellent husband. You *ought* to be proud of him. I *am* quite as much as you are. He is independent and manly as well as intelligent; and real manliness and independence are rare qualities in these days." Nevertheless, in spite of Chase's affection for his son-in-law, and he truly was attached to him, he always sees room for improvement. "I wish he were not so deeply immersed in business and could give more time to the reading and study necessary to qualify him for the part I hope to see him take in public affairs. Give my warmest love to him." [9]

From the time she had left school, when other girls were occupied with nothing more than beaux and fripperies, Kate had been her father's confidante, the person he turned to with all his problems, large and small. No detail of his day was too unimportant for him not to want to share it with her, no issue too great that he did not profit from discussing it with her, and she well knew in how many ways she had been able to help him. It was this kind of intimate sharing of everything that she longed for with her husband. And that, he could not or would not give her. He may have felt that the preeminently political climate of the Chases was not conducive to an appreciation or understanding of his business interests; undoubtedly he reacted to the public disparagement of himself and the sorry comparisons to the abilities of his wife and father-in-law; certainly he had a deep core in his nature that needed privacy and freedom. And part of this he found in his business life. Whatever the cause, he continued to exclude Kate from his affairs in a way that increasingly grew to be a source of tension and sorrow to her, all the more, perhaps, just because she was proud of him and recognized that in that area he was more truly himself than in any other activity. "Of his worldly success I am very proud, and the place of power and influence he has won, and would gladly follow all his interests with sympathy and encouragement," she related in her diary. "But I cannot make them mine, for his effort would seem to be to show me that I have no part in them, or as his wife he would have had a care to have defined, and protected me in that position." [10] Kate recognized her own abilities and it was frustrating to feel that her husband had no use for them in the work that interested him the most. But the new baby, of course, was a great resource and a delight to everyone.

Kate was tempted to have something of Chase in the child's name but he wrote her: "I long to see the dear boy, whom you must name William. It is natural enough that you should want to name him after me in some way; but my only tolerable name is my surname; and William is not only a better one; but it is the name of the one to whom *your first duties* belong . . . and it was the name of his father, was it not? and it *should* be borne by his first boy. So please consider that 'case adjudged.' " [11]

Little Willie Sprague caused a considerable stir with his arrival. Newspapers reported on his handsome christening robe, the large fortune he was heir to, the prominence and success of his parents, and pointed to a life begun in circumstances of extraordinary good fortune. It was a future full of promise that Kate saw for her son. She could not foresee the gradual erosion of her dreams for him nor his final tragedy.

The baby prospered that first summer, as did Kate too. "The baby is well and growing," Sprague wrote his father-in-law, "and so is its mother. All seem to be happy." [12] Chase was delighted with his grandson and greatly enjoyed a visit to Narragansett, and when he returned alone to Washington he missed the companionship and the pleasant company. "Give my dearest love to dearest Nettie," he wrote Kate, "and love also in full measure to your excellent husband and to Jenny, Allie and grandma, and everybody of the littlest sort." [13] Kate as usual had a houseful of relatives and guests staying with her. Chase realized that this could be tiring for the new mother and was concerned at Sprague's letter which informed him: "I fear she has been exerting herself too much at the pier and croquet and perhaps too much bathing. I think it will be well for her to find the warm climate at Washington as early as the middle of October." [14] Chase thought that it was not too much exercise which had tired her but her responsibilities as hostess. "You have had such a houseful that relaxation was impossible," he told her. "Three of one's own children create less anixety, because they can be better controlled, than one of any other body. I felt sorry for you when I was with you, and if I could be of any use would either have stayed or returned immediately. All I do here is to read, and attend to some little matters of no great consequence." [15]

Kate worried a little about her father alone in Washington, especially as the household arrangements there were a little confused by the illness of her usual housekeeper. But he assured her that he was getting along nicely and that everything was comfortable. Although Chase claimed that he was managing very well by himself, he was delighted when Kate and husband and Nettie and Grandmother and baby and nurse all returned to Washington and the house was filled again with activity of old and young.

That winter was a brilliant one in Washington. Even the tragedy of Lincoln's death could not dampen the excitement and activity of the new social season. Freed from the burdens and tragedies of the war, people threw themselves into an even greater round of gaiety than before.

Kate had wide scope now and with Sprague's enormous fortune was able to compete with any of her social rivals. She was the center of attention wherever she went. "Reveling in her millions, astonishing by her splendor, importing her gowns from Paris, she dazzled the drawing-rooms with her jewels . . . And yet she dimmed the splendor of her raiment and outshone the brilliance of her jewels. The correspondent of the *Chicago News* thought her the only woman with a vast number of gowns and jewels who rose superior to them all. 'Not a gown, not a chain, not an ornament ever attracted attention except in so much as it shared her beauty . . . She had more the air of a great lady than any woman I ever saw. She could make all the Astors look like fishwomen beside her.' " [16]

Kate, after the birth of her son, was more beautiful than ever. She liked to show the baby off at her afternoon receptions. One woman who so admired her that she felt that no husband was worthy of beautiful Kate found herself somewhat reconciled "when she sent for her lovely baby, at one of her delightful afternoon receptions and looked the picture of happiness with him in her arms." She went on to describe Kate's entertainments which "were elegant, lavish; her guests were perfectly at ease—she gave the impression that she was enjoying her party—and wished to prolong it. I recall a ball of roseate hue. The walls were lined with pink. The ballroom was a fairyland. Altogether it was the most beautiful ball I ever attended." [17]

Kate was not the only one who entertained lavishly, however. The most elaborate ball of the season was given by the French

Minister, the Marquis de Montholon, although it was asserted that it in no way was superior to those of Kate Chase Sprague. The Montholon party, given in Georgetown, lasted until daylight and ended with the serving of a sumptuous breakfast. The former Mrs. Stephen Douglas, now the bride of General Williams, re-entered the social scene with four "superb receptions." Mrs. Grant, wife of the General, gave several balls and some of the largest receptions of the season. All in all the estimate of a contemporary summed it up: "The long social depression and privation caused by the war, were followed by a reaction in the first year of the term of Andrew Johnson. Even the shock of President Lincoln's assassination and the mourning of the Nation, had no abiding effect in checking the gayety resumed when a few months had passed. The fashionable season of 1866 was almost a carnival. Washington seemed to have gone wild." [18]

Kate, as acknowledged queen of this society, shared the spotlight with her husband and father, and all three attracted public notice and comment. "The engaging manners of Mrs. Sprague gave her an ascendancy in society. Her slender form became a rich, ornamental style of dress, and her eyes, fringed with dark lashes, lighted her intellectual face with expression. The Senator had lustrous eyes, with small features and long hair rather carelessly worn. His manner was gentle, but he was said to possess a striking element of greatness—tenacity of purpose. The presence of the Chief Justice would grace a palace; his face expressed the most bounteous benevolence." [19]

In spite of her prominence and success and the busy whirl of parties, Kate was deeply troubled in her marriage. Sprague was drinking more heavily than ever and his conduct was often a source of humiliation to her. When he was drinking he grew coarse and sometimes even abusive and violent. But the drinking was not all. Sprague had begun to be openly unfaithful to her. Not only did he visit houses of prostitution, both in Washington and Providence, but, as she later asserted, "from the year 1865 . . . Sprague frequently attempted to have criminal intercourse with the female domestics and guests in the family, causing them to leave the house." [20]

What had happened to Kate's "glimpse of Heaven for purity and peace"; to her "hopes and dreams on a calm moonlight night" before her wedding; to the "security and trust" she had found in her husband's arms? Kate confided in no one, not even her father, who remained strangely blind to what was going on, bearing witness to what had so often been said of him that he was "nearsighted" in his judgment of men. What made it hardest of all was that Kate still loved her husband as he too, in spite of his weaknesses, loved her. With hurt pride, Kate threw herself almost frenetically into her social life, trying to blot out the reality of what was happening to their relationship. It was a superficial and frivolous reaction and it did not help at all, in spite of all her success at it. Nor did her explosions of temper, her attempts to win her dreams by force, to hold the broken image together by strength of will. Finally Kate determined to try a more desperate remedy—to leave the scenes of a home which had brought her such disappointment, to see what a period of separation could do, "hoping to find in absence fresh courage, and greater strength, and for a great deal more." [21]

CHAPTER
IX

THE FIRST WEEK of April 1866, Kate, accompanied by little
Willie, his nurse and Nettie, set sail for Europe. Her decision
to go had not been taken lightly and at the last moment she nearly
lost courage and wished that her husband or father were coming
too. The actuality of separation was not easy either for her or
Sprague and he wrote her after seeing them off on the boat: "The
tears came to my eyes when I saw you standing upon the deck and
Nettie holding out a cheerfull face. You attempting to appear
cheerfull. I was myself ready to drop out of sight as you did, but
you aided me by yourself doing as I was about to do. Well my
darling you are away. You are travelling. You would have your
father or your husband with you. This you cannot have." The
Chief Justice, he tells her, will have to hold court in the South
and he himself must try "to relieve those that have born the
burden and heat of the day in my absence from interests which
alone give me consumation." He plans to make extensive additions
to the house in Washington, which he hopes she will approve of.
"I am depressed past weakness. The result of a yielding to influences that came. When such influences possess and occupy, [they]
cause me serious trouble in my own reflections." He undoubtedly
referred here to his drinking. "I shall overcome them," he continues. He urges that she "not hestitate to go where you like to go,

and to live as you desire to live so far as the expenditure of money is concerned"; to buy what she desires, to dress "as becomes a refined intelligent lady of station, refinement and accomplishments" and to see that Nettie is not in any way less in this respect. He warns her that she must "expect to hear of my doing all sorts of things during your absence. You know I am fond of the ladies and you must not blame me for indulging in that fondness. I know that you will not if you reflect but will rather commend me for it." He tells her that he has been to the opera, to the theater and "I have taken to whiskey since you left also. I am still as sleepy as ever . . . We are miserable at home you know. I must I think get some young woman to live with me. Do you consent[?]" After touching briefly on a host of other subjects, from doings in the Senate to inviting his mother for a visit, he closes: "Do not cease to think that no matter what occurs, I am always your devoted husband and lover. If I may be permitted to try to love a little in your absence, it will be but to be stronger and stronger in my love to you when you return . . . Are you not sorry you have deserted me[?]"[1] Undoubtedly Sprague had "yielded to influences," as he euphemistically put it, before writing this long, rambling, and sometimes unclear letter.

Kate was more than a little lonely and homesick when she reached Liverpool. "You have now been in England 17 days," Sprague answered her first letters home. "No doubt you are more reconciled than when you wrote in Liverpool. I can realize the full force of your feeling when you leave ship and find yourself among strangers." He sends her letters of introduction to the Comte de Paris and the Prince de Joinville and his greetings to Ambassador and Mrs. Adams. At home he has given several dinners. Guests include the son of the Duke of Argyll to whom Sumner had given Kate a letter of introduction, and he hopes it will favor her friendly reception. He regrets that he has not a wider acquaintanceship abroad.[2]

Sprague and Chase seemed to be managing quite well at home and the household was running smoothly under the "kind and attentive" care of the housekeeper, Mrs. Crawford. Kate's Grandmother Smith "comes to the table to keep us company," Sprague wrote, "is well and appears happy." The two men did not stint themselves in entertaining: "Gen'l Ashley, Mr. Chandler and Nelson dined with us yesterday. We shall have four gentlemen with us today . . . We have had 4 to dine with us each day," [3] Sprague tells her.

In spite of the pleasant relationship between Chase and his son-in-law it seems more formal than intimate. Kate was eager to have her father join her for a while abroad, but Chase kept his plans to himself and she seemed hesitant to ask him outright or to press him too hard. Sprague attempted to find out for her what was really in the older man's mind. "I tried your father about joining you but no go." And with a rather penetrating observation, adds, "I [a] little think he is afraid. I don't know, perhaps a little bashfull." Chase had had an interview with President Johnson about the courts, and Sprague reported that "judging from appearances I think the interview was stiff." And he goes on to say with more political acumen than was usually ascribed to him: "The current is favorable for Grant for the next Presidency." He closes his letter: "Your Grandma continues in good health and reads your letters with great satisfaction. You have by this time given up all thoughts of home and we shall have to think of those who think seldom of us." [4]

Kate was beginning to get over her homesickness and to enjoy herself. Mr. and Mrs. Adams were cordial and welcoming to her and she had the opportunity to meet interesting and distinguished people. Even more important to Kate, however, was that her idea that a separation might help seemed to be bearing fruit. Sprague was evidently trying to control his drinking. His letters become more ordered and clear and a great deal more legible. A month after Kate's departure he wrote her: "I think I am past all temptations. I have gotten through and am safe without a scorch I think . . . But he added: "That I love my dearie this separation convinces me more and more and that I cannot get on at all alone and without her is quite as apparent." [5]

In spite of the fact that Kate was enjoying her first visit to Europe, her conscience still bothered her about leaving her husband and she offered to change her plans completely and to return home at once. "Your proposition to return and care for your disconsolate one is a proof of your care and communication and love that I shall not soon forget," Sprague responded.[6]

If Kate's hopes that Sprague might succeed in controlling his drinking and dissipation had been buoyed by some of his letters, they were soon dashed, as they had been so many times before. Within ten days the whole tone of his letters changed suddenly again. "I am glad you have been away during my troubles, as I should have visited it upon you. My mind is sadly disconnected," he writes. He complains of some petty family troubles in Providence and business worries. But the root of his disturbance is something else. Not only was he receiving more unpleasant anonymous letters, but various derogatory letters and comments had appeared in the newspapers. This was enough to destroy his precarious balance and shatter again any self-confidence he might have begun to develop. "I am more and more in the belief that I am unequal to my post," he told Kate. And in reference to his drinking: "I am afraid that my physical infirmities will prevent my being usefull. I don't want to resign. I don't want to again go into business. And I am quite sure unless I change my present habits I shall go down hill fast, or faster than I have. If I cast back, one, two or three years, and see how little I have accomplished, it is enough to discourage anyone. My weakness has place[d] me in very false and uncomfortable positions. I will *not* let you see the newspaper slips. I have shown the slips to your father, but get no satisfaction. He does not understand such weakness as *mine*.[7]

Here we see much of what happened with Sprague during the nearly three years since his marriage. His interest in business, which had given him such satisfaction earlier, seemed to be gone. He felt more inferior than ever in his political position. He had allowed himself to drink to the point that it was now common knowledge. Worse than that, his drinking had not only affected his drive and ambition but had begun to affect his health and his powers of concentration. His feelings of inferiority were more acute than ever as he looked at himself and saw what he was doing, yet was unable to control himself.

It did not add to Sprague's inner peace to be so close to someone of Chase's stature and self-assurance. He had worried before his marriage about the comparisons Kate might make between her father and himself but he had not reckoned on his own reaction. He could not help comparing himself to Kate either—Kate who was so universally admired and feted, who was considered so brilliant, so capable in every way, and he knew that many people found him increasingly unworthy of her. That might not have troubled him had he not himself felt it to be true. Sprague was honest with himself. He recognized very well what he had done and what he had failed to do. And he doubted his ability to do better.

Because she loved him, Kate understood far more than her father did about this wild, solitary man she had married. She had been ready to help him in any way. But why *could* he not do the things he ought to do? She knew he loved her. She knew he sincerely wanted to improve his ways. It was hard for her to understand why he did not.

Kate and Nettie made a visit to Paris and Kate, especially, was enchanted with it, with the Louvre, with the whole fascination of that unique city. Her stay there was a brief one, and they soon returned by way of Belgium and Holland to England where she thought they might try to see something of the countryside. Kate sent Willie and his nurse to the seaside for two weeks while she and Nettie went to Scotland and when she picked him up afterward was delighted to find him wonderfully improved and brown as could be after his fortnight by the sea.

Sprague was still doubtful about his chances for reelection and proposed that they might move to New York as "it has become almost indispensable for some one of us to be there. So your pride and position will be gratified. We will look at a spot sometime and set up ourselves conveniently, moderately and sensibly. I have come to that conclusion in advance of my being let to stay at home after my present term has past." [8]

Sprague often seemed bored and impatient at some of the Senate business and the endless speeches and arguments. "I have just returned from caucus. I am always putting my foot into it, getting myself into a scrape. I said to the caucus . . . that if they did not confine themselves to the subject matter of their coming together I should break and dissolve my connection with it. So I got the grunt from the old grunters . . . We are tinkering the constitution and every man wants some hand in it and I want to confine them to the subject." He was, however, deeply interested in the proposed Fourteenth Amendment, and his feelings against President Johnson and Secretary Seward were violent, especially after Johnson's veto of the Civil Rights Bill, even though the Congress had overridden the veto.[9]

Sprague was elated when the amendment finally was passed. "We shall be all right now very soon," he asserted. "We care nothing now for Presidents. We get on without him. From the field of battle we go on in triumph to victory in the council." [10]

But his interest in his senatorial role vacillated even during those exciting days, and when he received Kate's letter from Brussels, which especially delighted him by her "thousand kisses for your old man," he was tempted to join her abroad as soon as possible and questions "whether it is worthwhile for me to be in attendance" at the three months 1866–67 Congress. "I don't know as I am less useful than others," he tells her, "or some of them, but I am far from being satisfied with what I am doing or able to do. This much, my dear, upon a very threadbare subject of which you are reasonably tired of."

Sprague proposes several alternative plans for Kate, depending on how long she wants to remain abroad. He feels that she must give up the idea that her father will join them. Chase is making summer plans to travel about, following his usual routes in New England and Ohio but "he is reluctant to come in contact with strangers. He said today that if the Govt. would give him a ship as it did Seward he would have no hesitation, but he is unwilling to do so otherwise." And then in a touching and penetrating phrase: "He is a great proud man you see, and I am not prepared to say he is wrong." [11]

Sprague could not avoid twinges of jealousy, though he controlled it remarkably well. "In your last letter you gave me encouragement to admire beautiful women. I don't think I can be so liberal with you. Beautiful and intellectual women both, by my new education, are now necessary to my full appreciation. I am fully convinced that such would not reciprocate. But with you splendid men would fare differently. You would appreciate them, and it would be mutual, and the higher advanced, the more the appreciation. Now my darling take warning. I shall object to the proposition if you make it with a view of taking like liberty." He kisses the baby a "thousand times, and the mother a million." [12]

Kate was apparently trying to handle her husband now with a lighter touch, using a more teasing tone about his infidelities. "You send me note paper do you to write love letters thereon, and you want me to write love letters," Sprague observes. And he complains: "Ah my darling, does the privilege extend so far[?] Do you confine the love epistles to yourself that they may be further extended—and dearie, do you give me this liberty that you may enjoy similar liberty? What can I think? . . ." Now that Kate was giving him the freedom to indulge in affairs with other women, typically he did not want it and was eager instead to tighten the bond again between them. "I am glad I am not pleased any more with the rustle of other women's dresses," he announced to her complacently. "I am glad my mind and my heart is concentrated on my wife so far off as she is. I am glad I feel loyalty and devotion and do not mean to prove untrue in heart to it so long as I feel I can rely upon a response." And then he puts the burden on her. That she has loved him he does not doubt. His anxiety is "do you now love[?]" [13]

Kate's feelings of bitterness seemed to have become less poignant and she apparently responded to Sprague's uncertainties about her love for him with warm assurance. His reaction was immediate. "I have kept your last letter before me," he wrote her, "and the last thing I have done at night is to read them. I call it them because it was upon two sheets." [14]

Time and distance were doing their work. The memory of tensions and quarrels began to fade and the strong bond of affection to stand out clearly once again. Although none of Kate's letters to her husband at this period have been preserved, the tone of them is clear from his answers. When one of her letters arrived, he wrote her, "I immediately went up to my room and all alone feasted on the precious document. Two items compensated me. One the 'Precious husband' and the satisfaction you express that my last letters are more to you than any I ever wrote. The second that the tiara, the wedding gift of your husband, was more valuable to you than the Crown of the Princess Alexandra. A few words carry great weight and may I not my dearie feel proud that amidst all the splendors and attention, my little wife can keep her head and her heart for her husband. Will she hold steadfast to that[?] I believe so." [15] Kate had been presented at Court and had written him a full account of it. Sprague took great pride in his wife's brilliance and success and any idea that she was not getting the attention he thought was her due concerned him. "You must not fail," he wrote her. "We must not fail. No one with us must fail. Do you agree with me? Will we strive for that[?]" [16]

On the first birthday of his son, Sprague wrote a long letter addressed to him filled with noble precepts, hopes and plans for his future, and a great deal of affection. "I can see my little boy," he writes, "as he used to be in his little crib on Mama's side of the bed, and sometimes Mama would take him in to our bed and would lay him upon my arm and I would feel a holy feeling come over me. When I see my little boy again and fold him in my arms I believe I shall be a happier and a better man and with Mama we will love and cherish our little one and devote ourselves to him and to one another." [17]

As Sprague's health and habits continued to improve, one can imagine that Chase was doing his best to help instill a regular system of exercise and work in his son-in-law. Sprague informs Kate that, "We don't go out except between 6 and 8 to ride with two gentlemen. Then we walk till near ten, then we go to bed. We get up in time for 8 o'clock breakfast. We then work a little, go perhaps to the Dept. and then to the Senate and stay till adjournment and go home. This is *our* daily journal and exercise and you see dearie how . . . hugely we long for and wait for your precious letters." [18] With the progress in his physical and mental condition, Sprague's interest both in the political and the business scene began to revive.

He was considering a trip to Colorado where he had investments in a mine and felt an obligation to the other investors. He was concerned over the Prussion aggression against Austria and Bavaria and his ideas of the war and the burden of taxation foreshadowed some of the speeches he would later make in his one great wild moment in the Senate.

Most of all he was very concerned about the situation at home and highly critical of the President. He tells Kate that Johnson has completely alienated himself from the party that elected him and is making extraordinary efforts to insure its defeat. "He is, it is believed, the author of a call for a national convention. The call is from Democrats. But it will not prevail . . . Then the silence that broods over our foreign affairs is so humiliating that the people are becoming very sensitive. Seward plans for Johnson's downfall, that he may rise in his place. Of course if he can't get it himself, he will turn in with some one he can use, who will keep him in his place and let him rule them as has Lincoln and Johnson." [19]

Although his picture to Kate of life on Capitol Hill that summer of 1866 is hardly prepossessing, Sprague found it encouraging. "I inform you that there has been far less drinking and dissipation among our public men at the capitol than at any time I have been in public life. Even those who were usually drunk are not so now. It has become so unfashionable, so uncompanionable that none find it enjoyable. When such a condition of things exists look for wise action. The Congress of the United States never since its organization could stand the criticism that it now can, and have a verdict far in its favor for worth and superiority in all things that conduce to the national welfare, and the political and moral greatness of its people and government. I speak hopefully because I see signs of hopefullness. The cause may be the absence of all this in the Executive branch of the Government. Mr. Johnson is still a slave to passions and prejudice and to hate but it is like all other hate whether among the p[e]ople or in the governor, it injures only the possessor. He alone is the sufferer. None now care for the President. They do not propose to curtail his power but they mean to restrict his influence. A queer way this, you will say, but such it is. It is one of the anomalies of our time." [20]

In spite of the marked improvement in Sprague's general condition, his moods continued to shift between confidence and discouragement. Whenever he felt that he had not appeared at his best, his spirits would plummet and the whole carefully built edifice of security would crumble again.

Sprague was a man who needed continually to be encouraged, supported, and exhorted. And it was Kate who could bolster his spirits as no one else could do. But the job was never finished. It all had to be done over and over again. Kate could not have helped being frustrated and wearied by the constant drain on her courage and optimism.

Once again on the downswing Sprague was caught between his desire to be reelected to the Senate for a second term two years from now and his fear that he might be defeated. His fevered imagination could easily picture in all detail the humiliation of such a public failure and he finally built up the whole situation to a point that he even considered resigning before the end of his present term. He discussed the idea with Chase and wrote Kate about it at length. Her answer was the best therapy he could have hoped for. "I have read your note . . . received this morning, twice in two hours," he told her. "You are just right. I told the C. J. when I wrote you what I had written and he said that will not do. Katie will not think that right or we'll see what Katie says of it. It would be, I am compelled to say, a cowardly act to desert my post." Kate's letter had completely dispelled the cloud of gloom and depression that he had been under, and her encouragement worked like magic on his defeatist attitude. "Dearie I really think I have gained a little all the time," he expatiated happily. "I think my associates see in me a great improvement. Calm deliberate pleasant courteous obliging, I am and am getting more and more so. Withall an independence and self-reliance that cannot but command their respect. Dearie I thank you for your letter. It will give me strength to reach after good and great things. I am in good health now . . . Don't you get tired of all this personal talk?" [21]

On the wings of his encouragement from Kate and his renewed optimism, Sprague had the idea of studying law to improve himself. He wrote to the Chief Justice, who was vacationing at his birthplace in Cornish, New Hampshire and asked his opinion and advice. Chase wrote that he "thought very well of your idea of studying law. It is an excellent disciplinary study, but it will impose a very considerable tax on your time and patience. As you will not intend to practise, however, the tax will be tolerable." He suggests several legal books in addition to some reading in history and offers to read the books along with Sprague and discuss them with him and help as far as he can.[22] But as with so many of Sprague's projects for self-improvement, this one too never materialized.

Chase went to New England in mid-July and Sprague was planning to go to Providence shortly afterward. Chase did not want any arrangements made for himself for the summer in regard to the house and even, Sprague thought, might have "an inkling for a house of his own," he told Kate. "He spoke of one recently sold on 4th and C St. I think for 18000$." [23] Chase was not at all pleased by his daughters' absence and felt quite neglected. "He does not feel right to have you from him and alone in a foreign country," Sprague confided to Kate.[24] Chase needed attention and solicitous care and if his daughters, especially Kate, were not there to give it to him, he sought it elsewhere. Evidently he had been spending some of his time visiting several of his "fair ladies": Miss Susan Walker, of whom he saw a good deal, Mrs. Goldsborough, and he looked forward to seeing his delightful Mrs. Eastman at her place in Beverly, Massachusetts. Sprague invited him to visit in Providence in August but he wrote Kate that her father "has some fair lady I think up in the mountains so I can hardly think of his coming here." [25]

Poor Chase. His gentle flirtations were suddenly catapulted into public view. Rumors that the Chief Justice was about to wed a "Mrs. M. or a Mrs. E." circulated in the press. Chase was furious and instructed his secretary to deny all such reports "until you hear from me that I have actually determined to enter or have entered the bonds of matrimony. I don't absolutely renounce the idea . . . but I am still likely to remain a widower." [26] Undoubtedly Chase toyed with the idea of marriage during the summer but it was more a reaction to his feeling of being abandoned by his "children" than anything more serious.

He was even more unhappy when he learned that Nettie wanted to stay on for the winter in Europe and study art, and he wrote Kate, "It is bad enough to have you away seven months and it is hard to reconcile myself to the idea of either of you being away for another year." It took all of Kate's persuasiveness to gain his permission for Nettie's plan, but he did agree in the end to let Nettie decide for herself and promised to "do all I can to make the execution of her resolve gratifying to her." [27]

After all the publicity about his father-in-law's impending matrimony, Sprague was able to persuade Chase to visit him in Rhode Island. His own plans for joining Kate had been delayed not only by business affairs but by the death of his cousin Byron Sprague and the various obligations he had to assume as financial guardian for Byron's children. All these duties made him worry more than ever about Willie's future and how he would manage in a world where competition was worse than it had ever been before, where money and position counted for little and each man must make his own way.

While Chase was in Providence the two of them visited the farm at Narragansett. Sprague loved it there and was full of plans to improve the house and to make a fine estate of it. He was pleased at the changes Kate had ordered done. "I was afraid you would turn the farm into walks and shades so we should have to buy milk for butter for want of barn room to shelter our cows or mowing lots to provide them during the winter but I think we can show you how we can ornament the grounds and at [the] same time make them useful." Sprague's buoyant mood of self-confidence and optimism was still strong. He had finally almost finished with his business and family obligations and looked forward to joining Kate abroad very soon.[28]

He and Chase traveled back to Washington together early in September and stopped off in New York where Sprague, as delegate-at-large, attended a convention called by Southern loyalists. His antipathy to President Johnson is even more pronounced. "I am so disinclined to him that I almost refuse to take up a paper in

Kate Chase as the leading hostess of Washington, D.C.

Salmon P. Chase. From a portrait owned by The Chase Manhattan Bank, New York City.

Catherine Garniss Chase, who died as first wife of Salmon P. Chase and after whom Kate, daughter of his second wife Eliza, was named. COURTESY OF THE CHASE MANHATTAN BANK, NEW YORK CITY.

Henrietta B. Haines who ran the fashionable New York girls' school that Kate Chase entered when she was nine.

The home of Salmon Chase in Columbus, Ohio, when he was Governor.

Kate Chase photographed by Brady.

Salmon Chase as Secretary of the Treasury photographed by Brady or his assistant.

Governor William Sprague, leader of the dashing Rhode Island regiment at the time he courted Kate.

Kate Chase visits the Union troops.

Kate Chase after the war.

Wedding picture of Kate Chase and William Sprague.

William Sprague as Senator and his wife portrayed by Brady or an assistant.

The Chase-Sprague Mansion at Sixth and E Streets North West, Washington, D.C.

Kate Chase Sprague and her younger sister Jeanette Ralston Chase (Nettie), daughter of the twice widowed Chase's third wife Belle. THE CINCINNATI HISTORICAL SOCIETY

"Canonchet," the ill-fated home of Kate and William Sprague at Narragansett Pier, Rhode Island. RHODE ISLAND HISTORICAL SOCIETY

Senator and Mrs. William Sprague in the years when their marriage was threatening to be irrevocably doomed.

Roscoe Conkling, the powerful Senator from New York whose friendship with Kate Sprague prompted ugly gossip.

Salmon P. Chase as Chief Justice of the United States Supreme Court, photographed by Brady or an assistant.

which his name figures," he tells Kate. Sprague finds it hard to get back to politics after being involved with "machinery, buildings, water power, steam engines, ships, etc. You know how long it takes me to gather up after I have scattered myself abroad." He thinks he may bring one or two of his men to Europe when he comes to look into markets there for his mills. Sprague feels that Chase could very well have gone abroad "but he would have expected the attention due his position . . . and he would not have been fairly presented." [29]

As the time for his reunion with Kate approached, Sprague predictably grew more possessive and jealous. She had finally left England and had moved on to Paris with her little family and he was concerned about the temptations of that city, although some two weeks earlier he had written her that had anyone read her letters to him "they could have feasted on the words of wife to husband and might have said to all wives, go and do likewise." [30] But he found her first letter from Paris, "a little wanting in your usual fervor," and at once fell into a suspicious mood. "Have the temptations that surround you called up any unpleasant memories, and recalled pleasanter ones[?]" [31]

Sprague's jealousy of Kate was aroused not only by the sharpened focus on her that the prospect of soon being with her produced, but shortly before he was due to leave for Europe rumors that he and Kate were going to be divorced broke into the public press: "It is reported in Providence, R. I., that the wife of a (not very) distinguished Senator is about to apply for a divorce." [32] Sprague was upset. Chase was furious. "I hate to touch such filth in any way," he wrote his secretary as the reports continued to circulate even after Sprague had left, in October, to join Kate. A month later a denial was published in a few papers stating that the rumor was "an unfounded and malicious calumny, without one iota of foundation." [33]

Nevertheless the harm was done and it must have cast a shadow over the reunion. Sprague, excessively reactive to any kind of criticism, undoubtedly needed Kate to reassure him and boost his morale all over again.

Kate's dreams of a virile knight on a white charger had been swept away by the reality of this husband whose letters show that he turned to her more often as child than as man. She had hoped to find in him strength and protection. Instead, he called on her for hers. She did her best to re-create the image, to hold together the illusion, and sometimes for a while she almost succeeded. He had gifts and abilities, and charm when he wanted, but his whole inner life was fogged over by his intense neuroticism. Kate's strength of will and superiority were both a mainstay and a challenge to him and in merely being she aggravated his inner conflicts. He too had dreamed of being her virile knight.

CHAPTER

X

C HASE MET THEM at the boat in New York when they returned in early December—Kate and her husband and little Willie with his nurse, Maggie, and all looking "so well and in such good spirits." Kate had a new way of doing her hair. No longer did she part it demurely in the middle, drawn back into a low chignon behind. The new style demanded curls on the forehead in the fashion set by the Empress Eugénie. Chase was a little disappointed, having so long loved her in the old way, and Grandmother Smith, when she first saw a picture of the new style, could scarcely recognize her granddaughter. Kate had not stinted herself in the purchase of clothes and she had a fine wardrobe of Parisian fashions for the new Washington season.

Sprague went to Providence shortly after their return, and although Willie had an attack of croup, he recovered in time for Kate to join her husband for the New Year. Chase was lonely, but he was gratified that Kate had gone. "Your first duty is to your husband," he wrote her. "That duty unperformed or carelessly performed there is no chance of happiness in the married relation." Chase had been troubled by Kate's long separation from her husband and was glad to note how well they seemed to get along when they returned together. "I must tell you how much joy it gives me to see you possessed of your husband's entire confidence and affection" he continued. But he cautions her: "I hope that henceforth you will find less and less enjoyment in the society-whirl and more and more in making *home* attractive to husband and child." Kate had worried about leaving him alone for the big New Year's Day reception, but he tells her that "I got along bravely on New Year's" and he was obviously pleased that in spite of the fact that arriving visitors were told at the door that Governor and Mrs. Sprague were in Providence, "most . . . paid their respects to me— perhaps two hundred and fifty—quite enough." [1]

When they returned to Washington, Kate brought with her two young cousins of Sprague, Susie and Sarah Hoyt, and soon Kate was once again caught up in the social whirl in spite of her father's strictures about it. Chase could see that tensions were developing once more between Kate and her husband, following the same old pattern. Sprague was still drinking heavily and often suffered from "dyspepsia," Chase wrote Nettie. "Last night he felt so badly he could not come down. He takes more to *the boy* than to anything or anybody else. No woman could have a kinder and more indulgent husband than he has been to Katie. Sometimes I feel she don't feel it quite enough; though I know she loves him and is proud of him," he added anxiously. [2]

Kate did not confide in her father about her marital difficulties and even if she had, Chase would none the less have taken an unbending position on wifely duty no matter what the provocation. He had been thoroughly frightened that reports of a possible divorse had reached the press. For a woman at that time, divorce was an unthinkable disgrace, especially so in Chase's puritanical view. He had thoroughly disapproved of Kate's long European jaunt. A wife's place was at home with her husband, and he would bend every effort to persuade Kate to submit and carry out her obligations.

But Kate did not find it easy to submit, and often she was far from being proud of her husband. At one state dinner when he had been imbibing more than freely, his neighbor at the table, a daughter of President Johnson, suggested gently: "I would not take more if I were you. There are a pair of bright eyes looking at you."

"Damn them," said Sprague loudly, "they can't see me!"

"Yes, they can see you," Kate replied clearly, "and they are thoroughly ashamed of you." [3]

For Kate, with her pride, with her sense of decorum, such public humiliations were intolerable. During her long absence abroad she had begun once again to hope that things would go better, that Sprague would control his dissipation, that she would learn to check her own angry reactions. But the cyclic pattern was soon reestablished. There would be periods of tension when Sprague would drink and pursue his extramarital adventures, and Kate would be hurt and angry. But these periods were interrupted by weeks when he would be penitent and needing her, and she would respond and all would be smooth again. A friend who knew Kate intimately at that time, and who lived for over a year in the house, declared later that "I never saw the slightest approach to unpleasantness," and she was convinced that the early years of Kate's marriage were happy.[4] There were quarrels, undoubtedly, but the bond between them was still there. Kate had a strong will and fierce pride and she did not want anyone to see if she felt neglected by her husband. Mrs. Senator Sprague was the queen of Washington society and queens do not parade their private sorrows in public.

A description of Kate as she presided at one of her receptions notes first her eyes, "the most fetching eyes on earth. There is a slight saucy tilt to the nose, and the lips are very red and full, with fascinating tilts at the corners. The hair, richly golden. The form and feature of the most devastating and provocative of women. Perhaps the most expressive feature is the deep brown eyes that seem brooding in the shade of the veiling lashes. Her magnetism pervades the room. Maybe it is the mind behind the beauty that makes her stand out so regally among all the pretty women about her . . . She draws out the most reticent like strong wine; even the dull shine momentarily under her mysterious gaze. After all, it is not the mere physical beauty that makes her 'the enchantress,' but the distinctive intellectual charm of her manner, the proud poise of her exquisite head." [5]

It would have been hard for Kate to resist a social life in which she succeeded so pre-eminently and it helped her to forget the troubled relations with her husband. The Hoyt girls were enjoying themselves immensely and were sorry when the Lenten season brought the balls and dinners and receptions to a close.

When Nettie had decided to stay on abroad for the winter, it had been planned that Kate and Sprague would return in the spring to bring her home. Sprague changed his mind, however, and let Kate go without him. He had decided to stay at home and mend his political fences so that the state legislature would be sure to elect him the following year for a second term to the Senate. Both Chase and Kate agreed that he should seek reelection, and, at least to Chase, Sprague gave an air of confidence about his success.

Kate persisted in the plan of another trip abroad, once again hoping that the separation would work some sort of miracle in her marriage. She took with her, not only Willie and his nurse, and her French maid, but the two young Hoyt girls and their brother. She did not feel lost "among strangers" this time, as she had the previous year, and she spent money extravagantly. Worth, the great French dressmaker, thought she had the most perfect of figures and found her a delight to dress. French kid gloves were the finest to be had and Kate laid in a supply that should have lasted her for the rest of her life. Shoes, hats, ornaments, glass and china, porcelains and furnishings of all sorts—the beautiful Mrs. Sprague spent money like the wife of a millionaire. Which she was. Extravagant as Kate was, her husband's business empire could support it, even if his own tastes were not so inclined. When she returned in the fall it was with greater confidence in herself and her ability to be independent, but with an ever more faltering hope to find in her marriage what she would have given up every other advantage to possess.

The political scene in early 1868 was in turmoil. The country was split as fiercely as ever. As Sprague had pointed out to Kate already in the summer of 1866, Johnson was in conflict with the Congress, which simply disregarded him. The Radicals had a sufficient majority to do as they wanted. Johnson, with his tactless awkwardness and lack of political skill, was helpless. The Senate not only destroyed his whole Reconstruction plan, but they set a limit on his powers which rendered him politically impotent. He was deprived of control over the military and was debarred from removing any person who had been appointed with the "advice and consent" of the Senate. Rumors that Johnson was thinking of removing Secretary of War Stanton, with whom he found it impossible to work, had hastened passage of the Tenure of Office bill. The Radicals were determined to strip the President of power. Johnson was equally determined to maintain the power of the Presidency. When he tried to remove Stanton from office in defiance of the Tenure of Office Act, the House of Representatives voted to impeach him.

There were no rules laid down by the Constitution for the impeachment proceedings of a President aside from the specification that the Chief Justice of the Supreme Court was to preside over the Senate, and that a two thirds vote of members present was required for conviction. The Radicals were sure that their old friend Chase would be on their side and would do all he could to further their cause. But they reckoned without Chase's profound belief in the principles of law.

When Chief Justice Salmon P. Chase called the Senators to order for the start of the trial he knew that they had scented blood and were hot on the trail for the kill, that reason and restraint had long since been left behind. He was determined to maintain the dignity and power of law and the rights of his position as Chief Justice of the Supreme Court and presiding officer. This was to be a trial before a court of law and not a mockery of justice in a drumhead trial. Chase's adherence to principle, his dignity, his determination to see that reason and not passion prevailed did much to curb the travesty that had been inaugurated. He prepared an oath which he administered to each Senator: "I do solemnly swear that in all things appertaining to the trial of the impeachment of Andrew Johnson, President of the United States, I will do impartial justice to the Constitution and the laws—so help me God." And then he laid down the rules for the trial telling the Senators that they were now in a court of law as jurors and would be required to observe correct trial procedure with only specified modifications.

From the fifth of March till the sixteenth of May the impeachment drama was the focus of passionate attention throughout the country. The Senate galleries were filled to overflowing for every session, guards stood at each entrance checking tickets of the spectators. All of Washington society was there and the ladies outdid each other in the elegance of their attire. Kate and Nettie had seats in the front row of the gallery. Who is "that picture of delicacy and grace, arrayed in silk tinted with the shade of a dead forest leaf, with dead gold ornaments to match?" queried an observer. "Why, that is the queen of fashion—the wife of a Senator, the daughter of Chief Justice Chase." [6]

If ever Chase needed his daughters, and especially Kate, near him it was now. Newspapers were as hysterical in abuse as the politicians. An editorial in *The New York Times* stated: "The Republican Senators who have indicated a purpose to vote for acquittal, have done it in defiance of the most formidable battery of political denunciation ever brought to bear against the personal and official independence and integrity of men in high public station. They have been threatened with personal infamy as well as political ostracism." [7] Even Chase did not escape vicious personal attack. He was accused of openly favoring Johnson, of having made a deal with him to work for acquittal in return for support of his own ambitions for the Presidency; of using undue influence on various senators to affect their vote. Stories that, in an effort to win votes for acquittal, he had taken doubtful Senators for drives, and entertained them at home in lavish style were widely circulated.

Chase denied any such acts or intentions categorically. When his old friend Horace Greeley printed in the *Tribune* an accusation that Chase had played an unsavory role in influencing several Senators, Chase wrote him: "More lies seem to be afloat about me than I thought invention capable of . . . I have not exerted myself to influence anybody, one way or the other. The stories about dinner are mere bosh, and so are the stories about rides, except that there is a grain of fact sunk in gallons of falsehood . . . I had no information whatever how any senator would vote; I mean of those who had not read opinions, or declared them . . . I have kept my oath on the trial, and have done nothing from partiality or hostility." [8]

Chase found his position as presiding officer extremely difficult and he felt like a "foreign element" coming in to the Senate from the Supreme Court. "To me the whole business seems wrong, and if I had any opinion, under the Constitution, I would not take part in it." [9] He was determined "to do impartial justice according to the Constitution and the laws made in pursuance thereof." [10] Chase felt that the President had "a perfect right, and indeed, was under the highest obligation to remove Mr. Stanton, if he made the removal . . . with a sincere belief that the tenure-of-office act was unconstitutional, and for the purpose of bringing the question before the Supreme Court." [11] Although Chase's sympathies were for acquittal, he felt that the real test was that of justice and reason. "To me the most important thing seems . . . not that Mr. Johnson should be acquitted or convicted, but that his judges, the Senators of the United States, should render an honest and impartial judgement, according to [the] Constitution and the laws, upon the facts proved before them. In what I have done as presiding officer, I have endeavored to be, and I believe I have been, perfectly unbiased." [12] Chase did all that he could to raise the whole issue from the political into the judicial arena.

As the final vote approached, the whole country waited breathlessly for the verdict. Many of the senators had made their positions clear but there were a few who had not expressed any judgment, among them William Sprague. Some of the newspapers declared, and many observers felt, that Sprague's vote for acquittal was sure in view of the much-discussed sympathy toward Johnson attributed both to the Chief Justice and to Kate. One paper even professed to know that Kate had threatened to leave her husband if he voted "guilty." It seems hardly credible that either Chase or Kate would have had any illusions about Sprague's vote. His violent feelings against Andrew Johnson, about which he had been talking and writing to Kate for the past two years, would certainly seem to preclude any possibility that she could imagine that he would even consider voting against the impeachment. The pressures from the pro-impeachment quarters were extreme, and not a single Republican who voted for acquittal would be reelected to the Senate. It took a man of great courage and conviction to stand up against these forces, and all Sprague's convictions were strongly against Johnson anyway. Also he was up for reelection. He would hardly have been ready to risk his political future for a man and a cause he despised. The impeachment failed by a single vote, and that vote obviously could never have been Sprague's. He had been in favor of impeachment all along, and he voted for it.

With the overwhelming interest in the trial, Chase had been in the public eye as never before. It was a period of great strain for him and often he seemed tired and discouraged. Kate and Nettie did what they could to cheer him and make things comfortable for him when the day was over. But any idea that Kate felt so strongly about the outcome of the impeachment trial that she worked behind the scenes to affect its outcome can quickly be dispelled, for suddenly, right in the midst of it all, Kate packed up and left Washington, bag and baggage, for Narragansett. The reason? Another flaming row with her husband.

Chase was anxious and distressed and his concern for Kate was evident in the long letter he wrote her only six days before the vote was taken. He was "dreadfully frightened" about her cold, he told her. "How I wish you would take a different view of your social duties, and cease exposing yourself, by attending these wretched night parties.

"Most of all I long to see you an earnest Christian woman, not only religious but happy in religion.

"How I do love you my darling! My whole heart seems to go towards you while I write and tears come into my eyes. How wrong it is for those who love not [to] express their love. I remember how often you have felt hurt by my apparent indifference to what interested you; and I feel sorry that I ever occasioned such feelings to you. You have in your husband something of that which I blame in myself. But I know how strong my love really was, and I know how strong his is. And I am very glad that while you have sometimes forgotten that the happiness of a wife is most certainly secured by loving submission and loving tact, you generally conquer by sweetness. I never saw him so much affected as by the difference that occurred between you just before you went away. He was almost unmanned—near to tears. I have not thought it best to refer to it; but try to make my society pleasant for him and hope I succeed. You must *love away all his reserve*—and help yourself to do so by reflecting how generous, self-sacrificing and indulgent a husband he has been to you. How few husbands would consent to such absences; and be at once so liberal and thoughtful. If he was only a true Christian he would be nearly perfect." [13]

Chase was in the unenviable position of trying to walk a tightrope between Kate and her husband. He was sincerely fond of Sprague and he wanted more than anything for the two of them to live together in peace and harmony. He recognized the differences and the difficulties in both their temperaments and though he sympathized with Kate, he felt that she, as the wife and as the stronger of the two, had the greater obligation to adapt. He seemed hesitant, almost afraid, to intrude into the personal affairs of his son-in-law, worried, perhaps, that he might only make matters worse if he tried to interfere. Nor did Sprague show the slightest inclination to turn to him for help or advice. All Chase could do was to encourage Kate in the direction he thought best and pray that she would follow his counsels.

It was a time of deep introspection for Kate, alone at Narragansett with Willie and his nurse. Two brief pages, torn from a diary, give an insight into her inner struggle. "I feel today that I live once more," she wrote. "The opportunity was given me to do a good act and I performed it joyously, heartily, in something of the old spirit when doing good to others was the business and happiness of my life—not with the apathy and reluctance that of late years has characterized the performance of even an occasional or accidental act of kindness. O for some moral scourge (even though sympathy is denied *me*) to lash my better feelings into responsive quick action, to relieve others' distress— Selfishness grows daily more and more my ruling sin, since I dwell so constantly upon the absence from my life of a pervading, tender, devoted love. Perhaps I have no title to the only thing that gives real value

139

to all my other blessings— They are manifold and very rich, it is true, but oh how gladly would I exchange them all, and consider that I gained everything by that exchange, could I awaken and possess forever the great treasure my soul craves." [14]

Kate was clearly obsessed with her emotional life and she had reached a point where she was unable to be interested in much else. She was shocked at her selfishness in her absorption with her own unsatisfied emotional needs. But she still could not accept that Sprague could not or would not love her as she wanted to be loved in a warm sharing of life together. He still sometimes professed that that was what he too wanted, but it was perhaps the very strength of Kate's emotions that made him draw back and close her out.

Kate must have fought fiercely with herself those weeks in Narragansett and she won at least part of the battle and was able to free herself from her own emotions enough to take an active part in the affairs of others, this time of her father.

It was an election year again and the political scene was boiling as it had not done for eight years. Reconstruction policies were completely disordered; feelings North and South had not abated at all; after the impeachment trial Johnson was more politically impotent than ever; the country looked for salvation in a strong, popular figure. It was soon clear that the Republicans thought Grant this man and they nominated him on the first ballot. Although Chase had seen the strong current of Grant's popularity, he had naively hoped that the nomination might have been tendered him. As Lincoln had feared, the ambitions of the Chief Justice were not satisfied with his prestigious position and he still yearned after the Presidency. Carl Schurz thought he resembled a "wounded lion" who felt like a martyr as Chief Justice.

Chase was playing the old game again, trying to appear diffident about the nomination while at the same time doing what he could to secure it. Pridefully he did not want to appear overeager for the prize, in case it be denied him, yet he was tempted beyond resistance at what might possibly be his. There is something profoundly pathetic in the sight of that "great proud man," as Sprague had termed him, so obsessed with the one goal that nothing short of it could satisfy him. He was not blind to the press of his own ambition. Perhaps in his heart he was ashamed of it and what it led him to do, and from that in part sprang his efforts to appear indifferent: "It was without regret that I observed the preference of the Republican party gradually concentrating upon Gen. Grant . . . I, therefore, very willingly dismissed, long since, the subject of the Presidency from my thoughts; and am now, more than ever, satisfied with the dismissal," he assured a friend.[15]

At the same time, however, Chase was not only flirting with a new third-party convention movement but was stirred by the fact that he had been widely talked about for some time as a possible candidate—on the Democratic ticket. Yet he could feign surprise some weeks later at the "apparent strength and extent of the movement for my nomination . . . I think that it is pretty well understood now, that I want no nomination; and that while I should not feel at liberty to decline one which really represented the wishes of the masses, whether Republican, Conservative, or Democratic, . . . I cannot, under any contingency, abandon the principles of equal rights and exact justice for all, which I have heretofore maintained. This being understood, I am content to let the movement take its course, and shall be satisfied whatever the issue." [16]

The obstacle that rose between the Democratic party and Chase's nomination was not the question of shifting parties—after all he had done that several times before—but of his stand, from which he had never wavered, for universal suffrage. Chase stated that what had separated him from the Democratic party, the question of slavery, was now resolved, but the issue of suffrage was still in question. If the party would endorse universal suffrage there would be nothing to separate them. It was Chase himself, however, who shifted his position somewhat, thus opening the door to a compromise. He indicated that there might be two possibilities on the suffrage question: "either restoration on the basis of universal suffrage and universal amnesty . . . or, recognition of the fact that universal suffrage is a democratic principle, the application of which is to be left in the States, under the Constitution, to the States themselves . . . Upon a platform in either of these forms of expression, I might, I suppose, honorably accept a nomination;

and I have no doubt that this practical settlement of the question would be hailed with great satisfaction as the harbinger of restored union, and peace and prosperity." [17]

Chase could hardly have believed that state control of suffrage would result, in the Southern States, in the universal suffrage he had so long endorsed. It was the second of the possibilities he had outlined that the Democratic platform adopted, and although Chase wrote that the platform was "not exactly what I should like best," [18] he felt that he could accept it well enough. And so, Chase's race for the Democratic nomination became serious.

Kate came down from Narragansett for the Convention, which opened in the new Tammany Hall in New York City on July 4, ready to do battle for her father, who had been disappointed so many times before in his hopes for the highest office. She put aside her preoccupation with her own unhappiness and channeled her energies into this effort to win for her father the prize he so much desired. Here was a chance to show what she could do, to use her powers, to make up for the humiliations her pride had suffered in her marriage. It was unusual for a woman to take an active role in a political struggle, and her presence in New York at the time of the Convention aroused a good deal of attention and comment.

Inside Tammany Hall the heat and crush were incredible. People pushed and shoved to get in and find places, and the crowd, once inside, "experienced a martyrdom, resulting from that sanguine hope that two persons could be put into the space required for one . . . It was evident that the session was to be protracted suffering . . . The ladies were out . . . in full force." [19]

Women were not allowed on the floor of the Convention, but, as always, the real work was done before and after hours at the various hotels and headquarters where the delegates were. Kate stayed at the Fifth Avenue Hotel where also was installed the Ohio delegation. Amasa Sprague was a member of the Rhode Island delegation, and Chase's secretary, J. W. Schuckers, worked closely with Kate. Her father's old friends, Hiram Barney and John Cisco, who had held office in New York under appointment from Chase during his Treasury days, were staunch supporters of his candidacy. William Sprague, who had not changed his Republican affiliations, was nowhere in evidence.

The weather was insufferable, "as hot as weather can be. Too hot for the work on hand here," Kate wrote her father.[20] There was no pre-eminent candidate, as Grant had been at Chicago, and there was a great deal of jockeying for position. If Kate had hoped that her presence at the Convention would keep Chase from committing one of his naive indiscretions, she was mistaken. He sent a letter to a minor figure, Alexander Long, at Long's suggestion, in which he said that he was ready to support the nominee of the Convention if he himself were not named. As usual, Chase realized his mistake almost at once and wrote the same day to John Van Buren, who was acting in effect as his campaign manager, asking that the letter to Long be suppressed if Van Buren thought it went too far. The letter, however, was leaked to the press and a few days later Long pressed his advantage and asked Chase to approve a formal statement pledging support to the nominee. Although this put Chase in a dangerous position, endorsing a decision before it was taken, approving the nominee before the fact, he nevertheless complied, not exactly in the way Long had requested but by an open letter, which could be addressed later to anyone, and notes of a conversation which he hoped might serve the purpose without use of the letter. And then he added self-righteously: "It is my special request that no use be made of either, unless some real exigency shall require it . . . my self-respect is worth more to me than fifty Presidencies. Without the nomination I shall sleep more soundly than with it. To surrender my consciousness of doing right by binding myself in advance to, I know not what, is simply impossible for me. If it were possible, it would prove me unworthy of the trust and confidence of my countrymen." [21]

Here again we see the lengths to which Chase's ambition drove him and the dubious practices which he could not resist but which he tried to disguise under noble platitudes. And yet he was an honorable man and suffered from the compromises he made, trying to pretend to himself, and to others, that he had not done so.

There was an active Chase committee, but most of the work for his candidacy was done by the inner circle of supporters around Kate: Van Buren, Cisco, Smith, and Kennedy. Chase had a considerable following in the New York delegation, made up of prominent men such as August Belmont, and the hope was that former Governor Horatio Seymour would make the nominating address for Chase.

Chase stayed in Washington "where I take all things very quietly and play croquet nearly every evening," he wrote Kate. "I sleep as soundly as the heat will let me every night." And he told her piously, "I am afraid my darling that you are acting too much the politician. Have a care. Don't do or say anything which may not be proclaimed on the housetops. I am so anxious about you that I cannot help wishing you were in Narragansett or here." [22]

Chase was as contradictory as ever. At the same time that he was preaching to Kate, he was in constant daily contact by letter and telegram not only with her but with Van Buren and several other delegates to the Convention. One day he would write her: "You know how little I have desired the nomination and how averse I have been to making any attempts to secure it . . . and I am entirely satisfied with the opportunities for usefulness which my present position affords." [23] Three days later she would receive a letter in quite a different vein. "Do you see Mr. Van Buren? I think that he and Mr. Cisco are my best and most judicious and reliable friends there. Mr. v B. is the best posted and understands best how, and what and where to do. Please see him and give him all the information you can and let Mr. S[prague] furnish him a list of all my friends that will be useful, if it is not already too late." [24] But Kate knew her father better than anyone and was not at all confused by his contradictory attitudes. She understood how much he wished for the nomination and this time it looked as though it might really be within his grasp.

Kate was Chase's eyes and ears, but as a woman her role was limited. As she could not go on the Convention floor, neither could she go to the smoke-filled hotel rooms at night. But she could and did use her influence in so far as she was able, and tried to guide Chase's actions by her judgment of the general situation, the men who supported him, and her estimate of their motives and sincerity. But although Chase kept in daily touch with her and depended on her to keep him informed of everything that was going on, he simply did not believe that she could assess the situation as well as the men on whom he was depending for advice, and in at least one important matter, he did not follow her suggestion. When the party platform was adopted by the Convention, Kate, and some of her father's friends, thought that he should send a telegram about it such "as may seem advisable and necessary to read in open Convention." [25] Van Buren advised Chase to do and say nothing about it. To Kate's dismay, for she felt it to be a tactical error, Chase followed Van Buren's suggestion and remained silent on the subject.

Although Kate was hopeful that Chase might win, and determined to do all she could do to promote his success, her optimism was cautious. "I am glad you are not going to be greatly disappointed if the nomination is not for you. I should like to see this bright jewel added to your crown of earthly distinction and *I believe it will be.* But we can live and be very happy and just as proud of you without it. Will the *country* do as well?" [26] Kate finished loyally.

Chase's name was not put immediately in nomination. The strategy had been planned to hold off until the right moment and let the other candidates pit themselves against each other long enough so that a strong, new name in the lists would bring on a landslide. Pendleton of Ohio, who had followed Chase as governor, took the lead at once, but increased it only slightly during the first eight ballots. His strength then began to dwindle while that of Hendricks of Indiana increased. After eighteen hot, weary ballots, Pendleton withdrew, leaving the battle between Hendricks and General Hancock of Pensylvania. On the twelfth ballot Chase, although still not in nomination, received one half a vote from California. This set off a tumultuous ovation which buoyed Kate's spirits and made it look as though the strategy of waiting would succeed.

Although it was on the New York delegation, and especially on Governor Seymour, that the Chase faction had built its hopes, Kate had some doubts about them. On the second day of the Convention, she wrote her father: "Everything, as far as developed looked well—only New York—friends inside that close corporation say their action is cautious, and those outside call it timid." [27] Rumors persisted, and even appeared in print, that New York was really not for Chase but that their strategy of reserving their powerful strength, first for a favorite son and then moving to support Hendricks in order to weaken Pendleton, was really motivated by an actual purpose to nominate Seymour.

Nevertheless, on July 8, the New York delegation, in caucus, showed a majority for Chase and it was decided that they would put his name in nomination the next day as soon as Hendricks' strength, as was anticipated, began to drop, and it was expected that the Ohio delegation and several other states would follow New York's lead. The next day Vallandigham, of the Ohio delegation, an old friend of Chase, went to powerful Samuel Tilden of New York and asked that the long-awaited plan to nominate Chase be put into execution. Tilden refused, saying he could not remove support from Hendricks unless his position weakened. In the meantime, the Ohio delegation had split on the question of Chase and at a meeting the previous evening had passed a resolution refusing to support him. Once again, his home state failed him. Nevertheless, the Chase tacticians were not discouraged and felt sure that when Governor Seymour placed Chase's name in nomination, as they were convinced he had agreed to do, Ohio would quickly fall in line with the other states.

When, however, Tilden refused to remove New York's support from Hendricks, who seemed within an ace of victory on the twenty-second ballot, Ohio acted and acted with a vengeance. They placed the name of Governor Seymour in nomination. Seymour had already refused several times to be a candidate, the first time in November of the previous year. On the fourth ballot he had received nine votes and had declared categorically that he was not a candidate and could not with honor accept the nomination. Before taking this step, Vallandigham had once more begged Tilden to present the name of Chase and again Tilden had refused. Hurriedly, Ohio decided that if New York was reneging on the commitment to Chase, the only alternative to a Hendricks victory was to name Seymour.

The Convention went wild with excitement at this move. Seymour tried to make himself heard, tried to say he could not accept. A vivid picture describes "the touching scene" when Tilden saw Seymour standing all alone, tears streaming down his face. " 'My God, Tilden, what shall I do? This is terrible!' exclaimed the reluctant one. The placid Tilden was equal to the occasion and replied with something pertinent if not original: 'Sir, the Presidency has sought you, not you the Presidency and you must take it.' Consoler and consoled locked arms and sought more retired quarters mutually happy." [28]

The Convention had been in session six days under conditions of heat and overcrowding that were unspeakable. Tempers were short and patience even shorter. They had balloted twenty-two times and had not been able to come up with a candidate. Seymour seemed like an answer to a prayer and it was his name which came with the freshness that had been planned would bring victory to Chase. After Ohio made the nomination Wisconsin turned the tide announcing its votes for Seymour. After that, state after state changed its vote and Seymour was in. The Convention floor was a madhouse. The cannon outside started booming. Everything was in total uproar.

After a recess of an hour, the delegates returned to choose the Vice-Presidential candidate. It took no time at all for them to give unanimous approval to Chase's old enemy, Frank Blair.

Kate waited until the next day to write her father: "You have been most cruelly deceived and shamefully used by the man whom you trusted implicitly and the country must suffer for his duplicity. I would not write you yesterday in the excitement of the result of the action of the convention and until I had carefully gone over in my mind all the circumstances that had come under my knowledge of the action of Mr. Van Buren. When I get comfortably settled at Narragansett I will write out a full and detailed history of my knowledge of this matter that cannot fail to convince you of his bad faith. Nothing more would be needed than that since the result of the nomination was announced Mr. Van Buren, though

147

constantly at the Manhattan Club, next door, has not been near me . . .

"Had Mr. Kennedy had the authority to act for you, you would have been as certainly nominated on the wave of enthusiasm created in the convention by the half vote cast by California day before yesterday—as anything could be. Mr. Van Buren's telegraph to you to answer no questions in regard to the platform was the block he put in the way of your nomination, and when at the critical juncture he was at last found (for he had scarcely been seen in the convention) he refused to take the responsibility of speaking for you, and said he was not authorized . . . Mr. Tilden and Mr. Seymour have done this work, and Mr. Van Buren has been their tool. This is my honest belief, but I will write it out carefully. Do, dear Father, in the future be guided by the advice of some of those who are devoted to you, but who are more suspicious, than your own noble heart will allow you to be.

"With all this you personally can have nothing to regret. Your friends have worked nobly—and the universal disappointment today is amazing. Not a flag floats nor is the semblance of rejoicing visible anywhere. Your name is the watchword with the people and many have been outraged and deceived . . . You can form no conception of the depression here." [29]

Kate was far from being the only one who thought Chase had been deceived. Many of Chase's friends, and even outside observers, believed that the plan to put forward Seymour had been hatched long before the Convention and that Seymour had been a party to it all along. Others vehemently denied it.

The New York Times said that the entire affair was one of "dissimulation, treachery and fraud." Chase himself believed, however, that some members of both the Ohio and the New York delegations had contrived Seymour's nomination and in the end did not hold Seymour responsible for what had happened.

Could Chase have been nominated? Had he really had a chance? The answer is undoubtedly yes. Although early in the Convention *The New York Times* referred to a Chase nomination as "this chaff, which hardly suffices to show the way of the wind," [30] two days later the same paper found things looking very good for

Chase and a majority of the reporters covering the Convention so wired their papers. If before that fateful last ballot, Seymour had introduced the name of Chase; if, earlier in the Convention, Chase and his manager had not been so reluctant about publicly endorsing the platform; if, when he was given the ovation after California's half vote, if—if any one of several imponderables had gone differently, Chase might very well have been the nominee. And even won the Presidency. For in spite of the fact Seymour became an increasingly reluctant and ineffectual candidate, Grant won the election by only a narrow margin.

As it was, Chase emerged from the Convention with nothing except a last minute vote of thanks for the way he had presided over the impeachment. He had risked his reputation and the dignity of his high office on a gamble which he lost and he did not ever quite regain his former stature again. He was attacked in some of the newspapers in terms that ranged from outright insult: "Dishonoured, self-debauched, friendless . . . an example of the calamitous, disgraceful consequences of political prostitution," to jeering derision that he had flown in and out of the Convention like Wordsworth's cuckoo, not really a bird but only a "wandering voice." [31] Chase himself was, as usual, able to rationalize it all and to regret it "only for the sake of friends and country." [32] With such imperturbable complacency, self-esteem is impregnable.

And what of Kate in all this? When Chase first heard the news of his dashed hopes, it was reported long afterward, his first words had been, "Does Mrs. Sprague know? And how does she bear it?" And he was "relieved to find that the bad news did not overwhelm her. Mrs. Sprague," it was said, "manifested wonderful self-control, but evidently the blow was severe. She said little, but that little, albeit it was calmly spoken, showed the violence of the shock she had received." [33] Kate had hoped that the Convention would "have the *courage* to do right" and in an euphoric mood had ended the same letter to her father "affectionately and ambitiously for Country—the Democracy and its noblest Patriot and Statesman." [34] Certainly she was shocked and disappointed at the sudden disastrous turn of events that came so unexpectedly. But that she brooded in bitter anger over it for months, that it was the focal point of her thoughts and destroyed all else for her, as has so often been claimed, can hardly be credited in the face of her very intimate and revealing diary, written not long after the Convention. In it there is not one single mention of ambition or politics and only one or two brief references to her father which are strictly personal. Kate was in bitter turmoil that year but it related not to political ambition but to a single subject only—William Sprague.

CHAPTER
XI

"WELL my old friend," Kate begins her diary, "it is long since I have appealed to you for relief, as I used to do in the old days, when I was alone, and trouble over-took me. Now I am no longer alone. I have many to love, but none to talk with, no one to whom I can lay my heart bare. So I come back to you for that silent sympathy that even a listener may give. I shall not spare you ... You will have to receive and keep the record of all my thoughts, motives, feelings, desires . . . acting as a kind of Moral Telescope and Confessor, which while revealing the difficulites and trials of daily life will at the same time exhibit truthfully my own faults and short comings and help to relieve this weary disappointment that seems often more than I can bear."

Kate did not spare herself in what she wrote and there is something in it reminiscent of her father's rolling, pompous phrases of confession and repentance.

"Save me from further bitterness of speech and angry tempers," she pleaded to her diary-confessor," and when trouble comes, whether of my own making or that of others, let the expression I find here where no other eye can be offended by it, check at least the utterance of harsh and cruel words." She feels that in the volumes she wrote in the past there was far more to her credit than she can truthfully write now, "for during these later years, I have not commanded myself and struggled for the right, as then I did, but in my new relation, and with my husband I have striven to force conviction, and gain my desire by harsh words, when my life, its consistency and gentleness should have been my most powerful argument . . . But my punishment has come, and God knows it is heavy— Hence I am resolved to keep silence, remembering it is far better to feel the smart, than the remorse of having inflicted it."

An incident had occurred that morning, one that had "sorely tried" her. For a "simple act of carelessness," her husband had reproached her "most unworthily so far forgetting himself as to voice his reproach in the hearing of a cab driver, his servant and his child."

Correct comportment in public was important to Kate and she found any deviation from it humiliating. She had been strictly trained in manners and etiquette. Sprague had not been exposed to a similar background and training, having had to make his own way from an early age in the rough and tumble of the millhand world. "The Spragues were never received socially," an old timer in Providence is quoted as saying. "The truth of the matter is that Governor Sprague never had the manners of a gentleman, only the veneer of refinement, and in a mental lapse might put his feet upon a rose satin chair." [1] Sprague often exhibited a coarse streak which shocked Kate's fastidious taste.

The subject of the quarrel that morning was money. Sprague accused Kate of obtaining money from him "through artifice, 'managing to get money as he expressed it.' " At that, Kate refused to accept any from him, although she herself was without a cent. "I could not do otherwise," she wrote. "All my pride revolted at so unmanly, so unworthy a charge and the man who made it, though my husband, appeared small, and mean." And then she checks herself and adds, "But there, I judge himself hastily perhaps."

Although Kate had a small inheritance from her mother, it was scarcely enough for more than pin money, and she was wholly dependent financially on her husband. It is clear that this position of dependency rankled with her and she found it impossible to understand "the littleness of soul, that under any provocation could induce a husband, or a man feeling all the advantages of his position, to utter such a reproach. Can it be that he would keep this hateful thought of my dependency ever before me, forcing me to believe that every dollar given, or expended upon his home is begrudged." He is generous, in his own way, she feels, and when he gives, he does so liberally and quietly, but why would he have her believe that he is in straitened circumstances when he himself pours out hundreds and thousands of dollars "in channels that bring their own return"? She is bitter against the pursuit of power —strange thoughts for an ambitious Kate—" 'What shall it profit a man if he gain the whole world and lose his own soul,' " she writes, "or warp that soul in the pursuit of worldly power through the traffic in all that is implanted in our natures as sacred[?]"

Kate was so hurt and exasperated by her husband's "thoughtless expression of today, so uncalled for, so unworthy," that she felt as though she never could stoop to ask him for another cent again.

She was aware of her own reckless extravagance which increased constantly in proportion to her emotional frustration. "My fault, I know, is great in the other extreme and it is right and well that he should impose some check. *Money* as a possession I despise. Money as a means for usefulness for good and for happiness, I respect." And she makes the comparison with her own background and upbringing as opposed to the Spragues. Her father, she knows, compared to her husband was always a poor man, "but he felt himself rich when he was enabled to bestow a benefit upon the needy or a pleasure upon those he loved, and a treasure laid up in his home was money well invested. May that largeness of soul be my boy's heritage."

Sprague was extremely indulgent toward Kate in regard to money. She had exquisite clothes, marvelous jewels, fine houses extravagantly appointed in every detail. Sprague himself did not like luxurious living and the disciplines and formality which such a way of life imposed. Kate's extravagance and her concern with possessions were disturbing to his "old-fashioned ways," that he had written Kate before they were married he hoped eventually would "find favor with you." He enjoyed being generous with her, but he liked to pull the purse strings tight on occasion, not only

153

as a check on her extravagance, but as a reminder of his authority. The only area in which he was supreme was financial, and he would have been less than human had he not wanted to make his power felt. Trailing behind his brilliant wife and majestic father-in-law, "little Sprague" well knew how people regarded him. He needed to assert himself, to inflate the sense of his own worth. Any idea Kate may have had that he might some day free her from that "chain he forges" was pure illusion. Her dependency in this respect was the prime force that gave him stature with her in his own eyes. It was not the question of money in itself, but rather this need in him to put her down, to make her admit his ascendancy to which Kate reacted in such bitter rebellion.

"God forgive me," she went on, "that I have so often wished that I had found in my husband a man of more intellectual resources, even with far less material worth. It is all in his nature, but all wanting in his training. Life would be to him so different—and to me so precious." And then, in spite of everything, she reveals the depth of feeling she still has for him. "I love this dear husband, very much, some times I have almost worshipped him, and then some act or word will make him appear, for the nonce, so small that I wonder at its discrepancy."

Kate would like to share in her husband's interests, but he makes her feel excluded and neither does he seem to want to participate in the life of the home.

"Sometimes an awakening interest, or transient cordiality leads me to hope that my husband is really, at last, to become, in his own person, the essential element of his home," she wrote. "I fancy at times these things dawn upon him, he sees what he has only to reach forth his hand to grasp, and he resolves to try to fill and occupy the place, in the home circle he has created, as well as the position he has secured for himself in the world. But perhaps, on the other hand, he has never given it a serious thought, his only idea being to slip through these obligations in life, as easily and peacefully as he can. Then I feel rebellious. I ponder how with so little thought and consideration he ventured to take upon himself duties he so little appreciates."

As she continues to write, her thoughts penetrate to deeper

levels within herself, the unpleasant incident of the morning is put aside and she reaches far more serious problems that have occurred between them. The most painful are his recent accusations against her. "And far far worse than all, he has of late lent himself to some malignant tongue, seeking perhaps to destroy his peace, or mine, or both, and claims to know that *of me,* which if true, would make me unworthy to be a wife—*any* man's wife! Great God—is this the woman-hood, alone and singlehanded I fought for so jealously through long years. My Father's love, my Father's pride and confidence, my Father's happiness my motive and safe-guard through all!"

Kate's enemies were still at work and once again, as in the first year after their meeting, had made an impression on Sprague. He was jealous of Kate, and as so often happens, turned back to the time before their marriage and blamed Kate for favors she had granted to him, and to him alone, and made them the basis for mistrusting her now. "It is fitting perhaps," Kate observed bitterly, "that the only man who found me weak, though he be my husband, should reproach me with it and make it the excuse for withholding that love, confidence, and trust my heart has so ached to possess. Was my weakness, my sin deserving of this long punishment? Is no joy, no substance left in life for us?" [2]

Kate's despairing tone and obvious unhappiness present an almost hopeless picture of a relationship beyond repair. But the strange fact is that there were still periods, and even long ones, of happiness and communication between these two. Kate began her diary only a few weeks after one such happy time had ended. Sprague had been laid up with a broken leg and Kate had had him to herself during his convalescence. She liked to do for him, to take care of him, to have him want and need her. Such periods had always been happy ones for both of them. They had nothing to contend about, no jealousies, no dividing of attention, and then everything went smoothly. Only a few weeks before that, Chase had been anxious that they might be quarreling again. Without consulting Kate, Sprague had summarily dismissed her coachman for an accident to the horses when he had been drinking. Chase wrote her that he was afraid that she and her husband "had some unpleasant words about his prompt action," and he cautioned her: "You must reflect my darling that there can be but one head to a family, and that while a husband will always find the happiness of both increased by mutual counsels, yet that it is that wife's part after the husband chooses to act in any matter, upon his own judgement without asking hers, to acquiesce cheerfully and affectionately. This is a part of her marriage vow; and the best way, by all odds, to obtain and retain the confidence, affection, and consultation of her husband . . . Few wives ever had a more indulgent husband, and a husband to be more justly proud of than you. You love and honor him I know; but sometimes you complain when he thinks it unreasonable and contend with him when duty and prudence require submission. You can conquer only by love and sacrifice—not by argument and pertinacity. An end gained by pertinacity is really lost." [3]

With Sprague's injury, however, and the closeness that it brought to them, contention and pertinacity vanished and Chase was delighted with what he saw when he visited them at Narragansett in September. "It was a great comfort to leave you and the Governor so well; him apparently better contented and happier and you prettier and more lovely as well as more happy than I ever saw either of you." [4]

But Sprague's leg healed and the world impinged again. "After having seen my husband once more in his office, I come back today (to Narragansett) and feel as though my occupation were gone," Kate wrote her father. "The Governor has so far recovered that Dr. Perry says that it is now only as a precautionary measure that he keeps him still to use his crutches." [5] A month later Kate was so discouraged that she turned to her diary for consolation.

A week after Kate's first entry in her diary she took up her pen again, once more consumed with bitterness and frustration after a meeting with her husband. "Would I had something more cheerful to relate than the history of our interview today. I had so far conquered my hard feelings as to write him a cheerful letter, in reply to one consenting to our making the house more comfortable for the winter, rather ungracious and by no means an affectionate letter, and as soon as I could manage to leave the work which I watch as though a salaried overseer and find distraction in it, I went to the city. It was raining violently, but I would not be put off, for my errand was to secure some little token of remembrance for my husband, for the fifth anniversary of our marriage-day and I cannot let it pass unnoticed. I made sure that William had not come home on Sunday but was coming to celebrate this day." And she recalled how each year he had forgotten the anniversary and when reminded showed so little interest that she regretted having mentioned it. "Last year I hurried home from abroad, that we might not pass this day apart, but I try to forget my heartless welcome and the days that followed—but the human heart will cling to hope and once more I record a failure. This day of which I would make so much, is not even noted in passage by him. It is like all other days, one of affairs, it has no significance, it makes no event, it is worthy of no note. The disappointment is nothing new. Why should I feel it still?"

She went that morning to her husband's place of business and in order to save him the steps and the exposure, as it was raining hard, she went up to his office, something she always found distasteful for many reasons. Although ten days had passed since she had seen him last, she was allowed to wait in the outer office, among the clerks, although he could see her plainly, while he finished his conversation in the doorway and turned, in his own good time, to bid her welcome. "Welcome! if that be welcome it is surely not worth the seeking," she wrote. "William saunters indifferently into the room, looking shabby and unkempt, and with a careless nod to me, makes some remark about the weather. I answer as cheerfully as I can, but with my heart in my throat. I ask if he is coming home this week. Oh no, he has not thought of such a thing, and then picking up the papers upon his desk as though impatient at the interruption, turns again and asks me if *I want anything* of him, the thought of money again uppermost in his mind. Not a question of home, not an inquiry for the boy, not even the extended courtesy of a chair. I turn away disappointed, chagrined and indignant at this utter want of the commonest goodbreeding. A careless good-bye from William uttered in the same breath with a laugh, with a coarse, dirty boor (who is of course very interesting, he owns a *water power*), and I am allowed to find my way out in the rain, and to my carriage as best I can. This is a bald, hard picture, but true to the life."

It is not hard to imagine how Kate stood there in her husband's office, pale and tense, without a smile, frozen in awkward fury. A less passionate woman might have made light of the incident, might have tried to jolly him out of his rudeness, but Kate felt it too strongly to be able to use the arts and graces with which she was so adept in society. She must have boiled with anger all the way home in the rain and gone at once to set down her feelings. "It is a matter of wonder," she fumes, "that I feel so hard and bitter that I almost hate this man at times who calls himself my husband, and yet has so little title to the name. For five years my sensibility has been on the rack, impulses and feelings crushed back for the want of a response, tasks contemptuously ridiculed, motives impugned, acts misconstrued, charges both unworthy and unjust preferred, and finally with his own hand, William has added the drops which have caused my cup of sorrow to overflow, forcing upon me the knowledge, which a merciful enemy would have spared me."

Here Kate reveals the degree of rejection that she felt her husband showed toward her. It was not only that he made her feel her financial dependency on him; that he was bored with her ideas and her way of life; that he preferred to associate with his business companions rather than with the friends and relatives who graced her drawing room. It was she herself that she felt he was rejecting, all the deepest realities of her nature—her hopes, her impulses, her love for him.

What was the knowledge that caused Kate's cup of sorrow to overflow? Perhaps it was then that she learned the full story of his relationship with Mary Eliza Viall and that he had never broken with her completely. Although Sprague had refused to marry Mary Eliza, she continued in her adoration of him. After all, she looked on him as a superior being to whom the laws of ordinary mortals did not apply. But for him to marry someone else! She admitted that: "She was willing never to have been his wife; *but to give him up to another*—she had not dreamed of that." [6] From the moment that Sprague and Kate became engaged, Mary Eliza Viall Anderson was Kate's implacable enemy.

With Mary Eliza, Sprague felt none of the demands that Kate's mere presence imposed on him. She did not mind his drinking, in fact she joined him in it. She herself became finally an alcoholic and some years later Sprague was arrested in a drunken orgy with her. She did not mind his eccentric behavior, his slovenly dress, his wild ways. All she asked was to see him occasionally and to be able to adore him. Kate knew of Sprague's earlier infidelities, but they had been with prostitutes or servant girls—mere sexual adventures. But with Mary Eliza there was more than that, and it is not beyond the realm of possibility that Sprague, in a moment of anger, let Kate know that there was such a woman and that she had born his child.

In any event, Kate rode home that day before the fifth anniversary of her marriage, alone and distraught, and set down her feelings in a mood of such mounting despair that she had to interrupt her writing and it was several hours before she was able to continue. "I have laid down my pen and for hours I have been thinking—thinking. A wild tumultuous storm is raging without and my heart in attune with the elements was as turbulent and stormy. I have knelt down and prayed. Prayed that my mental vision might be cleared of these mists and clouds that mislead and blind me and I believe by the courage and strength I feel awakening within me, that my prayer will be answered."

She goes on to recall the night she spent in prayer before her wedding that she might be everything to her husband, "the messenger of every joy." And she remembered the feeling of security and trust that she found in his arms the next night, and how her every thought, every desire, every feeling merged with the one longing to make him happy. "And upon this bright treacherous stream we cast ourselves, to float without thought or care upon the current until through pride and prejudice we found ourselves at last drifting apart, until at length, this threat of difference became a strong deep stream, full of doubts, misunderstandings, and distrust. Oh my love, my love, may I not win you back! Is this fierce struggle with pride to go on forever! And embitter lives else so full of joy and beauty. My husband, pause, and look back, few men are loved as you were. But the vessel was unworthy of the wine. My hopes were too high. I could not attain to them and proud, passionate, intolerant, I had never learned to submit. Ah heart, remember your own stubbornness and cease forever these weak complainings, and bear patiently the punishment your wilfulness and selfishness has brought upon you. From this hour gird on again the dignity of your womanhood, and learn to bear what you may not control. Cry for no more, till you deserve it, and as you have much to be forgiven, have also to forbear and forgive. There will be backslidings and falterings, as you know poor heart, but take courage and God speed you!" [7]

Kate's prayers did bear fruit and in another of those amazing reversals the skies cleared and everything seemed sunshine and happiness again. "It has been a month and more since I have written here and oh such a bright, happy month, so full of gladness and delight and so fraught I believed with promise for the future," Kate noted. But the dark clouds had not stayed away long and once more Kate vented her hurt feelings in her diary. "And yet today has been spent in another long fierce battle with myself, in the effort to subdue and force back the old bitterness of spirit. I have not conquered yet, but I will strive! Am I so weak that I must yield to every passionate impulse, and display upon provocation the very qualities I protest that I despise—Yes, and I despise them even more in myself. The laugh of ridicule from my husband yesterday will do more to teach me self-control, than any amount of self-training. He shall never have occasion to repeat it. Whatever I may feel and what the aggravation, he shall not again witness my humiliations. Whether he respects me or not rests with me, and if there is that in me to command respect, he shall acknowledge it—so help me God!"

The trouble on this occasion had begun with a disappointment she had at Christmas, two days before. "W. was right though I had tried my best to conceal it. There was a pent up load upon my heart all the while which should not have been there, I knew, and which I hoped he had not discovered." The disappointment was in his gift to her, a "liberal gift of money." She would have been far more happy at a book or any trifle that he had chosen himself with care and affection. "I know it is wrong to feel as I do," she wrote, "and I would give the world to feel otherwise, and be able to adapt myself to my husband's irregularities and peculiar temperament, and accepting it as a condition I cannot control, make the best of it and keep all my disappointments and mortifications to myself."

She recognizes that in this instance she is peculiarly unreasonable for when her husband had asked her what she would like to have, she suggested money, as she had been in a mood of discouragement and indifference. They had been together at Tiffany's not long before Christmas and when he asked if she wanted one thing after another that she had admired, and his manner grew kinder, she became more interested. And finally when "we were shown the beautiful jewell which I did greatly wish to possess, I said, with some insincerity, I confess, 'Oh, it is too costly!' It seemed to me so like begging that I could not bring myself to simply say, what was the truth 'Oh yes, I do want it very much!' It was the only thing we saw that I did long to possess, as I do at times things that are rare and beautiful, and I fancied he saw how much I did want it and that he meant to surprise me with it as a treat."

Kate was still an incurable romantic and she woke on Christmas morning full of "glad anticipation at the belief that at length my husband had anticipated and prepared a pleasure for me and more than at the rich jewell I expected to possess, did this thought make me feel joyous and happy. And the *money* was a bitter disappointment. It may be all unworthy and womanish, I dare say," Kate comments honestly, "but I may confess it here without fear of ridicule, and now it is out, I feel the better for it—I would not for the world have my husband know of this, for he would think me ungrateful, and it would only add another to the contemptuous taunts he hurls at me when angry. Hypersensitive, as was her father also, Kate was easily hurt by criticism and outraged by ridicule. With her, however, it bit more deeply than it ever did with Chase. She did not have, at least in her marriage relationship, his imperturbable conviction of superiority. Sprague evidently saw how ridicule enraged her, and undoubtedly indulged in it freely when he wanted to strike back at her.

Kate was aware how petty and foolish she was being but was unable to control her reaction. She believed that Sprague must have felt that he had not behaved handsomely, for he asked her not to tell anyone what he had given her for Christmas, "afraid to let it be known, in his own family, what he had done for his wife." Kate had carefully and handsomely provided gifts for all his family and she did not feel that she needed him to caution her this way. She would not have been in haste to parade his gift. She tried to think what to do with the money he had given her. What she would like is to embody it "in some one thing which dearie can share and enjoy equally with my-self. I would like to consult him in regard to it."

She had made every effort to secure the pleasure of that day for those she loved. "I waived every personal consideration to do right and to please others, and I am almost ready to abandon all effort for the future," she wrote petulantly. She had denied herself in order to put aside money she could call her own to spend on gifts. "I wished to place something before my husband, to have him wear constantly some trifle to remind him that I had thought of and loved him, and my father and sister whom I have always remembered at this time." She had done everything she could to make home bright and attractive "to welcome dearie there." An accident changed all the plans and she offered to go to him in Providence, to his mother's house, to spare him inconvenience and discomfort and to give pleasure to his mother. "It was no trifling sacrifice for me to make. I dislike Providence extremely, and always go there with reluctance. It has an evil influence upon my happiness always and if I could have my way, I should never go there again. But I went this time cheerfully." She was encouraged by her husband's greeting, for she thought she saw some satisfaction in his face when he met her. She had evidently quarreled with his brother Amasa, and had brought herself to write him a letter that "would bring peace and good will. Such a step no power on earth would have induced me to take but the thought of my husband's pleasure." Sprague, however, merely answered in response to her inquiry "Will it do, dearie?" "Yes, send it, it is time there should be an end to such nonsense." Kate was hurt that he did not show any appreciation of the effort she had made nor the motive which had actuated her. Nor did he think of the offense that Amasa had given, and which he had witnessed without doing a thing. "Is this hard," Kate asks herself, "or is [it] what softens and sheds a charm over a wife's duties and makes them pleasures? Then came the disappointment (I am almost ashamed to think how great) of Christmas. And for the first time in my life my Father neglected me, and it grieved me. I could not help it. All my days I have so idolized my father, and now he seems so entirely gone from me and what have I gained in exchange?" [8]

On this note Kate ends her diary. The rest of the pages remain empty and blank. The image of Kate afforded by these three entries made over a period of some two months is as though one examined under a microscope a small piece of tissue from an organism. Certain traits of individuality are identifiable, but the relation to the whole organism, in this case the whole personality and life, is tenuous. Certainly she is revealed as having many contradictory tendencies—childishness and pettiness in small things, yet with deep aspirations for self-improvement; a longing for understanding from her husband but angry rebellion when she feels rejected. There is nothing here to confirm the image of the cold, calculating creature of social and political ambition which she is supposed to have been. Above all, Kate was a woman, intrinsically feminine in her reactions and feelings, passionate, proud, with an overpowering need to love and be loved.

CHAPTER

⚜ XII ⚜

KATE STAYED on at Narragansett through January of 1869, with Sprague continuing to go back and forth to his offices in Providence and Cranston. The house, which they had named Canonchet, after the Indian Chief who used to roam those parts, was altered beyond recognition by then, and Kate was deep in the long series of changes and additions which were transforming it into an imposing mansion rivaling those of Newport. The work was done entirely by day labor, and Kate supervised and planned as it went along, capriciously often, changing what she had already created more than once, building and spending with a lavish hand. Sprague was fond of the original house, which had once been the home of Governor William Robinson, and he asked Kate to preserve it, which she did. When the new house was complete, or almost complete, for actually she never really finished it, around the original farm house Kate had added a three-story mansion with wings and turrets and balconies and sixty-three rooms inside. The hand-carved staircase from Italy was a work of art and worth a king's ransom. Mirrors, chandeliers, paintings, tapestries, vases, marble busts—each room was filled with art objects from all over the world. Even the tiled dairy in the basement boasted a marble table.

Narragansett was a fashionable summer resort with several large hotels and a casino, but Kate stayed on long after the season was over and the summer visitors had fled. She enjoyed outdoor life, the beach, boating, walking, and horseback riding. She had been called the finest horsewoman in Washington in the days when she used to ride through the countryside around Rock Creek. In spite of her pleasure in social pursuits, Kate was no product of eastern drawing rooms and her childhood days on the farm outside Cincinnati had early set patterns of outdoor vigor.

In the building of Canonchet, set on land that extended from the ocean front through lakes and fields to the farm beyond, Kate found an occupation for her restless energy, and an outlet for her extravagant tastes too, although it was no more elaborate than many houses of that period, vast white elephants that seem anachronistic in the modern world. Frustrated in her emotional life, Kate sought satisfaction in material things, yet was never satisfied, looking always ahead to the next object, the next plan, the next addition to the house.

The Spragues were back in Washington in time for the new session of the Senate to which Sprague had been reelected for his second term. Although he had always felt out of his depth in the Congress and had remained in the background as much as he could, something had been fermenting in him during his years as senator, something that was to lead him into an explosion of ideas and feelings in a series of startling speeches in the spring of 1869. He had always resented the way he had been brushed off as "little Sprague" and he wanted to show his colleagues, to whom he felt inferior in education, that a businessman could see more clearly than they what the country needed. Undoubtedly too, he wanted to prove his worth and importance in front of Kate and her father.

An apocryphal story still makes the rounds that after a Senate debate Sprague approached Kate and asked if there was anything he could do for her. "Nothing," she retorted, "but go in there and make a speech—and that, you *can't* do." It sounds like Kate even though the source is a more than dubious one—Sprague's old love, Mary Eliza Viall Anderson.

Whether the anecdote is true or not, it is certainly true that Kate, and Chase too, had been disappointed in their hopes for

Sprague during his six years in the Senate through which he had passed like a shadow without substance.

Sprague's letters during the summer of 1866, when Kate was in Europe, show that underneath his detached and often bored exterior, he was seething with ideas and feelings, with resentment and ambition. And suddenly, at the start of his second term, it all boiled over in a series of speeches that attacked everything from the President, the Congress, businessmen, financiers, to the material and moral condition of the country. No one and nothing was spared.

At first, nobody paid much attention to him. He had so long been a silent partner that his first speech aroused almost no interest at all. It was during the discussion of a money bill that Sprague got up and issued a warning to the country. The economy was like "a mad horse in full run with broken reins," he warned.[1] Unless the financial policies of the Government were changed, disaster lay ahead. He attacked the concentration of capital in the hands of the few, the sky-high interest rates, and the scarcity of ready money and laid the blame on Government policies which were dictated by the bankers. Money at reasonable rates should be available to small businessmen and manufacturers. He proposed a study of the English system and the formation of a national bureau which would furnish capital at a low rate of interest and would insure that cheap money could be had by the people. The senators were not impressed.

Sprague had waited six years to make a major speech and he was miffed that no one seemed to pay any attention to him. Nine days later he rose to his feet again. This time his attack was aimed straight at his colleagues. The Senate was not unused to personal invective and abuse. The vicious animosities of the pre-Civil War period were still fresh in everyone's memory. Preston Brooke's physical attack on Senator Sumner had not been forgotten. Fist fights were not uncommon, and there had often been talk of duels. But Sprague's attack was not launched against some individual with whom he had a personal or political quarrel. His was a general indictment of the Senate itself, of all of them, and of the United States Government, describing it as a tyranny of "lawyers and judges . . . educated upon the quarrels and exhibitions of the worst passions of human nature, practised in the dissensions, influenced by the vices of the people." [2]

This time his colleagues did listen to him and were less than pleased with what they heard. Senator Nye of Nevada rose to answer the young whippersnapper. With heavy sarcasm he mocked his younger colleague while gusts of laughter passed through the chamber and the galleries. "The Senator from Rhode Island says he has been puzzled to understand the legislation of Congress. Is that a lawyer's fault? Perhaps if he had been a little more of a lawyer he would not have been puzzled so much." [3] Nye was evidently enjoying himself and anticipated an easy annihilation of the insignificant Sprague. But Nye's attack did not accomplish what he had expected. Far from being cowed by the irony and the patronizing amusement at his expense, Sprague seemed to gather even more strength. "You have been educated to laugh and to make light of the most serious things," he flung at the galleries. "You have been indoctrinated into a frivolous, thoughtless, senseless disposition." The country was on the brink of a financial precipice, he asserted, and unless the people could be roused from their apathy, all was lost. Not only did he find the financial condition in dire distress but the social conditions of the country quite as bad. "It is the striving of those who are rich to be richer and the striving of the poor to imitate the rich, and in that process virtue is lost." He charged that there was less virtue and morality in American society today than in any other civilized society on the face of the earth. The prevailing demoralization was frightful. What mother could send her son out in the world with any confidence that he would be able to resist the temptresses that would surround him? What husband could close his door with satisfaction? [4] This produced gales of laughter. The galleries were enjoying themselves hugely. But Sprague was not daunted. He had begun to talk and nothing could stop him. He told of his own life, and boasted of his wealth stating that he had given more money to his party than all the other senators put together.

No one was ignoring Sprague's speeches now. His accusations of immorality, of corruption, of legislators as tools of the bankers, of imminent financial disaster drew sharp retorts from his colleagues and the press. But not all the comments were critical. *The New York Times,* although disagreeing with Sprague's black picture of the state of the nation, editorialized: "Mr. Sprague is entitled to the credit of having the courage to say what he believes to be true:—and that is about the highest credit which any American statesman can claim or crave, nowadays." [5]

No one could understand what had happened to the modest, silent Sprague. Stories circulated that he was on a drinking spree and under the influence when he spoke and these rumors were widely published. Sprague did not ignore this and again leapt to his feet. About the newspaper reports, the people "may be assured that my words and courage do not rest on wine, or whiskey, or any other stimulant, but upon the knowledge of the shrinkage of property, and the loss of virtue going on around me. My great anxiety is to effect a cure now. The remedy is now accessible; a year hence it may be beyond reach . . . I utter no words that are not deeply considered . . . The general purpose is to restore to the market for the use of the people all the capital in the country, in contradistinction to the method now in use of keeping the source out of reach of the people . . . I wage war on the legislative and executive power as exercised by this body, and on the disastrous results of its action." [6]

Senators may have breathed a sigh of relief after this latest speech and considered that at last the young man was finished with his nonsense. If so, they were much mistaken. Five days later Sprague rose again to address them. It was another blast. Against the Senate, the office of the President, even the Supreme Court did not escape. And "the example of the Government in arrogating to itself superior powers is followed by the people," he asserted. "I have aroused the attention of the country to their affairs." And then in a defense of his sincerity and purpose he explained, "I have not come before the Senate or the country for any idle display, or for any purpose of sensation . . . It has always been my nature to hide myself from the public gaze. It was my boyish nature . . . there must have been a strong power that could have forced me to the expression of my views and reflections . . . Were

I to consult my own convenience and pleasure alone I would continue, as I had done, silent and apparently inattentive . . . But, sir, I could not do it. I could not resist the pressure that compelled me to speak that which I thought, that which I knew to be the truth." Senator Nye had criticized him, he said, for attacking Congress when he himself had had a part in their work. But, Sprague stated, it is "not only the right, but the duty of every man . . . when new light breaks upon the mind, to follow that light, even though it lead him to conclusions very different from those he has hitherto held." [7]

The press did not escape his attacks either. Looking straight at the press gallery he told them that they were a great power in the land but that they had not used this power to promote the prosperity of the people. "I believe you assume to be the champion of liberty. Freedom of the press is said to be the synonym of freedom for the people." But he speaks of the difficulty for journalists to live on the pittance doled out to them and adds sarcastically that they "are of course never tempted by the great corruptive influences about them into words or deed[s] contrary to justice and the good of the people." And then he challenges them directly. "If you are truthful and do stand truly by the liberties of the people . . . why slur my utterances? Why try to underrate the person who utters them, his arguments, his facts, or his position?" [8]

Heady with his new-found freedom of expression, Sprague grew more personal in his attacks. "There is in my state a great capital centered in one family, and that family has a newspaper organ, and that newspaper organ is conducted by my colleague." And he accused the firm of Brown & Ives, to which he was referring, of having suggested to him to join forces and break their business rivals. This was bad enough and drew down on him the wrath of his colleague from Rhode Island, Senator Anthony, and the newspapers in his state, especially the powerful *Providence Journal,* the paper to which he had alluded. Not satisfied with that, however, Sprague aimed the final blow which shocked everyone almost more than anything he had said heretofore. Striking at the honor and pride of his whole state, he excoriated the First Rhode Island Regiment, its commander, General Burnside, and their whole action at Bull Run, and in scathing tones accused them of cowardice.[9]

Rhode Island was outraged. The *Providence Journal* fulminated against this insult to the people. General Burnside, having read "with profound indignation Sprague's charges," published an item by item refutation of them. Senator Abbott of North Carolina was one among many who was furious at the attack on Burnside and spoke in his defense. Sprague retorted with insinuations about powerful "mastiffs" to which "mongrel puppy dogs" attached themselves and took courage. Abbott took this personally and threatened to horsewhip the Senator from Rhode Island. Sprague replied in kind and Washington was abuzz with excitement over the next round in the battle. Important senators, however, intervened. Sumner and Sherman took it upon themselves to pacify Sprague. Others dealt with Abbott and the incident was allowed simply to peter out.

The interest and excitement aroused by Sprague's speeches was not wholly negative, however. A great many people supported his attacks on the concentration of wealth and power and he received masses of mail and requests for copies of his speeches from all over the country. The working men of America felt that here at last was someone on their side. In Washington they organized a torchlight parade and marched to the house on Sixth and E streets to serenade the Senator. After speeches and cheers and hurrahs, the shout went up for Sprague as President. In spite of his own wealth, and the extravagance of his wife, to which one newspaper alluded, Sprague had become the popular champion of the underdog when he challenged: "Who that is a poor man dare attack one that is rich in any court in the land? Is there protection for the rights and liberties for the citizen in this boasted land of freedom?" [10]

To some, Sprague was a hero; to others wild Don Quixote; to many a laughing stock. Everyone was interested in this man who had so unexpectedly leapt to center stage. The *New York Herald* published an interview with "Little Rhody" at his home. "He says he is crazy, like all great reformers," the headlines proclaimed. "He is not after the Presidency, but if he got it he would give office hunters 'Jessie.'" The reporter quite obviously enjoyed his assignment. Sprague's attack on newspapermen had evidently not ruffled his feelings unduly. "Senator Sprague," he wrote, "being the lion of the hour, if not the coming man of the Nineteenth Century, your correspondent, as in duty bound, paid his respects to him yesterday afternoon at his splendid residence on the corner of Sixth and E streets . . . Going upstairs we passed the grand old form of the Chief Justice, whose presence alone would grace the handsomest palace in the world. He tripped lightly downstairs, wearing that inevitable and charming look of bounteous benevolence that bespeaks one of nature's own noblemen. We found the Senator from Rhode Island in his study, reclining before the fire, wrapped in a loose and well-worn dressing gown, and apparently lost in thought beyond hope of awakening. The study appeared in itself a study, with all kinds of curious traps laying around loose. Books on top of Bohemian vases, wonderful carved paper knives, odd-looking ink bottles, pen wipers, and a host of other articles of stationery on the mantelpiece . . . Near the Senator's chair stood a small tray holder, laden with the abstemious fare of a student, consisting of coffee minus milk and toast minus butter.

"We took a long look at the Senator's face to see if we could find therein any trace of the malady called craziness, which his enemies conveniently attribute to him. There was none in the eye at least, and the other features are not generally known to offer any sure indication of the complaint in question. Sprague looks old on near acquaintance. He has a small head, small features, large, lustrous eyes, slightly dashed with dimness that necessitates the wearing of glasses . . . Sprague might have been a fast young man at some period of his life or he might have been a very hard-working student of business; for on the outer edges of his face there are furrows that one of his age should not have. He wears his hair somewhat long and with extreme carelessness as though the comb that nature provides in the fingers had been the only one he ever made use of. It certainly presents a very dishevelled appearance; but it shows at least he is above the small vanity of lavishing on the outside of his head the time that is better bestowed in cultivating the inside." [11]

Sprague was riding high. He had at last shaken off the inhibitions that had held him in check for so long. He saw himself as the orator he had longed to be, the man of power and influence in government, the center of attention throughout the country. There was much that was absurd and outlandish in Sprague's speeches: the exaggerations, the intimate personal references, the pathetic readings from history, the obvious personal vindictiveness. But he had an idea and he had the courage and the sincerity to express it. The Grant administration had only just begun. The years ahead were to prove Sprague prophetic, years that Herbert Agar describes as leading to a "breakdown in government which came close to discrediting American institutions." [12] But the people did not want to listen to Sprague's words. They were indulgent toward the venality and the rapacity of the times. "Rich and poor alike joined in throwing contempt on their own representatives. Society laughed a vacant and meaningless derision over its own failure." [13] Four years of such conditions led to what Sprague had foreseen and the terrible depression of 1873.

No greater contrast could have been found than in Sprague's speeches and those of Salmon Chase. No matter how passionately he felt a cause, Chase always used reason instead of emotion, light without heat. His speeches were masterpieces of logic, consistent, well ordered, and objective. Sprague, on the other hand, was diffuse, disjointed, painfully personal and emotional. The bombast, the lack of dignity, the invective and personal revelations were hardly of a kind or tone that would be expected to please Kate, brought up on her father's quietly reasoned posture. She knew that most of his colleagues in the Senate, if they were not too furious to be amused, were laughing at him. She knew too that many people had interpreted Sprague's remarks about the absence of morality of the country and of its women as an attack on his wife.

One of the people who found great pleasure in this was Sprague's old flame, Mary Eliza Viall Anderson. But even in her book she denied that Sprague had really had any such thought of Kate in mind. And Mary Eliza, in view of her continuing relationship with Sprague, was in a position to know the facts. "Hamlet had not thought of his wife in his speech,—being in that exalted frame of mind peculiar sometimes to intense natures which disdains personalities, and loses itself in midforest of grand themes; certainly he had no idea of offering the public a cap to crown him with; and he was the last man to heap reproaches upon women, when he had borne more than any other from one, just because she *was* a woman." [14]

Mary Eliza describes the speech and Kate listening to it in one of those passages of purple prose which illustrates the pathological jealousy she felt toward her lover's wife: "My lady comes down to the House of Senators, looking from her place in the galleries like some haughty lily bending its head, and sending forth a sweet fragrance. This time she has come to listen to her husband who has been speaking for several days, and better than formerly, only with the rankest revolutionaryism . . . He is about to throw the last shovelful, when he abruptly pauses and looks towards the galleries . . . and gravely hints at a more vital corruption, and shrinkingly exposes the 'decaying *heart* of the Republic' . . . it was like a hot cannonball hissing into the Chamber . . . Fathers, brothers, husbands were outraged . . . and there was a general imaginary leaping of swords from their scabbards, to the defense of American women,—to the defense of the insulted queen of the Capitol . . . That languid humility of haughtiness (the fashionable pose of the period) is abandoned . . . Some women are glorious in wrath; the lily was not; its face now bolt upright on the stem is reddening fast, and begins to look like the face of any other angry red-faced woman . . . For almost the first time in her life the Statesman's daughter has dropped her mask (she is no longer lovely); and as she clutches at the lace shawl and quickly struts up the narrow *calle* (her seat has been in the first row) you are at a loss to know how she could ever have won that encomium of *la grace personifiée*. An eyewitness from the corridor laughingly remarked, 'I believe, 'pon honor, she's capable of hitting him with the coral stick of her parasol.' " [15]

This sounds singularly like an eyewitness account. Was it possible that Sprague had brought Mary Eliza to the Capitol to share in his moment of glory? The Sprague who delivered those five flaming speeches was a man in the throes of an enormous excitement, compulsive, arrogant, cocksure. He was obviously in a frame of mind not to care what anyone thought. Intoxicated with a sense of his own power, in a fighting mood, he was ready to ride rough shod over everything and everybody. Whether the presence of Mary Eliza was a contributing factor or not, the relationship between Kate and Sprague reached a crisis before his final speech, more serious than ever before, and Kate left Washington, with Nettie and Willie, for Aiken, South Carolina.

That there was some real offense on Sprague's part is shown by Chase's letters to Kate which, for the first time, do not merely preach to her about wifely duty, but show an understanding of what she had suffered.

"I was very glad to receive your letter," he wrote her, "and to note the indications in it of a more tranquil mind than you carried from Washington. You have been sorely tried, my precious child; but much of your trial is as you acknowledge brought upon you and continued by yourself . . . Have you written to the Governor? I hope you have and in the best of spirit . . . He has been so busy with his speeches, and letters, and I so busy with my records and opinions, and the business of the Court that we have seen very little of each other, only meeting at table. The Court adjourns today and I hope to have opportunities of a conference with him before the week ends. I have no great expectation of benefit from what I can say, but what I can I will do. You can do more than anybody else. Naturally you say 'Must I do all? It is hard to be loving and affectionate when met by unkind words and unkind acts.' I know it is; but I know too that she who thus acts will have her reward. There will come after a while a sweet internal serenity which will make duty easy and almost certainly assure a return of love and affection."

Chase did not seem too upset at Sprague's speeches, although he admits that he has not considered them sufficiently to have any definite opinion as to the merits of what he proposes. But, he feels Sprague undoubtedly "has gained a very prominent position; and if your old mutuality of affection can be restored you will be happier than ever; for, if I am not mistaken, you have been always ambitious for him. But with his new position, new responsibilities

will come. How I wish you could be at his side bearing all things, believing all things, hoping all things, a real helpmeet." [16]
· Nettie sent him cheerful letters with a sketch of the house they were in and stories of Willie and his mud pies and the pretty garden and the strawberries. It must have been a relief to Chase to have this breath of freshness to lighten his concern about Kate and her husband.

This was by far the most serious quarrel they had ever had, and Sprague, in his moment of triumph, was in no mood to be bothered by any peace-making overtures from anyone, including his father-in-law. It is a strange sight to see the self-confident Chief Justice hesitant and unsure about approaching Sprague, although he wanted to do what he could to help the situation and was clearly extremely eager to accommodate the son-in-law. "My heart is full of sympathy for you, my precious child," he wrote Kate, "but I pray earnestly and hope humbly that out of this great trial may come true peace for you. I have not yet seen the Governor, there has been no opportunity. Have you written him? You can do far more than I probably. I do not know how he will receive my unasked interference. But I shall try, and try before I go to bed tonight if I find the least opportunity. Let me entreat you to indulge no hard thoughts of him. You have both erred greatly; and each *ought* to do all that is possible towards reconciliation. If he won't you must, my darling. Humble your pride—yield even when you know you have the right on your side—remember the sacred obligation of your marriage vow. Read it over and pray for strength and affection to keep it *fully*, in spirit as well as in act." He has asked his secretary, Mr. Schuckers, to tend to some financial matters for her but regrets that she did not ask her husband to take care of it as usual "for any little (thing) may now help to heal the breach, and it would certainly please him, I think, to attend to your matters as usual." He reproves her quite emphatically at the end of the letter. A letter she had written to a Mr. Ward was returned to him, as she had forgotten to put postage on it. He sends it to her with the comment, "I am rather glad, for I don't want to have you write anything to anybody of the male variety of the human species." [17]

Kate herself was deeply troubled by the estrangement, and at times almost frightened. And she had more than normal reasons to be fearful of the future, for she was pregnant again. Although she confided many of her worries to her father, she did not tell him this, hesitating perhaps to put this added burden on him.

Chase tried to keep Kate informed of what was going on at home. He wrote her some of the background of Sprague's row with Senator Abbott, "a meanly concocted affair," he thought. But Sprague did not discuss anything with his father-in-law. When Chase's old friends, Senators Sumner and Sherman, called on Sprague, Chase could only "suppose it was with a view to compose the affair with what I do not know." And he goes on a little plaintively, "The Governor does not consult me at all on his matters; and I do not feel myself at liberty to obstrude unasked counsels; though I would not hesitate to volunteer, if I had any reason to believe that good would come of it. I fear the contrary." [18] Chase must have been very uncomfortable living in Sprague's house at this time. The old cordial relationship between him and his son-in-law was stretched very thin. "I have seen very little of him," Chase wrote Kate. "He is visited a great deal and is almost constantly engaged. The newspaper men are, of course, eager to get something for their papers; and a great many want to see the man whose speeches have made such a stir. Besides callers he has ever so many letters."

Sprague must have reveled in being kingpin at last; Chase almost humble toward him; Kate isolated far away in Aiken. It fed his ego to triumph in this way. All eyes were on him. All those great names, Sumner, Sherman, Fessenden, Chase were taking a back seat. It was his triumph and he did not intend to share it with anyone. Chase felt keenly the change in his son-in-law. "He does not seem as cordial towards me as formerly," he wrote Kate, "but it may be that I am more sensitive to his natural reserve and abruptness. I am anxious for a good opportunity for a frank conversation, and must have one before I leave for Richmond."

Nettie had written him about a visitor, a Mr. Charles Leary, who was staying in Aiken and acting as Kate's escort to nearby Granitville. "Does she mean that Mr. L. is your guest? I hope not." And he cautioned: "You cannot be too careful, my child. I have learned more of the slanderous propensities of men within the last few years than I ever knew before. Only this morning I received a most abominable note from New York. I seldom read these anonymous libels, but I read enough there to find that it was full of the most detestable abuse of you and the Governor not sparing either me or our innocent Nettie. Of course I destroyed it. For Heaven's sake, for my sake, for your own sake avoid all possibility of occasion for evil eyes and evil tongues." [19]

Kate had been away nearly four weeks and things at last seemed to be improving a little. "My hope and belief is that all will come out right," Chase wrote her, "but you must use all your tact and discretion guided by a sincere affection and duty." [20]

Kate and Sprague had started writing to each other and Sprague for the first time mentioned a letter of Kate at table. "He seemed much gratified by something you had said; but not greatly satisfied with some of your criticisms," her father wrote her. "What pleased him I don't know; but one thing he did not like was your disapproval of the mastiff and puppy story." Kate predictably would not have liked that story which provoked the row with Senator Abbott. Chase felt that the dog story finally turned out very well and had a good effect, but he does hope that the Governor will say nothing more of a personal nature. The Governor assured him that he would not, that what he said was on purpose and had effected its object and that nothing more of the same kind would be needed. Kate too was receiving anonymous notes, as always, and she sent one on to Sprague, written on the margin of a newspaper clipping. Sprague showed it to Chase who recognized neither the handwriting nor the initials. "But the writer was very impertinent and it angered him (Sprague) that it should have been sent to you. And I am sorry that you sent it to him," added Chase, who had always thought such attacks should be utterly ignored.[21]

For the first time since his marriage, Sprague, in his euphoric mood, was completely independent of Kate. The need for her support and confidence which had been so manifest before was gone. And the young Senator who had looked to his father-in-law for guidance was transformed into the cocksure, bombastic orator who asked advice of no one. Chase was bewildered and anxious over the new state of affairs. Always so sure of himself in the past, so righteous, he seemed almost cowed in this new situation. All he wanted was a reconciliation and he seemed ready to do almost anything if that end could be achieved. He even took steps to liquidate his debt to his son-in-law, who had advanced him nine thousand dollars toward Nettie's education. He wrote Kate that he wanted to reduce the three thousand that remained of this to two that month and that it would keep him short of funds to send her and Nettie in Aiken.

The clearest example, however, of Chase's hesitant attitude toward his son-in-law was his reaction when Sprague brought one of his mistresses into the household. This man who had been so sure of his ability to direct the affairs of the nation could not bring himself to speak of it openly. And yet his conscience did not let him ignore the situation completely either. And so he compromised on a letter, extremely mild in tone. "Mackay dismissed Annie yesterday as he said by your order, and has put in her place a very fine looking English woman who appears very well and seems to understand her business. But is it not a little risky to bring such a woman into the house while there are not other women here?" [22] Chase did not write Kate about this. He did not need to. She had long known about Sprague's affairs.

Chase had tried for weeks to find an opportunity to have his "frank talk" with the Governor. But Sprague kept him dangling and Chase did not want to force the issue. He kept counseling patience to Kate and faith in the will of God. It was some weeks after Kate's departure for Aiken that he finally wrote her of the long-awaited talk with Sprague. "I found him under some excitement. He said he . . . could not do anything but it was not misinterpreted by you, and you seemed all the time to be wanting to make a case against him to defend yourself against him. That very morning he said that having missed something for several days, he had gone into your room and found the small trunk or box in which they and other things—papers I understood—were and packages taken out of it which had been sealed up and one in particular which contained your letters from Col. Crosby broken open and the letters taken away. He then spoke of your coming into his room when you thought he was asleep and searching his pockets. This matter you explained to me, and I tried to make the same explanation to him but what had just first occurred made it impossible to get a hearing. He then went on to say that he could not be controlled by you . . ." [23]

In spite of his not very satisfactory talk with Sprague, Chase was beginning to be hopeful that things would turn out well in the end and he was pleased, at least, with Kate's attitude. He read her last letter "with profound interest and the deepest sympathy for you. It is my firm faith," he assures her, "that you have only to carry out the purposes you express with patience and perseverance to win a happy issue . . . cherish every wifely sentiment whether now reciprocated or not, have no disagreements with your husband, let your conduct be as the day, and all will come right." He advised Kate "Not to criticize your husband's public antics even in your thoughts . . . He cannot take criticism from you, now particularly. Let him take his own course without any words but cheer and approval." [24]

The ice jam was at last beginning to break. Sprague wrote Kate a letter which she sent to her father who found it, "not what I wish it was; but it is far from being as unsatisfactory as it might have been." And he advises her to "make the best of it and not the worst." [25]

Sprague's speeches were over and the excitement about them died down quickly. It was like a firecracker which burst briefly on the scene and had now fizzled and gone out. Sprague sank back into his former political apathy and did not rouse again. Reality came back into focus and windmills receded into the mists. His big moment in the Senate had come and gone and he found that he was the same "little Sprague" he had always been. Nothing had really changed at all. As so often had happened before, his euphoric mood evaporated and uncertainty returned and with it came his need for Kate again. A few days after Chase left for Richmond, Sprague decided to journey South too. Kate was still in Aiken with Willie and Nettie, and Sprague joined her there before taking her home again. Kate was subdued and conciliatory and determined to try once again to make her marriage work.

Summer at Canonchet passed as usual with Nettie and Willie and the customary flock of relatives and guests. After a pleasant visit there, Chase was vastly relieved by what he noted in the improved relationship. Once again, the happy cycle had returned. "It was a great delight to me," he wrote Kate, "to see the restoration of the old affection between you and your husband. God grant that it may never be interrupted again. How happy it seemed to make you both." [26]

Kate had not told her father of her approaching confinement, and incredibly he had not noticed her condition although the baby was due in a matter of weeks. "It was wrong in you to leave me to be informed by others that you expect to be a mother again in October," he complained in mid-September just after his visit. "I cannot help being anxious about you; but trust that our Heavenly Father, whose mercies have ever exceeded our *ingratitude,* will give you safety and blessedness in your confinement, and give us all love and obedience to Himself." [27]

It is possible that Kate had wanted to spare her father the anxiety she knew he would feel about her approaching confinement, as his health had not been good that summer. He had had the first intimations of real heart trouble and she was concerned about him.

Chase was feeling a little sad and nostalgic that autumn. He had finally decided that it was time for him and Nettie to move to their own house. Undoubtedly, the events of the spring and the Governor's coolness if not coldness toward him had brought about this decision. By now, the tables were completely turned and it is Chase who complains that Sprague does not answer his letters. "I wish I could feel his loving me and trusting me," he tells Kate. "But his nature is reserved and he has been always in the habit, as I have been myself, of acting on his own judgement and saying little of his matters to anybody. If he could only feel towards me as a son how glad I should be." He regrets the move away from the familiar house on E Street and especially away from Kate. "I am sorry—very sorry—to part even so far as to have a separate house in the same city; but I really think it will be for the best. You know how I like comparatively early hours and regularity;

and you are late and irregular. This, to be sure is not much." And then he indicates something of the real reason for the move. "I could easily conform, and would if you and the Governor really felt any need of me." But Nettie quite naturally feels that she wants a house of her own, he goes on rationalizing, "or rather that her father should have a house and that she should be at the head of it. And I think I ought to gratify her. You presided over my house some five years and did it admirably. I rather shall like to have her try her hand." But again come the qualms. "The worst is that we find no house near you, and shall probably have to go on to I St. . . . Nothing, however, is yet definitely settled. Fortunately the street cars abridge distance." [28]

Chase feels it almost as a parting of the ways, that now Kate will never be as close to him again. As a final paternal advice he exhorts her: "As a wife your duty is clear—not to expect him to change his nature, not to complain if he is reticent, or to feel like complaining—but 'to love, honor, cherish and obey,' and this cheerfully, heartily, and perserveringly asking God's blessing, and God's blessing will come." [29]

Chase felt the chill of old age approaching. He and Nettie were getting along very well, "in our plain way. Very few come to see us, but we are not lonely." [30] Life with Nettie, who was gay and natural and who cared nothing for the political or social whirl, would be very different than it had been with Kate. It would be a more reasonable and quiet life for a man whose health was beginning to fail. But Chase found it hard to withdraw from the excitement and stimulus that Kate drew around her wherever she went. And he felt he was no longer needed or wanted.

CHAPTER

❧❧❧ XIII ❧❧❧

KATE HAD BEEN profoundly affected by the estrangement from her husband in the spring of 1869, when she had passed weeks of anxiety and apprehension about the future for herself and her children. She knew now that there was no changing Sprague, that his character and habits were firmly set, and that she would have to accept him as he was. She must either adjust to her husband's difficult nature or leave him, which was unthinkable. Not only did divorce in those days often mean ostracism and disgrace, but Kate had absorbed much of her father's attitude toward marriage and wifely duty. She recognized the difficulties of her own character, her pride and temper, and her wilfullness. She had never been ready before to accept a compromise or to put up with humiliation and disappointment patiently. But after the crisis in her relationship with her husband there was a definite change in Kate. Her marriage had come very near to the breaking point, and when she returned home it was with the determination to accept what she could not change and to make the best of what she had.

Kate changed in other ways, too, after the crisis in her marriage. The social scene lost much of its former attraction for her. She was spending now more and more time at Narragansett, where the building and furnishing of her magnificent house afforded her a great deal of interest and occupation. Washington society missed

Kate and the society columnists wondered who, "since the absence of Mrs. Senator Sprague from fashionable society," could possibly take her place.[1] A few malicious gossips charged that Kate's relinquishment of her social leadership was due to the humiliation her husband's erratic Senate speeches had brought upon her and to his often wild and drunken scenes. But there had been no real change in Sprague's behavior during the last years. Had she wanted to, Kate, the "acknowledged queen of fashion and good taste," could have maintained that position indefinitely.[2] Actually, she did not retire from all Washington social life, she simply participated in it far less frequently. But Kate Chase Sprague would still retain her sway in Washington society on the rare occasions when she felt like asserting it.

Kate's baby was born in October 1869, a daughter this time, whom she named Ethel. Chase was very relieved to hear that Kate was doing as well as could be expected, even though she had shown some imprudence, according to Sprague and her cousin Eliza, who undoubtedly had difficulty in keeping restless Kate as quiet as they thought she should be. Eliza had written Chase a description of the baby, for which he had evidently waited with some impatience. "I congratulate you on being the mother of such a dear pretty little one," he wrote Kate. "And I am glad that the baby is a girl. For my part, I like girls rather better than boys, though I would, I believe, have put up with one boy—perhaps two—for the sake of having a brother apiece for you and Nettie. But *girls* are *nice,* and it will be so good for little Willie to have a little sister. It is a great thing to have a little sister. It is a great thing to have charge of a little mortal, and to know that the character of all its life here below depends so largely on the direction given to the setting out. How much more to have charge of young *immortals,* with all the influences that mothers necessarily possess." [3]

Kate was extremely anxious about her father's health that year. He was almost visibly failing before her eyes. When he and Nettie started off on a trip to Minneapolis and St. Paul the next summer, everyone hoped that the rest and change would benefit him, although he himself was rather pessimistic about his condition. He had been having chest pains and weakness for some two years and he knew that his health was deteriorating.

On the return trip, he and Nettie stopped off at Niagara Falls and he undoubtedly told Nettie of his first view of the Falls as a boy on his way to Ohio. It was afterward, on the train from Buffalo, that Chase suffered a mild stroke. He insisted on staying on the train until it reached New York and managed somehow to reach his hotel and get up the stairs in spite of the fact that his whole right side was affected to some degree and his speech was scarcely intelligible. Kate and Sprague came at once from Narragansett and stayed with him until he was well enough to be moved, a week later, to Canonchet.

Chase's condition improved gradually under Kate's watchful and solicitous eye. His dietary regime was strict and he was supposed to exercise as much as he could without fatigue. Within six weeks he was walking a mile without stopping to rest and could ride eight to ten miles without difficulty. Soon his walks increased and he was able to manage as much as four to six miles at a time. But in spite of the improvement in his condition, Chase was still far from well. "My health is quite precarious," he wrote his old friend Henry Cooke, "and I feel that I ought to make some permanent disposition of property." [4] But Chase was ready, as he had always been, to "commit the future, in this respect, as in all others, to Him who has so graciously cared for me." [5]

Chase's appearance was very much altered after his stroke. His hair had whitened and he had lost a great deal of weight. But "even in ruin, he retained his old impressiveness of presence," his secretary, J. W. Schuckers, wrote of him. "He was patient under suffering, and, though the natural imperiousness of his temper would sometimes flame out for a moment, there was something inexpressively pathetic in his resignation, and the constantly gentle, uncomplaining way in which he spoke of his sickness." [6]

Chase liked his fine room at Canonchet, which Kate had furnished especially to suit his tastes. Relations between him and his son-in-law seemed far better than they had during the previous year and something of the old affection was restored. When Kate was away briefly to consult with his doctor in New York, Chase wrote Nettie that, "the Governor, as long as Katie was absent, was very constant in his attendance, coming down (from Providence) every night. Since he went up on Wednesday morning, he has not returned, but we expect him tonight as usual. His place is well supplied by Katie." He enjoyed the family life and getting to know his new granddaughter who "grows in grace and beauty day by day, and I look soon to see her walking and talking. Willie improves constantly." [7]

Chase was not able to return to his duties on the Court that winter, and when the Spragues returned to Washington, he moved with Nettie to New York where he underwent treatments for the slight paralysis which remained from his stroke and was particularly evident when he was fatigued.

Although the therapy may have helped, and the rest from his Court duties certainly did, it was a fresh interest that gave Chase almost a new lease on life. Years before, when he had been a young teacher in Washington, he had seen and fallen in love with a property, called Edgewood, outside the city. There was a handsome old brick house, set on some fifty acres of land, and although he had to borrow part of the money, and the house would need considerable remodeling and repair, Chase had bought it a few months before his stroke. Edgewood held memories for Kate, as it had been on a ridge nearby that she had visited the camp of the First Rhode Island Regiment and had galloped over the neighboring hills and fields on her magnificent horse, Atalanta, the dashing young War Governor at her side.

After his stroke, and in spite of being as usual hard pressed for money, Chase determined to go ahead with his plans for remodeling Edgewood. He may originally have caught the building fever from Kate, and her work at Canonchet, but it provided him with a real source of interest and pleasant anticipation at a time when he most needed it.

There had been another shock for Kate in the autumn of 1870 besides her father's stroke. This one concerned her husband, and though not personal in some ways it was more serious than any she had yet faced in regard to him. It was only a few weeks after they had brought Chase to Canonchet after his stroke that she learned of a sensational speech made by Thomas A. Jenckes of Rhode Island, at a political meeting in Providence where he opened his campaign for reelection to his fifth term in the Congress. He accused Sprague of violating "in the darkest days of the war . . . the Articles of War of the United States in holding commerce with the enemy, and aiding them with money and munitions of war." [8]

His audience was stunned. Sprague, the fighting Governor, the first volunteer of the war, the hero of Bull Run—dealing with the enemy? "I know you cannot believe it," Jenckes told them. "I do not ask you to do it upon my statement." And he proceeded to read to them a report from the Judge Advocate General to Secretary of War Stanton which told an amazing story.

In the first year of the war, a man named Harris Hoyt, from Texas, arranged a meeting with William Sprague in Washington. He had a plan for getting cotton out of Texas. Four Rhode Island firms took an interest in the venture, including the Reynolds Company and Sprague's firm, each of the four putting up twenty-five thousand dollars. Ships were bought and loaded with a cargo of machinery and arms and cleared for foreign ports. Proceeding by a circuitous route by way of Havana to Mexico, sometimes under a changed flag, the ships reached Texas. Hoyt carried with him letters of introduction to General Butler and Admiral Farragut, written by William Sprague. The cargoes were sold in Texas and the proceeds invested in cotton, part of which got out while some were seized by blockade cruisers. It was the capture of one of these vessels carrying cotton in November 1864 that led to the discovery of the whole plan. Byron Sprague, a cousin who had since died, and William Reynolds, an old friend of Sprague, were arrested along with Harris Hoyt and another Texan, Charles Prescott. General John Dix was in charge of the Army Department of the East under whose jurisdiction the case originally came. According to the Advocate General's account, William Sprague wrote "several letters to General Dix in regard to the case, in none of which does he admit, and in one of which he denies a knowledge of Hoyt and of the details of the operation, such as is indicated by letters from him found on Hoyt, who expressly declares William Sprague to have been cognizant of the progress of the business, and to have advised and aided it to the utmost of his powers." [9]

In view of the importance of the people involved, a United States senator and son-in-law of the Chief Justice of the Supreme Court, General Dix decided discretion was in order and he referred the whole case to the Secretary of War. Hoyt had panicked and allegedly had made a full confession, involving William Sprague, his cousin Byron, and William Reynolds. The two other partners in the enterprise, although they put up capital, were considered unaware of the manner in which it was going to be used. General Dix's report stated that: "The high social standing of these gentlemen makes the case one of great delicacy and I regard it also as a question of importance whether the proceedings against them should be by a military Commission or a civil Court, whether the facts charged, if proved, constitute a mere violation of the laws of war, or a higher crime under the Constitution of the United States. There are at least two witnesses to the fact of illicit trade and ample written proof. Harris Hoyt and Charles L. Prescott, who were parties in the interest, are willing to testify to all the facts in the case providing their doing so shall not inure to their own conviction.

"It appears that among the articles purchased in New York, to be taken to Texas, were some arms and ammunition, and on the invoice of the cargo with which Hoyt went from Havana to Matamoras were thousands of cartridges and percussion caps. From an examination of all the papers, this Bearer is of the opinion that the persons who were engaged in the unlawful traffic may be brought to trial before a general Court martial . . . for relieving the enemy with money and ammunition; or by a military commission for violating the laws of war in trading and holding intercourse with the enemy. It is for the Secretary of War to determine whether . . . their trial shall be ordered." [10]

Reynolds and Byron Sprague won immediate parole and would soon be released even from that, and Hoyt's lawyer was asking and getting parole for his client also. Weeks lengthened into months, William Sprague had disclaimed any involvement in the project, Hoyt's confession mysteriously disappeared and the whole thing, incredibly, never went any further. Lincoln's death, the end of the war, and the abrasive new problems helped to turn attention from the affair and the various documents were left to gather dust in the files of the Secretary of War. Until Congressman Jenckes stumbled across it and found in it a potent weapon against his political enemy, Senator Sprague.

Sprague answered the charges at once in a public statement that was unusual for him in its reasoned tone. He admitted having met Hoyt in the early war years and stated that Hoyt had come to him armed with a "general letter of introduction from the late President Lincoln." The letter was, in fact, from the White House but it was signed not by Lincoln but by his secretary, John Hay. It was rather noncommittal saying merely that Mr. Hoyt had been recommended to the President, as a "true and loyal citizen" and commended him to the "kind offices of Union people on his way back home." Sprague stated that the letter was sufficient authority for his "entertaining any proposition with respect" that Mr. Hoyt might make. Sprague described Hoyt's plan as one to furnish relief to loyal men in Texas, by obtaining funds through which cotton could be purchased from these people. "I heard his statement," Sprague declared "and the details of his scheme, and in view of the credit which the letter of President Lincoln gave him, I had no reason to doubt the feasibility of the plan, and had no reason to entertain the slightest suspicion of Hoyt's good faith." After hearing his plan and perhaps giving him letters to General Butler and Admiral Farragut, though Sprague claimed to have no recollection of that, "my connection with the subject entirely ceased," Sprague stated. He claimed to have had no knowledge of any arrangements his cousin, Byron Sprague, might have made in this regard due to the pressure of his public duties which compelled him to leave all details of the business of the firm in his cousin's hands. He stated he had no reason to suppose that his partner or any of the other gentlemen had any suspicion that Hoyt was concocting "a plan for defrauding them of their money, or to pursue a treasonable scheme for his own advantage." He claimed that the investment A. & W. Sprague had made was wholly lost. When the matter came under investigation in 1865 he had forgotten all about it and was surprised to hear that Byron Sprague and Col. W. H. Reynolds were arrested by military order of General Dix. He himself was asked for information at that time and replied with all the facts within his knowledge. He heard nothing further of the matter and in due time Byron Sprague and Col. Reynolds were honorably discharged. In closing he inquired, with some of his old bombast, by whom such an "atrocious charge" is made, and he described Mr. Jenckes's war record in which he preferred to go in the capacity of a Representative to Congress rather than a soldier in the field. Jenckes's record in Congress "will sufficiently indicate to all thinking people the selfish ends which he has in view . . . From such an assailant I can safely appeal to the protection of the people." [11]

General Dix, in answer to an inquiry from a Providence newspaper, also saw fit to answer the charges brought by Jenckes and in a letter for publication he wrote that as it was through him that the attention of the Government had first been called to the Hoyt affair, "I deem it a simple act of justice to those gentlemen to say, that on a full investigation of the case, no ground was discovered for instituting proceedings against them before a civil or a military court . . . The case was one of those which sometimes occur in times of civil strife, and which leave only the regret on the part of the government that it has acted on mistaken information, and that unjust suspicion has, for the moment, been cast on those whose high character and conspicuous patriotism are sure guarantees of their integrity." [12]

Newspapers through Rhode Island, even those like the *Providence Journal* which were not friendly to Sprague, were shocked at Jenckes's attack and cautious in their comments. There were many areas in which Sprague had been vulnerable to criticism, but not in his patriotic war record. In spite of Sprague's statement, and that of General Dix, Jenckes continued to press the charges against Sprague, talking at rallies throughout the state, reading excerpts from the statements made by Byron Sprague and Prescott at the time of their arrest to support his argument. Sprague's power and prestige were on the line and it became vitally important for him that Jenckes be defeated at the polls. Once again, as in his first campaign for governor, the press accused him of spending large sums of money to this end, and after Jenckes's inevitable defeat the *Providence Journal* commented: "Nothing so disgraceful, certainly nothing since the time when Sprague was first elected ... in 1860, has ever occurred in our politics as in this election." [13]

Sprague realized that he could not let matters rest with Jenckes's defeat. He had to try to clear his name officially of the charge and so he asked the Senate to investigate the affair. A committee of five senators was named, but after much time-wasting and delay the whole thing petered out the day before the session ended. The senators had shown a very half-hearted interest in the investigation, and had not demonstrated any energy in following up evidence or in calling witnesses. The office of the Secretary of War had dawdled unaccountably in furnishing the documents to the investigating committee, and Hoyt's confession allegedly implicating Sprague was still missing. Somehow, Jenckes did not receive the first request to appear before the Committee and it was only a few days before Congress was to adjourn that he presented his testimony. As proof of Sprague's involvement he had photographs of the letter signed by John Hay, Sprague's letters to General Butler and Admiral Farragut, and another from him to Secretary Welles describing the whole venture. *The New York Times* commented cynically as to what happened then: "In answer to a direct question, Mr. Jenckes stated he had no information to show that Sprague had any improper object in entering into the transaction. This testimony may modify the report of the Committee, but probably not in a manner prejudicial to Mr. Sprague." [14] The Committee, at the end of their desultory investigation, concluded that there was nothing in the evidence to implicate Sprague and asked to be relieved of further responsibility about it. The war was over, what was done was done and the senators, like members of a private club, liked to stand by their own.

Fortunes had been made during the war as never before, in goods and services and in speculation, and the textile mill which could be assured of a supply of cotton was in a position to make tremendous profits. Sprague had claimed that the minor involvement that he admitted to was motivated only by two factors: the relief of loyal Union cotton men in the South and the advantages to the Government in maintaining employment and the supply of textile goods. Serious as the evidence against him was, Sprague managed to emerge unscathed and the affair was never to be questioned again during his lifetime.

One can only imagine the effect that the grave charges brought against Sprague had on Kate and her father. Undoubtedly, they put the best face on it and tried to convince themselves and Sprague that they did not believe there was any truth in them, but it must have shocked them both deeply. Chase had always stood so foursquare for honor. And now to have the son-in-law of the Chief Justice of the Supreme Court investigated for holding treasonable commerce with the enemy! Sprague was bound to feel at a disadvantage again vis-à-vis his wife and her father, and as so often happens, especially with weak characters, when there are feelings of guilt toward someone, there is resentment and vindictiveness too. In the middle of the Senate Committee investigation of himself, Sprague found a way to take out his feelings against his father-in-law, and Kate by extension, in a calculatedly mean and petty way.

For many years, the salaries of the members of the Supreme Court had been woefully inadequate. Chase received only $6,500 a year and already in the summer of 1866 regretted that the salaries had not been increased. "No judge can now live and pay his travelling expenses on his salary," he had written Sprague that year. "Its amount practically is not as large as it was at the organization of the Government. That of the Chief Justice should be at least 12,000 and that of each Associate 10,000." [15]

Five years later, Congress had at last decided to do something to remedy the situation. The hope was that the salaries would be raised at least to $10,000 for the Associates and $10,500 for the Chief Justice. The Appropriations Committee, of which Sprague was a member, voted favorably on this amount and everything boded well for passage when it came to the floor. Chase undoubtedly waited anxiously for news of the increase. He was eager to get on with the work at Edgewood and he felt he had waited a long time for a reasonable reward for his arduous services. The sum finally voted, however, raised the salaries only to $8,000 and $8,500. The higher original figures had failed to pass by a single vote. And "that vote was given by Gov. Sprague," Chase was informed by a friend, the marshal of the Court. "Why would he not help us in this emergency?" the writer complained. "Had he left the Senate or *not* voted, we should have won the day. I am really distracted about it." [16]

Sprague well knew how much the larger increase would have meant to Chase, who was still far from well. His vote against it was more than an unfriendly act. It was a pointed and cruel one toward a man who had been unfailingly understanding and indulgent toward him. In his action one can see clearly what Kate had referred to in her husband when she wrote: "I love this dear husband, very much, sometimes I have almost worshipped him, and then some act or word will make him appear for the nonce, so small, that I wonder at its discrepancy." [17] But this was more than small. It was a vicious blow at Chase, and through him at Kate. And it came at a moment when his own honor and fate hung in the balance.

Kate needed all her new resolution and self-control not to let this latest aberration of her husband affect her, and it was not the most cheerful climate for a happy event—Nettie's wedding. Nettie was engaged to William Sprague Hoyt, no relation at all to the Texas adventurer, but a cousin of Kate's husband, and grandson of the founder of the A & W Sprague Co. Kate was a sentimentalist, and she would not let anything spoil Nettie's wedding. She gave several pre-wedding parties for the engaged couple and saw to it that Nettie's wedding was every bit as brilliant as her own had been. The ceremony took place at St. John's Church on Lafayette Square and the reception afterward was at the house on Sixth and E streets. Everyone of any importance was there, including President Grant, members of the Cabinet and the Supreme Court. The Marine Band played for Nettie as it had for Kate, and the whole reception was an enormous success. Kate was as much admired as the radiant bride, if not more so, in a turquoise velvet dress with a train of pink silk. The ladies of the press raved over the affair the next day, praising Kate's superior taste, her patrician air and regal manner. Nothing was mentioned about Chase, who had returned to Washington for the first time since his illness and whose thin and haggard appearance shocked his friends in the capital who had not seen him during the eight months he had been away. Sprague was not noticed either for it was the ladies, as usual, who drew the attention and caused all the comments. Everyone prophesied happiness for the young couple as they always do. In Nettie's case they were to turn out to be right.

The newlyweds took a honeymoon trip abroad and Chase spent the summer at health spas in Michigan and Wisconsin, where he found the waters and the treatment beneficial. He began to gain weight from a low of 145 pounds, which was cadaverous for his huge frame, and generally began to feel well enough to contemplate resuming his duties on the Court at the fall session.

Kate was at Narragansett "with a houseful of company" and her two very active children. Very few of Kate's early letters have been preserved, but the ones that do exist show the pleasure and interest she took in her children. "My little curly-headed girl came to me Friday," she wrote her father, "with the paperweight containing your photograph (and which I always keep on the table before me, though Willie claims you gave it to him) and said, 'I want Grandpa Chase to prum (read come). I hurrah fer Bubnor Sprague, and I hurrah for Chase!' Her sentence was a little less connected but that was what she intended . . . She is only twenty-two months old and she has many of Mother Goose's Melodies, as well as such epics as Good-Bye John, Up in a Balloon, quite pat. Willie has been made proud and happy by having received from his Aunt Nettie a miniature mitrailleuse which I have the honor to be saluted by most every morning before I am up and find ready cocked and elevated for the purpose at night, at the foot of Willie's bed, beside my own." [18] Kate found, in these little people, the warmth and unquestioning love she had always wanted and she looked forward to the new baby she expected in February.

Besides giving news of the children to her father, she enclosed an article from the *New York Herald* "advocating a mutual friend of ours for the next Presidency—If you meet him in your travels, advise him not to make too many speeches, or attend too many celebrations of one sort or another, but to devote all his energies for a while to getting quite well, that he may yet live a long while to gladden the hearts of his children and if need be serve his country." [19]

Incredibly, thoughts of Chase for President were again simmering and once again he was receiving various letters from people advocating his candidacy. Ohio was reported to be in his favor and there was the same old stir and maneuvering as in the previous years. Chase at first showed no interest at all. "I pay no attention to politics," he wrote "except to form my own opinions and give my own vote." [20] After his return to Washington, however, where he was well enough to take his place on the Court, his old blood began to stir again one last time with dreams of glory. Although he wrote of the Presidency, "I do not desire it," admitting that there had been a time when he did, he could not bring himself to put away his dreams wholly. "If those who agree with me in principle think that my nomination will promote the interests of the country, I shall not refuse the use of my name. But I shall not seek a nomination, nor am I willing to seem to seek it." [21]

Chase's letters in all the years that he had hoped to be chosen were interchangeable. He might as well have made carbon copies of them from the first and simply sent them out on demand. He wanted to be President. But he wanted the office to come to him.

This time, Kate did not involve herself at all in the contest. Her new baby, another girl, had arrived on schedule in February of 1872. Chase must have been pleased that Kate named her Katherine and she was always known affectionately as little Kitty. As far as her father's prospects were concerned, Kate did not seem either hopeful or even favorable toward them. She was more concerned with his health than his ambitions. She did, however, give a reception for him in Washington in the spring to which she invited all the important political figures. The question in everyone's mind was whether a man who had suffered a paralytic stroke as Chase had done and who had not been able the last year to fulfill his duties on the bench, was able to assume the onerous duties of the Presidency. Chase himself evidently felt, or hoped, that his health was sufficiently good to accept the nomination if offered him.

Kate's reception for her father was a signal success and the lady journalists as usual went into ecstasies. They found Chase vastly improved in health and appearance, a "miraculous change'" compared to the previous year. Carl Schurz, who had first seen Chase's Presidential fever back in the Columbus days, saw more deeply below the surface, and thought that Chase's "futile efforts to appear youthfully vigorous and agile were pathetically evident." [22]

The result of the Democratic Convention was predictable, at least in so far as the rejection of Chase as Presidential candidate was concerned, though no one had ever dreamed that the fantastic Horace Greeley would be the one to receive the nomination. To pass over Chase—that had become too ingrained a habit to change now.

A great deal has been written about Kate's ambitions for the position of First Lady and it has been repeated more than once that it was she who was behind her father's ambition for the Presidency. Certainly she had shared his hopes, but no one needed to spur on Salmon P. Chase. Everyone who knew him recognized his driving ambition. Carl Schurz had spotted his malady years ago, when Kate was only just emerging from childhood. Mrs. Eastman, who came closer than any one else to ensnaring Chase and who knew him well, once wrote him discerningly: "I have a feeling nowadays that my letters to you give but little satisfaction, as they can do nothing to advance the object for which it seems to me you live—Now shall I be frank and perhaps offend you—and tell you that I am jealous! And of whom and what? Of your ambition and through that of yourself, for doesn't ambition make the worshipper the god of his own idolatry?" [23]

Carl Schurz had wondered why the "disastrous, crushing, humiliating defeat" Chase had suffered at the Convention of 1860, when Lincoln was nominated, had not cured him of his Presidential fever. "Alas, it did not. He continued to nurse that one ambition so that it became the curse of his life to his last day. It sometimes painfully distorted his judgment of things and men. It made him depreciate all the honors and powers bestowed upon him. When he was Secretary of the Treasury and, later, Chief Justice of the Supreme Court, the finest opportunities to enviable distinction were open to him, which, indeed, he achieved, but he restlessly looked beyond for the will-o'-the-wisp which deceitfully danced before his gaze." [24]

Chase infected Kate with his burning ambition, but hers was a pale shadow beside his. As attested to by Schurz, and proven by his refusal to give up his dream even when his health was broken and his physical condition grave, Chase never let go his ambition until he died. Kate showed no such tenacity. She relinquished it all without a backward look or a complaint.

Chase's health, which had remained stable, even improving a little through 1872, began to worsen with the spring of the next year. At the last session of the Court in May, he felt so badly that he asked one of his Associates to preside.

A few days later Chase left for New York with his Negro servant, William Joyce, who had been with him for many years. Nettie had had a baby girl in January and Chase stayed with her and her husband at 4 West 33rd Street. He seemed in good spirits and happy to see his little granddaughter, and he discussed his plans for the summer. After a visit with Kate at Narragansett, he thought of going to Boston for special treatments, applications of "magnetism and electricity," which he hoped might help his condition. He had always been sensitive to any mention of the paralysis he had suffered as a result of his stroke and which was still sometimes apparent in a thickness of speech and awkwardness of movement, and he tried to pretend that it was due simply to overwork. In spite of the moderate improvement in his condition the previous year, his appearance had changed markedly. He had grown a beard in his later years and he was so thin and his face so altered that many of his friends did not recognize him when they met.

Four days after his arrival in New York, on Tuesday morning, May 7, Chase had another stroke and lapsed almost at once into unconsciousness from which he did not recover. Kate and Nettie, and their husbands, were at his bedside until the end.

Funeral services were held at St. George's Church in New York. There was a tremendous crowd both inside and outside the church. Great and simple people had come to pay their last respects. Telegrams and messages poured in from all over the country and newspapers eulogized the late Chief Justice.

From New York the body was taken to Washington where it lay in state at the Supreme Court chamber. A funeral service was conducted at the Senate Chamber at which every prominent political personage in the city was present from the President on, and many from other cities. It was estimated that fifteen hundred people attended and eighty carriages bore the mourners to the cemetery at Oak Hill—not far from Chase's beloved home, Edgewood.

Kate had known the end could not long be kept at bay, but anticipation of such a loss does not mitigate it. Gossips, as always, fluttered their vicious tongues about Kate, even presuming to know that her father's death was more a blow to her ambition than a grief at his loss.[25] Kate had shown all her life a wonderful devotion to her father. She had loved him and been proud of him, and after the often degrading experiences of her marriage, she had found support and confidence in his presence. There would be no one to whom she could turn now.

CHAPTER

❧❧❧ XIV ❧❧❧

IT WAS September 1873. On the surface all seemed well. President Grant was at Philadelphia visiting Jay Cooke at his fabulous estate, Ogontz, where Kate and Nettie and their father had often stayed. It was opulent beyond belief and bespoke security and wealth. Jay Cooke's private telegraph line was unusually busy that evening, but the financier did not seem at all disturbed. Grant puffed on this thick black cigars in perfect relaxed enjoyment.

The next morning, after driving the President to his train, Jay Cooke went to his office. There he received the news that his New York office had closed its doors. The reality he had tried to stave off during the President's visit caught up with him then and tears poured down his cheeks. Within a few minutes he closed the Philadelphia office and by noon the Washington branch also. The great Jay Cooke & Company had failed. Panic hit Wall Street and stocks plummeted. By the next day the failure of other firms was announced; there were massive runs on banks; money was almost unavailable. At first railroads were among the hardest hit, but soon industries, great and small, were caught up in the vortex of panic and depression.

No one was surprised when on October 30 the imminent collapse of A. & W. Sprague was predicted. On that same day the failure of Sprague, Hoyt and Company in New York, buying and selling agents for the A. & W. Sprague Manufacturing Company, was announced.

Sprague had recently returned to Washington with the family, but he hurried at once to Providence arriving there on the thirty-first. Amasa had been bearing the brunt of the trouble alone until then. In Providence, Sprague found things very quiet and under control. In contrast to New York, where there was near hysteria, there was no panic and even the banks holding large amounts of Sprague notes did not face any massive runs.

The company was wholly owned within the Sprague family: Fanny, William, and Amasa, their two sisters, and the Hoyt cousins who were grandchildren of William Sprague, Sr. One of these, who had been in charge of the New York office, was Nettie's husband.

Sprague tried hard to raise money on loans that would tide them through the crisis, but all efforts were unsuccessful. Although the firm still had tremendous assets, actually assets of $25 million with which to carry liabilities of $11 million, further credit was denied them. Why this was done is still a matter of difference of opinion. The pro-Sprague factions claim that it was the result of vindictiveness and jealousy; that rival firms and competitors were out to ruin the great Sprague empire; that Sprague's vituperative speeches in 1869 had aroused hostility among powerful factions in Rhode Island that were determined to put an end to his influence; that Sprague's financial theories were mistakenly reputed to be radical and unsound. Certainly, Sprague's attacks on the rival firm of Brown & Ives had earned their undying hostility.

The New York Times considered the suspension of the firm inevitable and analyzed the reasons why they were in trouble. First, that they lacked reserves, having put back money earned into the business, or into land, or other business enterprises. Second, that they had too many irons in the fire. Instead of concentrating on their business of textile manufacture, they had expanded into a mass of unrelated enterprises such as street railways, intercoastal steamship lines, sheet iron, steam engines, foundries, horse shoes and nails, mowing machines, land speculation even as far away as Texas and Kansas, and so on. Third, the *Times* pointed out that one of the partners, they did not name him but undoubtedly they meant William Sprague, did not give regular attention to his business. Banking circles in Rhode Island which refused the loans found still more reasons why the Sprague enterprises were no longer considered a good risk. Among these reasons was the extravagant way of life of the family, particularly that of William Sprague. This seemed to point directly at Kate, especially to her large house at Narragansett, which was reputed to have cost over $600,000.

Kate did not accompany her husband on his hurried trip back to Providence, for a very good reason. She was expecting another child at any moment. She was unwell and understandably depressed as she waited alone in Washington for the new baby.

Kate's third daughter, her last child, was born on November 3, 1873 and she was named Portia in a kind of salute to her grandfather.[1] Kate must have fretted at her enforced idleness and her inability to help in the disaster which had struck the Sprague family business.

It was a grim time for everyone. Banks were failing all over the country, businesses crashed, factories closed, railroads went into bankruptcy, hundreds of thousands of people were out of work, over half a million due to the limitation of new railroad construction alone. Although the Spragues could not get the loan that might have enabled them to carry on as usual through the crisis, they were allowed, in order to avoid the expenses of bankruptcy and forced liquidation of properties, to execute a trust mortgage to secure payment of the outstanding notes. Zechariah Chafee was named trustee and William Sprague, under the new arrangement, became in effect an employee of the company which he had controlled for so long. It must have been a bitter blow to his pride, but at least his situation was not desperate. Every day the newspapers were filled with stories of failure and bankruptcy. Tragedy stalked the streets with poverty, unemployment, and hunger. There were reported to be ten thousand homeless men and women in New York City alone.

An unfortunate side effect of the situation was the strained relationship that developed between the Spragues and the Hoyts. Kate and Nettie had always been very close and Kate was devoted to the younger sister whom she had mothered ever since she herself had grown up. Now, there were two areas of discord. The first was connected with the failure of Sprague, Hoyt and Company in New York and the plight of the parent company. Nettie's husband was not at all satisfied with the arrangements and he grew increasingly to blame his cousin William Sprague for the financial difficulties in which he found himself. At the same time, certain problems about Chase's will became apparent. Chase had left everything to his two daughters, whatever money or investments to be divided between them and the real estate given to them jointly. Nettie was undoubtedly influenced by her husband and his suspicious attitude toward the Spragues, for a little more than a year after Chase's death it became evident that an impartial advisor and adjudicator was necessary. Clarkson Potter, a New York lawyer, was agreeable to both sides, and he wrote Kate that he had had a talk with Mr. Hoyt who "stated Mrs. Hoyt had a letter from you suggesting that I might serve as a friend to value the Real Estate left by your Father with a view to its division and added their wish that I should do so. Mr. Hoyt explained to me in a general way the situation of the personal Estate and that nothing was likely (now at least) to be realized from it and his wife desires for an amicable division of the real property stating she did not want Edgewood and that perhaps, you might want it and generally treating the subject with entire frankness and firmness." [2]

Kate did want Edgewood. She did not want to part with this place her father had so loved and where he had spent his last years. But with the Sprague failures and the absence of any cash assets from her father's estate at that time, due partly to the depression and partly to the claims against it which delayed settlement, it was difficult for her to raise the money to buy her share from Nettie.

Kate must have been extremely depressed at this period. She missed her father's affection and support; her relationship with her sister was strained; the financial failure of the Spragues had driven her husband into even more than his usual taciturnity and moodiness; her lovely little Kitty, the only child who possessed the promise of her own beauty, was extremely fragile physically and it began to look as though she was not developing mentally quite as she should; Willie, already nine years old, was undisciplined and sometimes uncontrollable. He had always had a mischievous disposition that sometimes went beyond the bounds of mischief. On one occasion when he was playing with his sister Ethel, he took hold of her and held her over the window sill threatening to let her fall the two stories to the ground below. Sometimes he would bring firewood into the house and chop at it with an axe, paying no attention to the damage he was wreaking on the polished floors. Like his father, but even more so, he was disorderly and slovenly in his dress and he would often maliciously tear his new suits.[3]

Kate may have felt that she saw in her son all the worst traits she found in her husband. Many of these she had blamed in her own mind on his education and early training, and she was determined that Willie would have a better opportunity for a fine education and strict discipline. There were undoubtedly two reasons why she chose Europe for this. She believed that a knowledge of languages would be a great advantage to all her children and she hoped that Willie's wayward habits and lack of application to his studies would be cured by the strict discipline of a German school. The other important factor, in view of the straitened finances of the family, was that a European education was far less expensive and she herself could live there modestly with her other children. And so, in October of 1874, Kate set out for Europe once more, this time with what Nettie used to call her "dear little flock."

Just before she left New York, she and Nettie had come to a tentative agreement about the disposition of Edgewood. Each had written an official letter to the other agreeing to Kate's purchase of Nettie's share for $16,875 to be paid in full within a year at 6 percent interest.[4]

Kate's statements of intent included a letter to Jay Cooke, who was executor for the estate, which would allow him to proceed with the settlement. There was only one problem. She had given the letters to her husband just before sailing to be delivered with her instructions to Mr. Potter, but Sprague was evidently not at his most alert, for, as he wrote Potter, "whether I was confused or in the confusion of getting off I don't know I did not understand her instructions." [5] Mr. Potter was a careful lawyer and responded that without Mrs. Sprague's express instructions, he was hesitant to deliver her letters.[6] Sprague decided to be cautious too. There were claims against Chase's estate by the Hoyts and also by Kate which he felt should be settled at the same time as the property. With masterly obfuscation he tells Mr. Potter that "I could however in case such a settlement was made advise you to deliver the letters though now I do not advise you to withhold them." [7]

The result of this confusion was that the Hoyts, not having been given Kate's letter, believed that she did not want to go through with the arrangement, and Kate, not knowing what had happened, imagined that the Hoyts were refusing to carry out their end of the bargain. Mr. Potter evidently wrote Kate several times enclosing copies of Nettie's letter and her own, and asking for a clarification of her instructions. Kate undoubtedly felt that the instructions she had left with her husband were perfectly clear, for evidently she did not send Mr. Potter the authority he felt he must have.

The furniture at Edgewood presented a further problem, for evidently Nettie did not agree to the sale of more than the house and land as being covered by her agreement. "As regards the furniture," Mr. Potter informed Kate, "Gov. Cooke was anxious that you should divide it. No sale except at a great sacrifice could be effected. But the Hoyts don't want it and are unwilling to make any arrangement except to have it sold . . . you can bid in half of it at the sale if there must be a sale."

By midsummer there was still no settlement, either of the Edgewood problem or of Chase's estate. The financial depression had greatly affected the holdings of the estate and there was a debt owing to Jay Cooke & Co. which also helped to delay the closing. Kate finally decided to make a quick trip home in an effort to bring things to some sort of conclusion, but evidently with little or no success. After her return to Europe she wrote Nettie, telling of a letter she had sent to Mr. Potter which he will show her and then goes on to explain: "My object in going to America was twofold—to reach if possible a final settlement of our affairs and to which end I did my utmost with the material I had to work with and the impediments I found in the way. That I made no greater progress was no fault of mine. I might perhaps have remained longer but my expenses were heavier than I could well afford, and my children were alone among strangers . . .

"My other object was to make myself thoroughly familiar with the actual position of the affairs of the Concern in which we all have interests. Comprehending the situation as I believe I now do, and after careful thought, I have decided to make a very plain appeal to your husband. It can in no event do harm, God grant it may do some good!

"I hope your little ones are quite well. Mine have improved amazingly. This winter we spend in Paris. The children will add French to their other accomplishments, and I shall see and learn all I can. Believe me always dear Nettie, in the affection of your truly attached sister." [8]

The trip home had not solved anything, either in legal matters or personal ones between the Spragues and the Hoyts. As delays and misunderstandings continued, feelings began to rise and Mr. Potter was hard put to it to find a solution that would be agreeable to all parties. Sprague, nettled perhaps by Hoyt's attitude, and not at all sure that Kate was receiving her due, entered the lists on her side. "I received a letter from my wife a good deal unnerved at a note received from her sister and possibly in her haste and perplexity directed that which was not best for her," he wrote Mr. Potter. "I do not know about the other lands belonging to the estate (Mr. C.). Some of them I believe have an income. This property at Edgewood will not enjoy an income. Still Mrs. Sprague seems to want to hold it. That she should give $16,000 in money for it is quite inadmissible. So to[o] is it that the two sisters should hold property together. Therefore, I advise you to settle the real estate matter as you propose.[9]

Mr. Potter was still as careful as ever not to move without complete written authority, especially in a case like this one, where a good deal of emotion was involved and finally, he was able to secure from Kate the kind of document he wanted. "On my return from Germany this morning whither I went to see my boy," Kate wrote him, "I found yours of the 5th inst. I confess it surprised me. Leaving as I did full power in your hands to decide and act for me, any such renewed appeal to me I considered unnecessary. The moment my sister made any offer to part with her half of Edgewood on terms that you considered fair and equal I expected you would 'close the negotiation on that basis' and without again referring the matter to me, only reporting to me what *had been done*. My desire for a settlement is probably as great as Mrs. Hoyt's, although I have not a proclivity for trying to reach it through the Courts or by means of law suits.

"Following your suggestion I name the 1st of January 1876 as the date for the transfer of the Edgewood Estate to me, to be delivered over free of all liabilities, taxes and encumbrances up to that date. The Estate has been even pending the division, a great care and heavy expense to me personally, and I consider its valuation now, under the depressed condition of all Realty at $30,000 excessive. If you are satisfied, however, that this is its fair market value I agree that sufficient of the balance of Father's Real Estate shall be turned over to Mrs. Hoyt to meet her half interest in Edgewood—viz. $16,000. On the other hand there is no reason that I should be forced to pay more than any other purchaser would pay for the property. This I believe covers the essential points of this matter."

She assures him that her not seeing Nettie again before her departure from New York was not at all his fault, as Nettie was informed of all her plans and knew the date of sailing and the name of her ship. It was a "great disappointment" to Kate not to see Nettie again, as Nettie had assured her that she would come "and I confidently looked for her coming." [10]

Chase could never have imagined that his daughters would quarrel about his estate. Nor could he have dreamed that "dear little Nettie" would insist on a public sale of his belongings at Edgewood. Kate somehow managed to arrange to buy in advance some of the things she wanted especially to keep, but the public poured through the house, tramped through Chase's library, peered into the bedrooms and examined family portraits and personal mementos.[11] How he would have hated these prying eyes. Kate, fortunately, was in Europe and did not have to witness any of it.

Nettie, quite evidently, had completely transferred her loyalty to her husband and had taken over all of his attitudes and ideas. What he looked for from the Chase estate was cash value and in spite of Mr. Cooke's opinion that the Edgewood furnishings could be sold only at a great loss, he and Nettie did not let that or any sentimental considerations stand in their way. That kind of practicality was totally alien to Kate.

Although Kate did not adopt the hard, practical attitude of the Hoyts, she too did not find it easy to manage on the greatly reduced allowance she was given. "Finding my little people like so many Locusts have eaten up my substance during my absence, I am forced again to overstep my allowance," she informed her advisor after her return from America. "We have a modest simple little apartment in the Rue Duphot close to the Madeleine, and very central." She found "no end of Americans" in Paris and had already seen several Washingtonians.

Among the new material which has become available about Kate Chase is a letter book in which she kept copies of several letters she wrote from Europe that year. These letters afford a rare insight into the quality of her mind and temperament. Kate did not lose her interest in the political scene while she was abroad. She followed the news from home eagerly and reacted with her old fire when she thought an injustice had been done. On one occasion, when she learned that General Sheridan had been ordered to New Orleans to settle the disputed elections to the Legislature in late 1874, without any prior consultation with General Sherman, head of the Army, she wrote Sherman in high indignation at this slight by the administration in Washington.

How does it happen (even if we admit that with the conditions existing in Louisiana interference was necessary) that Executive authority proving insufficient; and we having constituted a General in Chief of our armed forces, that *he* is not the one called at such a critical juncture to exercise his functions, and issue his own commands? Perhaps my view of the situation from such a distance is incorrect, but I can not passively entertain even the suspicion of such an outrage upon the *first Soldier* in our country, and a proved Patriot and Statesman like yourself.

The Situation in Louisiana, and indeed in the South generally, is truly deplorable, and brings our boasted *Republic* into ridicule if not worse, before a world too ready to see its faults.

My husband wrote me of his meeting with you in New York and of your conversation. Don't dear General withdraw from politics in disgust, because of the blindness and corruption you see. If good men and true do this, what is to become of our country in her present desperate throes? We need a *great* General now, more than we have ever done.

I write and plead with my husband not to remain silent. He takes a very comprehensive view of the situation. No man perhaps is more familiar than he through *actual* knowledge and experience (dearly bought) with the crushing incubus under which the Industrial Masses of our American people, are at present staggering. Governor Sprague is a brave, independent, public-spirited, deep-thinking man and such a remedy as he would offer for the relief of this prolonged financial stress would at least be worthy of a hearing. But I have bored you too long. I meant only to write five lines and I have covered as many pages. Again I crave indulgence.[12]

Here we see something of that penetrating mind which had so impressed Senator Sumner when she was still a school girl, and also her passionate interest in the affairs of government. Her loyalty to her husband, and her confidence in his business acumen is striking. Kate was not unaware that General Sherman's brother was a powerful Senate leader and she may even have nourished a faint hope that Sprague's ideas about the critical financial situation in the country might find a hearing.

One of the qualities that was so appealing in Kate was her sincere interest in people, in their lives and their concerns. As someone said of her once, she was able to make each person she talked to feel that they were the very person she wanted to meet.

No matter how much Kate was interested in people and politics and the new and different experiences she was having in Paris, her thoughts were never far from home and what was happening there.

In 1873 when financial ruin had threatened the Sprague corporations with bankruptcy, it had been arranged that the new notes issued against the trust mortgage were to run for three years. In effect this represented a three-year moratorium based on the hope that within that period conditions would have improved to such a degree that there would be no further financial difficulties or embarrassments. But the depression of 1873 did not end as soon as had been anticipated and conditions remained very precarious throughout the country. The textile market had not recovered and the hope that the financial troubles might be over for the Spragues was illusory. The situation, indeed, began to look even more serious than it had and it seemed possible that the trustee, Mr. Chafee, might not be able to meet the payment of interest on the trust mortgage in January of 1876. Sprague and Chafee were at loggerheads about everything, each distrusting not only the other's ability but his intentions. Kate was in constant contact with her husband by letter and looked for every opportunity to help where she could. The birth of a son to Amasa gave her the opportunity to plead her husband's cause with him:

> Your brother is entitled Amasa to all the confidence and support that can be given him. He has a rare fund of strength and wisdom which when rightly appealed to, is at your disposal, and *in him* is your best, your only real hope of ultimate success. You must now realize this. Do trust him entirely. Give him your unqualified support, and together, and in perfect accord, you may confidently attack the complications you have to meet, with a reasonable hope of overcoming them.[13]

In spite of the disappointment and grief Kate had experienced in her marriage, she did not let that affect her loyalty toward her husband. She still strove to find qualities in him that she could admire, and she was ready to do battle with anyone on his behalf. For the first time, it appears that Sprague turned to her for specific help in his present business difficulties. The Hoyt faction was pressing for a separate settlement of their claims on the basis that when the A. & W. Sprague Manufacturing Co. had been incorporated in 1865, they were infants and they each claimed one twenty-fourth of the whole property that had been transferred to the corporation from the original firm at that time. Hoyt was planning to take these claims to court.

Mails were frustratingly slow and Kate waited anxiously for word of what was going on. When she received a letter from her husband in November asking her to write Hoyt and see what she could do to soften his position toward the settlement of the affairs of the company, she responded immediately.

"A copy of the letter to Wm. Hoyt you have herein enclosed. It is not what I wanted it should be. I have re-written it several times, but finally let it go as it was. If there is a point to be gained it would not do to excite further opposition by being bitter or too aggressive. Therefore I have toned my letter as quietly as I could with the hard truths with which I had to deal. I hope you will find nothing to disapprove in it." [14]

Knowing Kate's strong protective reaction toward members of her family and her dislike of the Hoyts' habit of seeking settlement in the courts, her letter to Hoyt is a model of restraint and tact. She reminds him that years ago she told him that he could count on her if ever an emergency arose in his life wherein she could do him a service. "That emergency presents itself now. My position is difficult, but thank God it is to be just and true to all alike. The interests of those whom I would serve, do not conflict. They are identical.

"Hitherto I have been sanguine as to the final issue of the embarrassments of A. & W. Sprague. But the prolonged depression in all business so universal and so unprecedented makes their case extremely critical."

Kate goes on to tell him that she had believed his course, even considered strictly from his own interest, to have been a mistaken one from the start for two reasons: "First, it appeared to me you were proceeding on the ground that a fraud had been perpetrated against you, while in point of fact, none was attempted or intended. Secondly, your case being even all that you claimed for it, there was a better, shorter, surer way to meet it than the one you chose."

When she had been at home the previous summer, she had made it her special business to inform herself thoroughly upon all the questions at issue, she tells him. She saw his bill in Equity and talked with the lawyers. She did not believe it valuable to take it up point by point, that is the lawyers' business. "The vital question is, how much more of the substance which should be yours are you will[ing] they shall consume, or in other words are you not taking the risk of losing everything you are contending for (and more if you have it) by seeking under the existing conditions to exact what you claim through the slow and costly processes of the Law? It is through the Rhode Island Laws you must seek redress, and will not the powerful Credit Interest there, first protect itself as against your poor claims, as well as against those of the Principles in the Concern."

Hoyt was trying to arrange to have his own claims satisfied regardless of the others involved or of the condition of the firm itself. "That you have certain rights, no one denies," Kate assures him. "So have we all if they can be secured. What is justly yours in the division, if anything remains, no one could withhold, and if it were attempted *then* the Law would come to your rescue."

Kate pleads with him to trust Sprague. "Unless your object is to destroy, your only hope lies in him. He is peculiar and difficult to approach, but he is honest and he is capable. Trust him instead of suspecting him, cooperate with him unreservedly, and see if some plan can not be devised at once by which the Creditors may be kept at bay, and these interests in which there is still so much life and vigor if preserved intact, can not be made with wise management, to protect their owners and shake off their encumbrances."

Kate makes this appeal, she tells Hoyt, from her profound interest to see this done. "It may be too late. It may be that Gov. Sprague may be unwilling at this late day to lead a forlorn hope or to assume the enormous burden. It is worth the attempt however and it lies greatly with you to inspire and aid it.

"I only wish I was a man with such a chance. Aside from the benefits to be derived it would be one of the greatest social triumphs of the age." Kate closes by suggesting that he subject her opinions to the sharpest criticism of any one who has his interests at heart.[15]

She enclosed this letter to Hoyt in her answer to her husband. Sprague was evidently greatly disturbed not only by Hoyt's intransigent attitude but by the whole state of affairs with his company. If Mr. Chafee was unable to meet the interest payments in January, then all would be lost, as the creditors would not sit idly by in such an event. From Kate's letter to Hoyt, it seems as though Sprague was in one of his moods of depression and lack of self-confidence that attacked him so regularly. When he was in that condition, action became impossible for him and he remained frozen in an attitude of outward apathy which belied his tremendous inner conflict and which Kate knew from past experience could explode into violent action at any moment. Sprague's second Senate term had ended that year and he had not tried for a third term. His business interests were all that was left to him now and Kate recognized clearly what the Sprague company had always meant to him. She believed that the only hope to save it was to get him out of his depression and on the upswing again into one of those states of confidence and euphoria when everything seemed possible to him and when he was able to think and act vigorously. She had succeeded many times in the past to break his cycle of moods, to disperse the winds of depression. As she sat in front of the fire with his latest letter, which was obviously filled with black thoughts, she worked out her response carefully. She must formulate a plan, and try to give him the encouragement and confidence to carry it out. Yet she must be careful not to wound his already battered self-esteem. Gradually, through that long night, her ideas took shape, and she wrote:

> Now let me give you this drift of my thoughts.
> I gather there is danger that Mr. Chafee will not be able to pay his interest in January. If this is imminent why is it not the *golden moment* for *you* to seize the dilemma by the horns, and strike your blow? If it fails there is nothing lost beyond what was inevitable, if it succeeds you take command of the situation. Your prompt self-abnegation when disaster came, your patience and forebearance while everything that promised any favorable issue was being tried, sufficiently established your integrity and commands every consideration in return. It gives emphasis to any course you may

now take, while entitling you to the confidence of the business community.

How does a program like that strike you? You to call in advance of a crisis (forseeing it, and showing the moral courage to proclaim it, which few men would have) a meeting of your Creditors. Flatter their choice and satisfy Mr. Chafee by giving him as much credit as you can, for his administration; explain plainly and forcibly the true reasons for his failure to fulfill what he undertook in the best faith; try and make your Creditors see and understand the existing conditions at large in the country, as *you* see them. This gains their recognition of your forecast and prescience. Then show how unreasonable it is to expect any man not familiar through long habit and actual contact, or held by that *personal interest* and *accountability,*—which would sharpen the wits even of a dullard,—to grasp and manage to the best advantage a Concern of the vast magnitude of yours. Point out what a magnificent groundwork as an Industry and in favorable times, it is constructed upon, and how little it would render if broken in pieces.

Offer to assume the *entire* management of the Interests of the A. & W. Sprague Manufacg. Co. with the full co-operation of the Hoyt faction, if it can be obtained. Here would be the most powerful leverage to apply, to bring the latter to terms.

There would be your debt to carry awhile longer and the interest to pay. You would have to protect yourself at every point possibly exposed to irregular or malicious outside embarrassment, trusting to your great sagacity and business ability to carry you through. But thus reinstated in a position of power you stand ready when the right time comes, to influence more forcibly than words could do it, those vital measures, which must determine the prosperity or anarchy of our country. It is not with the idea of advancing anything new or that you have not already considered, that I write. Something impels me to plead with you. If I am impracticable you will be quick to detect it, while at the same time you will see how earnest I am in my convictions, and in my desire to help you. Rest assured that the Hoyts are taking advantage of and misconceive your apathy, and that your Creditors will do the same unless you anticipate them.

If you take up this burden I go home at once to help you bear it with heart and soul. I provide the children with proper instruction, and settle them in the country and you may make me General Inspector of the Factories, or the head of a Corps to gather up the waste, and fragments that nothing be lost, everything of use.

Kate then goes on to discuss a few more specific items advising him to consult Mr. Potter on the legal aspects and telling him of the great markets for print cloth that exist in Italy and Spain. And she closes:

> But there must come a halt. When I become interested, I see no stopping place. Good-night. I cast my crumbs upon the water, and I expect bread before many days. Faithfully always your wife.[16]

Here at last we see Kate in full flight with all her powers—the incisive mind, the delicate tact, her remarkable energy and response to a challenge; the desire to contribute to some positive achievement, not merely to let life float by in passive enjoyment.

Kate must have been bitterly disappointed that Sprague did not act on her suggestions. His discouragement and apathy were too great for him to overcome at that time perhaps, and it was only some years later that he tried to follow Kate's advice. For the present, the status quo remained with Chafee as trustee, Sprague powerless in his own company, and the relationship between them deteriorating rapidly.

The Hoyt faction did go to court and their case dragged on as interminably as did everything else in connection with that once great business empire. The obstinacy with which they pressed their claims was unusual, for they continued through court after court until the United States Supreme Court, in 1881, turned down their final appeal.[17] The expense of this battle must have been great and the tenacity with which they pursued it would seem to show more than a little vindictiveness. Nettie was undoubtedly as loyal to her husband's cause as Kate was to hers and the whole unfortunate situation could hardly have contributed to an unclouded relationship between the two sisters.

CHAPTER

❧❧❧ XV ❧❧❧

KATE RETURNED to America with her three daughters in the fall of 1876 and apparently went directly to Narragansett. She left Willie at his school in Germany. He had made remarkable progress in the two years he had been there and though she dreaded the separation from him, she considered, and so did his schoolmaster, Mr. Lautern, that it was best for his development that he should stay on for at least one more year.

Kate's letters to her son show the deep affection she had for him and her interest in everything that concerned him. She writes him of all the happenings at Canonchet, the fire that started in the chimney in the Reception Room and how "Papa fortunately was at home, and with promptness and coolness, our Extinguishers which stood already charged and ready and plenty of water we soon put out the fire." [1] It was the third time that great wooden structure had been threatened with destruction by fire and she hoped it would be the last. She sent Willie a Christmas box full of presents, and turkeys for Christmas dinner hoping that they arrived in time. "How we have all missed you during the Holiday times," she tells him. "Our children have had a very simple, old-fashioned Christmas but a very jolly one. Their stockings were hung and they found them full of goodies and trifles that served to keep them amused all day." [2]

Kate undoubtedly spoiled her children and indulged them in every way that she could. Her evident delight in them and in the simple pleasures of home and family life radiate from her letters to Willie, "beau boy" as the little girls liked to call him, and she tries to bridge the distance from home for him with her accounts of what they are all doing.

"Thanks, thanks, thanks, the thanks of the whole family for your New Year's greeting," she exclaimed delightedly.[3] The little girls missed their brother even more than usual during the holidays:

> Oh, how happy the little sisters would have been to have their dear brother with them. There is not a pleasure they enjoy that they do not miss and regret you and wish they might share with you. During the snow and ice Ethel would exclaim continually "If beau boy was only here what fun we could have!" She did not skate or slide upon the ice—but both she and the little ones enjoyed the snow. They each have Rubber boots, then in their little white fur coats and hoods they defy the weather, and turn out looking like little Polar bear's cubs and come in with the brightest of cheeks. So far the babies have not had the least cold this winter and they seem to have forgotten the croup—although the winter with us has been unusually cold and snowy.[4]

Kate also tried constantly to impress on her son the importance of habits of neatness and order, of hard work and truthfulness. She did not weight down her precepts in the grim puritanical way her father had done with her, yet she urged most of the same things on Willie, sometimes even quoting from her father. "I repeat his advice to you my dearest Willie. Never be afraid of speaking the truth, only be careful not to say what may wound another person's feelings and seize every opportunity to do little kindnesses that you may be beloved by all who know you." [5]

Another of the many misconceptions about Kate which new material has clarified is that she was, so to speak, a mother in name only, so preoccupied with her own pleasures and ambitions that she turned over the entire care of her children to nurses and governesses and concerned herself very little if at all with them. In point of fact, she was in every respect truly maternal. She supervised and shared in her children's pleasures, she took over a great part of their instruction herself, and when they were ill, she nursed them. "For one week now I have scarcely been in bed," she informed Willie. "Portia and Kitty have both been very ill and one or the other of them have been almost constantly in my arms, night and day." [6]

Kate did not let on to her son that things were not as easy and happy at home as she made out. Sprague had not improved in his habits during her absence abroad and even the presence of his growing daughters in the house did not induce him to control his behavior. Kate was no longer emotionally involved with him but she felt the obligations of marriage and wanted too to keep up appearance for the sake of her children. But his conduct became so flagrant that she could no longer stand it and she realized that it certainly was not good for the children either. Later, Kate charged that Sprague's "indecent advances to female servants, and other violations of decency, which had increased in frequency and enormity," had made Canonchet "an unsuitable abode" for herself and her children and that in February 1877, "with the assent of said Sprague," she left that home with her three daughters.[7]

So Kate moved once again with her daughters, this time back to Edgewood. She did not break with Sprague, however. They corresponded regularly, and he visited her occasionally at Edgewood, but at least she was no longer subjected to the constant humiliation of his conduct and the girls were spared the sight of their father's excesses.

The best news for Kate was Willie's continued progress and she received excellent reports about him from his schoolmaster. "Mr. Lautern gives me a most encouraging account of you, my darling boy. What happiness this is to me, it would be difficult to give you an idea of, and if this long separation proves, as I certainly believe it will, to your advantage, we will have great cause to be grateful for the courage and resolution which sustained us both, in consenting to it, and a good solid foundation laid now, in health, in education, will render your future course so much simpler and so much more successful.[8]

The girls, especially Kitty and Portia, continued to be almost continually ill with colds and earaches but Portia's "spirit does not droop," Kate tells Willie. "She is as bright and saucy and wild as ever, and is greatly admired by all her old friends here. Dear little Kitty wears always her serene smile, and is as cheery and musical as a bird." [9]

A few weeks later Ethel was taken seriously ill with diphtheria, "a disease which in all its phases is alarming," Kate wrote Willie in answer to his letter which came at a time "when it could do me the most good." She had chosen to take care of the child entirely herself. "We were quarantined, she and I for my dread was very great lest the epidemic should spread through the family but thus far God has been very good to us, and only Ethel and I have had it and both lightly and are both now rapidly convalescing." [10]

No sooner did Ethel and Kate recover than Kitty came down suddenly with scarlet fever and the child "lay for several days at death's door," Kate wrote. She telegraphed Sprague who came at once and stayed until the danger was passed. "During such anxiety and constant watching I could not write—besides, I would not have wished to leave you in anxious doubt. Now thank God I believe we may feel quite happy and hopeful about our darling Kitten." [11]

Another good report of Willie's progress "fills my heart with joy," she tells him. "Both your Grandpa and your Papa have filled very high and important places, in the History of our New Country, and you are the only boy to keep their record open, and untarnished through their descendants." [12]

Kate had high hopes for her son and planned his education and training with great care. School in Germany was succeeding beyond even her expectations and the change in Willie was remarkable. Even Sprague agreed that it had been wise to leave the boy for the time being in Europe. "Mama was right," he wrote his son, "in keeping you in Europe. It was a great sacrifice for her to do it. Cling to your Mama. Love her and your sisters." [13] Grandmother Fanny also approved of Kate's decision and believed that although Willie was a long way off, in the present unsettled state of affairs it was for the best.

Although Kate sent off letters to Willie every week and enclosed photographs, poems, newspaper articles, anything she thought might possibly be of interest to him, Sprague wrote very rarely to his son. "I have received all your letters to me," he wrote Willie after a long silence, "I am very thankfull to you for continuing to write to me although not having your letters replied to." He is pleased at the evidence of Willie's improvement and says that he himself at the same age could not write and express himself as well by a great deal. "I had difficulty; from want of concentration, and habits of order instilled into me. My mother, your grandmother was quite rigid with her sons. Your father and Uncle Amasa. A good deal like what your mama feels and acts towards you. Constantly reminding us of defects, and worrying us into obedience." And then he shows something of the divisive attitude of competition with Kate for his son that was to have such disastrous effect on the boy later. "You are a long way off and a long time away. I must make a bargain with you before your Mama bribes you away from me. Your sisters Mama takes with her, and leaves me here alone. She complains a good deal because I have so little to do with the family. Now you must make me a part of your family by joining me when you come home." He describes how hard he is working and how his business has been "measurably broken up" since Willie left. And in rather stilted fashion he exhorts him to study and to get "habits of industry . . . Never be idle . . . Idleness is the cause of all the evils in life. Be industrious no matter so much, what it is in, but be industrious. Hate idleness . . . I will write you again. Remember that you cannot be forgotten that I love you my boy. Keep up good spirits and courage." [14]

Kate tried going again to Narragansett during the summer but soon beat another hasty retreat back to Washington. Sprague one night in a drunken fury had broken into her room at Canonchet, seized her and dragged her to the window, which was in an upper story, and attempted to throw her out. This was not the first time that he had attacked her physically, but his wild moods were growing more uncontrollable all the time. The little girls were no longer infants and could not so easily be shielded from scenes of such violence and disorder.

Another winter at Edgewood passed slowly. Kate hoped and planned to be able to go abroad to bring Willie home or at least to be with him for this thirteenth birthday, but as time went by she grew increasingly discouraged. Her health was not very good that year and she began to suffer with her eyes, something that was to give her great trouble in later years. She writes Willie in February that for the past two weeks she was not permitted to use her eyes at all. "I have practised every self-denial for these past weeks in order to recover my eyes," but she hopes for a real cure. "I enter thus into detail now that all danger seems to have passed that you may quite understand why your Mamma, in whose thoughts you are uppermost every hour of the day, has not committed those thoughts of late to paper but has had to deny herself that satisfaction." [15]

In March Kate was sufficiently recovered to take a two-week tour with her husband "through the Factories and Print works in New England." One of the chief objects she had in view in going to New England "was to thoroughly canvas with Papa a plan for you, my dear boy, for the coming year, and this seems to be the result so far as I can foresee. If I can rent this place, by the first of June, I hope to start for Europe taking certainly Ethel with me, the two little girls if Papa will consent." She hopes that they could stay long enough in Paris to see the Exposition, then spend the hottest season in Switzerland or the Tyrol, after which she would like to take them to England and find there a good school and stay near him for as long as possible. "For myself, I should like it extremely to remain in England for two years to come and then return all of us together to our American home, and settle down quietly here while you make your way through College." [16]

Sprague, evidently, did not either withhold permission for this plan, nor did he do anything to suggest he would allow it. The weeks passed. Kate apparently did not succeed in renting Edgewood. By the time summer came, she was not looking further than somehow managing to see her son either by going abroad herself or bringing him home. But Sprague evidently said nothing on the subject until the very last moment, by which time Kate was nearly frantic. "The weeks are rolling by and summer is well upon us," she wrote Willie, "and both you and I are suffering a bitter disappointment. When I found I was not to be with you as I so confidently expected upon your birthday I begged your Papa who was here at the time and only announced it at the last moment, and after I was all ready to start to write and tell you. I had not the heart, and it made me ill. *Still* I have hoped almost against hope, that each day I should have some good *news to send* you and have *waited* anxiously for each mail to come—confident that your Papa would find a way either to send me over or to send for you to come home even only for a short time and even if you *were* to return. I have offered many suggestions, but all have failed. Now, after receiving *this morning* again a letter, and no plan proposed I have determined to find a way for myself. *The times* here are hard beyond *description* and your Papa's business does not prosper. *We are living with the utmost economy* and have *never* ceased to hope for improvement. But with my failing health and my poor eyes I have been much crippled and discouraged. In the past fortnight, *however* there has been a very favorable change in my health and with returning strength I feel renewed courage and have hit upon one of *two plans* which I hope will work after submitting it to our good Mr. Lautern." She hopes to manage to go to him in August and if that is impossible to have him go first to the Paris Exposition and then come home. "So set your heart at rest my boy you *shall* either be with your mother or your mother will go to you in August." [17]

This agitated letter shows how much the separation from her son and the uncertainty about seeing him again had cost her. Kate's financial position was very precarious. The business affairs of the firm had not improved and Sprague was receiving still only a compensation from the trustee, a part of which was paid over for the support of Kate and her children. Edgewood was a financial burden that Sprague did not feel obligated to assume and Kate watched the arrears of taxes and other expenses accumulate. Kate had no more financial sense than had her father and all her plans to make Edgewood pay for itself somehow fell through. How she managed to bring back Willie in the face of Sprague's lack of cooperation, is not clear. Undoubtedly she enlisted the aid of Fanny Sprague who visited her at Edgewood with Sprague's sister, Almyra and her husband. Fanny, with her ideas of how much a woman sacrifices when she marries, would be sure to have assisted

Kate in bringing home the grandson she herself was eager to see. In any event, in July Kate wrote her son happily, "How I shall count the days until your coming and will, God willing, be on the wharf myself to see the Steamer bearing its precious freight make fast and receive you into my arms once more." [18]

Kate moved once more to Canonchet with her children after Willie's return. It was, after all, home for the children with cousins and uncles and aunts and Grandmother Fanny, and was a marvelous place which had everything to offer in the way of activity and recreation for a growing boy. Willie had been away from home for more than three years and Kate must have been hopeful that the whole family could spend at least a few months together in peace and harmony. But peace and harmony were soon shattered when Sprague was arrested in a drunken orgy at Nantasket, Massachusetts, with none other than Mary Eliza Viall Anderson. The scandal was all the more acute as Mary Eliza had published her little book less than two years before and, though privately printed, it undoubtedly had been widely read in and around Rhode Island. The savagery of the thinly disguised attack on Kate was rich grist for the gossip mills. "Look," she writes in describing Kate, "while she stands before the Venetian mirror to fasten one white camellia in a braid of chestnut hair . . . It is a regular face you see reflected there, a handsome face—*fine*, but not intellectual, nor tender, nor true. Involuntarily one shudders whilst he admires and admires whilst he shudders. Could Catherine de Medici have looked like that; but what need—did not the tender-mouthed Cenci murder her own father?" [19] When Kate decided to marry Sprague, or rather, in Mary Eliza's terms, when the "Statesman's daughter" decided to marry him, "In that hour the evil eye lit upon our Launcelot. In that hour the bow was bent, whose arrow was to pierce both heart and life . . . Ah, better for him had it been cannon shot from the enemies' mouth—from the jaws of Death." [20]

The pages of pyschotic ramblings of Mary Eliza's book, the intimate revelation of her own love affair with Sprague are all vicious in the extreme. To be the object of such an attack would have been painful enough in itself, but for her husband to be intimate with this woman, and his relationship with her publicly exposed in a flagrant scandal was more than Kate could bear. She had "striven hard," as she herself later stated, "through untold humiliation and pain, to hide from the world, for my children's sakes, the true conditions of a blighted, miserable domestic life." But after Sprague's arrest at Nantasket Beach, "I then sought with my little girls, the neighborhood of old friends, and the shelter of my honored father's former home. There, dwelling almost within the shadow of his tomb, I felt more secure, less unprotected." [21]

Fourteen-year-old Willie evidently chose to remain with his father in Rhode Island and Kate must have despaired as she saw all her efforts to inculcate in him habits of discipline and application vitiated. The boy's natural inclinations and his father's example and encouragement, allying himself as he did with Willie against his mother and her efforts to discipline and direct him, undid in a few short months what she had watched with so much hope during his years in Germany.

She was finally able to prevail upon Sprague to send the boy to school, and after the first of the year Willie went to a naval school not far from Washington, in Maryland. He came often to Edgewood for weekends and Kate's hopes revived a little that he might again make progress with his education. "I feel especially desirous that you shall pursue both your Latin and German with more diligence," she wrote him. "Write as often as you can and go in now, in dead earnest dear boy to improve yourself. Through your own industry and resolve you can accomplish wonders." [22] But her concern for him is clear. "I shall send you a list of words that you misspell which I want you to return to me with the correct spelling . . . Again I must say I want you to take the utmost pains with your letters. Certainly you can obtain *ink* if you will take the pains. Do not write again with 'Saratoga Dressing.' " [23] He wants a gun, but she is hesitant. "It makes me feel very anxious to think of you handling fire arms with the little experience you have had in using them and I beg you to be cautious." [24] Although Willie was not yet fifteen he was already smoking and Kate hoped that in his next letter he would tell "of your firm resolve not to smoke at all any more." [25]

The few letters that exist from Kate to her son during his

months at naval school reflect the change that had come over the boy since his return home. There is none of her former delight about encouraging reports at his progress. He had evidently slipped back into all his slovenly habits of study and of dress, and showed very little interest in improving himself. Knowing his inheritance and the influence his father evidently had with him, she realized that it would not be easy to hold him in any kind of reasonable discipline.

All this time while Kate was so clearly occupied with her children and her domestic affairs, Washington society was busy. It fed on gossip and it is not surprising that Kate, who had always been talked about ever since her early days in Columbus, should be one of the prime subjects. Kate, in her late thirties, was as beautiful as ever, more so, many people thought. Living as she did most of the time alone with her daughters, her husband coming for only occasional visits, it was natural that the tongues of scandal would soon begin to wag about her.

What was the beautiful Kate Chase Sprague doing at Edgewood? Where was her husband? Why was she not with him in Rhode Island? These were the questions whispered in busy drawing rooms. It was not long before another name began to be mentioned in connection with hers—that of the influential Senator from New York, Roscoe Conkling.

Senator Conkling was a magnificent figure of a man. And he knew it. Over six feet tall, with broad shoulders and deep chest, he was a picture of sartorial elegance. His waving reddish gold hair and beard was a foil for the carefully chosen colors of his ties, his fancy waistcoats, the spotless white of his shirts. He was known as the Apollo of the Senate and ladies simply swooned over him. To Conkling this seemed perfectly natural. Already richly endowed by nature, he had worked hard to improve himself. Temperate in his habits, in a day when that was rare, he exercised regularly, was an excellent horseman, enjoyed boxing and swimming and paid loving attention to what was jokingly called "the finest torso in public life." As a speaker he was tremendously effective, and he had made a point of perfecting himself as an orator. Standing ramrod straight, one foot slightly before the other, head thrown back, a supercilious lift to the eyebrows, mellifluous voice carefully modulated and each syllable clearly enunciated, Conkling gave the impression of unstudied command when he spoke. Actually it was all carefully worked out in advance. Few men ever spent so much time preparing their speeches as Conkling. Although he was far from ineffective as an extemporaneous speaker, his set speeches were thoroughly memorized and rehearsed, often in front of a mirror, to calculate the best effect. Conkling left nothing to chance, took nothing for granted.

He had started his career as a lawyer in upstate New York and soon began his rapid upward climb that was to lead from Mayor of Utica to Congressman and finally, in 1867, at the age of thirty-eight, to Senator. After the death of Salmon Chase, he was offered the position of Chief Justice, but turned it down. Not only was Conkling undisputed leader of the Republican party in New York State, but for the two terms of Grant's administration he had been extremely close to the President and wielded enormous power. Although some of his colleagues derided his supercilious, vain manner, and laughed when one of his enemies referred to his "haughty disdain, his grandiloquent swell, his majestic, supereminent, overpowering, turkey-gobbler strut," no one underestimated Roscoe Conkling.[26] For with all his flamboyance, his airs, his conceit, Conkling was a serious, hard-working man of real ability. He held himself aloof from ordinary mortals and disdained the kind of amiable contact that is usually expected in a political party leader. He loathed being touched or even having any one sit too close to him and he despised any sort of easy intimacy or rowdy carefree company. He was fastidious and had a horror of any kind of disorder, mental or physical. He had very little if any humor and absolutely none where he himself was concerned.

Conkling married, in his twenties, the sister of Governor Seymour, a young woman of unusual intelligence and modesty. She produced only one child, a daughter, and very rarely appeared in Washington, preferring Utica and the life there to the capricious atmosphere of the capital. Rumor had it that she and her husband did not get along and that the reason for the rift was the Senator's irresistible attraction for the ladies. His name was linked with dozens of them, a whole line extending from upstate New York, where in later years gossips liked to point out a young man bearing a startling resemblance to the handsome Senator, to New York, where a public official was rumored to have divorced his wife because of her liaison with Conkling, to Washington, where he was supposed to have conquered a multitude of fluttering feminine hearts.

Small wonder that soon after Kate's return to Washington, in 1877, gossips began to watch the handsome Senator and beautiful Mrs. Sprague and whispered that they were showing more than a casual interest in each other. It was reported that every time Conkling spoke, Kate was in the Senate gallery listening with breathless interest and attention. No matter how dull the argument "the voluptuous form and bright bewitching face of Mrs. Sprague were rarely missed." [27] It was said that Conkling seemed to make every speech for her benefit. As soon as she would enter the gallery he would leap to his feet and start to speak under any pretext. On one occasion, Mrs. Sprague was supposed to have stayed on during a Senate debate until three in the morning, and this disclosure caused such a furore of gossip that it was noticed that for a while after that she brought with her the wives of two senators, impeccable ladies whose company might dispel any gossip about her actions. On several occasions she was supposed to have scribbled notes to the Senator which he received in discreet fashion, standing with his back to the door, his hands folded behind him so that the note could be unobtrusively slipped into his grasp. His notes to her would be equally ineptly camouflaged, folded inside another piece of paper, then inserted into a large official envelope and given to a messenger who would wait a discreet period and then appear in the gallery and hand the large envelope to Mrs. Sprague. That lady would let the note lie unnoticed for a while and then most casually open it and read it. On one occasion, it was reported, after Conkling finished an important speech and had duly received his congraulatory note from Kate, a colleague went up to him and nudged him in the ribs with a broad grin as if to say: "Oh, you lucky dog, you!" Conkling was reported to have turned red and furious.

Whenever she would leave the gallery, Conkling would accompany her to her carriage and several times it was even said she had been closeted alone with him in his office. The pair were reported also to hold meetings at the house of a friendly Southern senator and on one occasion, when they were both invited to a dinner party, the Senator shocked everyone present by his attention. Arriving before Kate, he inquired for her in a loud voice in the hall and learning she had not yet arrived, waited for her outside in the vestibule, in spite of the very bad weather. When she arrived, and the doors to the drawing room were thrown open, the assembled guests watched while he presented her dramatically with a large bouquet of rare flowers.

Another incident that people declared was true occurred on the occasion when Conkling got into a heated argument with Senator Lamar. Insults flew and the Senators approached each other obviously in a rage. A fight appeared imminent. Kate was reported to have turned deathly pale and slumped back in her seat in a near faint.

There was even more talk when Conkling introduced a clause in a bill to exempt Edgewood from all past or future taxation as long as it was in the possession of any child of the late Chief Justice. Although the Senate passed it, the House limited the period of tax relief allowing it only until June 1880. Wagging tongues pretended to be outraged that Conkling should show such utter disregard for the niceties of conventional behavior as to introduce a measure for the help and support of the woman they claimed was his *chère amie*. From all this it was only a step to suggest that the strong-willed Senator from New York was completely under the control of Mrs. Sprague.

When Kate returned to America after her two years abroad, the country was in the throes of another Presidential election. Grant's Administration was petering out, Grant himself managing somehow to escape the opprobrium that the frauds and scandals of his Administration had earned. Things looked hopeful for a Democratic victory. The country was sick and tired of the Republicans; the depression maintained its strangle hold on business and individuals alike; Rutherford Hayes, the Republican candidate, was little known and less admired; Samuel Tilden, the Democrat, was a most impressive candidate. Conkling disliked Hayes and thought he could not win. An illness, real or feigned, prevented him from making more than a single campaign speech for the candidate of his party. All in all, the campaign was a quiet one and election day passed off with fewer than the normal disorders. Certainly there were no signs that this election was to be the most scandalous in American history. By nightfall almost everyone was sure that Tilden had it and went to bed with complete confidence in the outcome. But during the night the picture changed and by morning nothing was clear except that the results were in doubt. The electoral vote was close, so close in fact that the election might in the end hinge on a single vote. Four states were in question with conflicting results being claimed by each side. South Carolina and Oregon sent in two sets of electoral votes; Florida sent in three, and Louisiana, where fraud was the most open of all, two. In order to win, Hayes had to carry all four of these states. There was no real problem for him in Oregon, but Tilden had received a quarter of a million more votes than Hayes and had clearly been elected in the popular vote in the three Southern States. With each side claiming fraud everything depended on which set of electoral votes would be accepted.

Feeling ran high both North and South. The situation was explosive and might ignite at any moment. Dangerous talk of armed men and armies was made by the hotheads. It was to his old friend Senator Conkling that Grant turned for help in finding a solution. A bill was finally agreed upon after fighting it out, in Conkling's words, "not only section by section, but line by line and word by word." [28] It provided that the election should proceed as prescribed by the Constitution with the president of the Senate, at a joint session of both houses, opening the election certificates and announcing the votes. The significant point was that any question or disputed vote should be handed over to a commission made up of five members of each house and five from the Supreme Court. The proportion of Democrats and Republicans from the Congress would be even, but as there were only two Democrats on the Supreme Court it was inevitable that the odd member would be nominally a Republican, even if his position on the bench had detached him from partisan politics.

Although Conkling had not been in good health for some months, he outdid himself in his speech for the bill. He spoke all one afternoon and later collapsed in the cloakroom. The next morning he arrived late, and after his usual dramatic entrance he took the floor again and spoke almost till midnight. Finally, in spite of powerful opposition, the bill was passed.

Proceeding alphabetically, Florida with its three sets of electoral votes was the first disputed state to be reached. The question was referred to the commission which decided that it would accept the first returns that had been sent to the Congress and that it had no right to look beyond these or to intervene in the rights of the states. These first returns were in each case Republican returns. The commission had voted 8–7 strictly along party lines. It was February 26 before the last of the disputed states was reached, South Carolina. Like the others, it was declared for Hayes. All was over now but the shouting and there was plenty of that. Rumors began to fly that someone was going to stop the whole farce at the last moment and that someone was Conkling. It was reported excitedly that he detested Hayes, that he planned a filibuster, that he would demand a new national election and arrange to keep Grant in the White House until the issue was decided. Conkling was the man, they said, who would throw everything into a turmoil and demand that it all be started over from the beginning.

The night of March 1 the Congress was to complete the count and announce the final result of the election, unless something happened to stop them. The scenes of disorder in the House chamber took on the air of a circus. The "riotous demonstrations and threatening attitude of the filibuste[re]rs caused intense excitement . . . Many ladies fearing that a free fight was about to take place on the Democratic side left the galleries." Congressman Beebe, a New York Democrat, "worked himself up into a terrible pitch of excitement, and out-shouted the madmen who were howling all about him . . . Finding the Speaker paid no attention to him, Beebe mounted his desk, and running over the tops of four desks in front of him denounced the rulings of the Speaker as unlawful and unjust." A semblance of order was finally restored by the Sergeant at Arms.[29] Everyone looked for Roscoe Conkling. He was nowhere to be found. Quietly, he had left Washington and was visiting friends in Baltimore. The election of Rutherford B. Hayes to the Presidency was announced by the Senate in the early hours of the next morning without the imposing presence of the Senator from New York.

Among the many stories about that explosive and sordid election battle was one which developed only some time after the event: Senator Roscoe Conkling's failure to lead a movement to throw the Senate vote to Tilden was the fault of Kate Chase Sprague. Kate is supposed to have harbored a resentment against Tilden, blaming him for her father's defeat at the Democratic Convention in 1868, and here at last, had her revenge. In effect, Tilden's defeat was the result of the nasty vindictiveness of a woman. This story has persisted in the face of many denials and of all logic.

Conkling may not have liked Rutherford Hayes and may have regretted his nomination, but he would never have worked so hard to frame and pass the bill setting up the election commission had he either the plan or the desire to upset their decisions and throw everything into turmoil again.[30] Conkling was a party man above everything else. As undisputed boss of one of the most powerful states in the Union, he wielded great power within Republican ranks. That he would, in effect, defect to the Democrats seems completely incredible. In January, as reported in *The New York Times,* Conkling in a speech declared that "he was thoroughly convinced that Rutherford B. Hayes had been fairly and legally elected to the position of President of the United States . . . Senator Conkling then clearly for the first time since the election publicly expressed his opinion as to the result. For weeks past his probable conviction upon this point has been much discussed in Washington. Had he announced it sooner, he would have been saved from much severe and, as the event proves, unjust criticism." [31] Conkling never made a public statement without having thought it out to the last detail and he certainly would not have assumed a position and then switched to its diametrical opposite within a matter of some three weeks.

As to Kate's role, Conkling was the last man to be influenced against his own judgment by anyone, least of all a woman, even a woman of Kate's stature. Furthermore, Kate had been out of the country for two years and had not participated either politically or socially in Washington even before that, due to her father's death and the birth of her two youngest children. If she stopped off in Washington at all after her return from abroad, it could only have been very briefly. Kate's last letter from Narragansett to her son that has been preserved is dated February 12, 1877, the very day that the Commission began to discuss the Louisiana case and several days after their vital decision about the Florida votes. Kate mentions nothing in that letter about moving, something that was not undertaken those days without considerable and lengthy preparations. Let us imagine, however, for the sake of argument that she managed to arrive in Washington toward the end of February and that somehow she succeeded in settling into Edgewood with her household effortlessly and that the violent scene where her husband had tried to kill her and all that followed in the way of outrage and grief was completely forgotten, and she was in fine fettle, ready and eager for only one thing—revenge against a man she might or might not have looked upon as an ancient political enemy. And let us even suppose that she happened to meet Senator Conkling again after her long absence from the city. Even Kate Chase could hardly be expected to gain supremacy over any man, let alone a man like Conkling, during the brief period she might have been in Washington before the final count on March 1.

One more point. To imagine that Kate, who was intensely patriotic, who cared passionately for the welfare of her country, would for reasons of extremely dubious personal pique want to throw the country into disorder and see the very real risk of new civil war erupt is preposterous. It makes a good story. It has all those exciting elements of libel, sex, and sensation which people relish. But all the facts are against it.

Both Kate and Conkling were people who aroused interest no matter what they did or where they went. And as always, with that kind of attention, there was a great deal of envy and jealousy too, and all sorts of malicious gossip. It is generally believed that they had a passionate love affair which they flaunted before everyone. It would be nice if it were true. Kate deserved a rich ripe romance after all she had been through with her husband and Conkling was certainly a handsome figure, a powerful and adept politician, which was something she would have loved, disciplined and temperate in his habits, a strong-willed rock of a man, proud and self-confident, a total contrast in every way to the self-doubting, dissipated, introspective Sprague. There is, however, not a single proof that they actually did have an affair in spite of all the gossip and newspaper comment about them.[32] The final scene was played out in full view before a greedy public and the private lives of the distinguished Senator Conkling and proud Kate Chase Sprague were exposed to penny-thriller notoriety coast to coast.

CHAPTER

XVI

IT WAS a warm August morning in the summer of 1879. The rocking chairs on the wide hotel porches at Narragansett were moving a little more animatedly than usual. Eager tongues were clacking and eyes were bright with that kind of special avidity which indicates scandal is in the air. As one paper later described it, the rumors were "as thick 'as leaves in Valabrosa' and as divergent in particulars." [1] No one knew exactly what had happened, but that something thrilling and scandalous had occurred was sure.

Some people claimed to have seen Governor Sprague, gun in hand, dash madly into a restaurant at the Pier and search frantically there for a German professor who had been engaged as tutor for his children by Mrs. Sprague. "Was the Governor going to shoot you?" the lady attendant was reported to have asked Professor Linck, who had taken refuge in a back room. Foiled in his attempt to find his prey, the Governor was said to have driven off at a furious rate.

Other people asserted that the incident had not been between Governor Sprague and Professor Linck at all, but that Sprague had been after Senator Conkling. These reports had it that Conkling was in a restaurant eating Little Neck clams when Sprague rushed in and advancing toward the Senator exclaimed in a loud voice for all to hear, "Let me get at the damned scoundrel!" Thereupon

Conkling bristled and it was only the interference of friends that prevented bloodshed.

Within a day newspapers from all over the country were inquiring by telegraph as to the event and sending reporters to the scene. A reporter for *The New York Times* wrote that he "wished that mysteries would not happen in hot weather. With the thermometer at ninety, investigation becomes intolerable and process of thought a prodigious strain upon the intellect. The Narragansett mystery is a case in point. Had it happened in cool weather, a coherent explanation of it might have been possible, but in August heat the mere thought of it wearies the mind and wilts the shirt collar." [2] He might have added that nation-wide interest in the affair might not have been so avid had the heat not taken the starch out of people and left them panting for something stimulating which would require no effort on their part.

Wilted with the heat or no, reporters filed thousand of words about the incident that appeared in almost every newspaper in the country. The confusion about what actually had happened lasted for several days and there were all sorts of conflicting reports. The first dispatches were brief and matter of fact, stating that Mr. Sprague, in a moment of excitement, had ordered Professor Linck to leave the house and attempted to shoot him. "This he was prevented from doing by Senator Conkling and some other friends." Conkling was described as having stopped off at Narragansett on some legal matters on his way to Providence. [3]

The first statement by any of the parties to the incident, and it was a long one, was issued by Professor Linck some three days after the event. Under the unflattering headline, "The Missing Link," he explained that he had been engaged in July by Mrs. Sprague as tutor for her older children, especially for Willie. He and the boy had been sent on ahead to Canonchet where no one seemed to have been informed of their arrival. Governor Sprague appeared from time to time, but although he seemed pleasant, Linck declared that the Governor "did not impress me favorably . . . his ideas seemed mixed-up and muddled." Linck was horrified one late afternoon to see the Governor and his son scaling the garden wall and disappearing into the twilight. A few days later, father and son simply vanished, leaving a note for Linck that he had better move to a hotel as Sprague did not know when he would return with his son. Not knowing what to do, Linck stayed on at the house waiting for news from Mrs. Sprague to whom he had communicated what had happened. She agreed that he should move temporarily to a hotel and her letter expressed outrage at Governor Sprague's "apparent discourtesy" and congratulated him for "the manner in which you treat Governor Sprague's erratic proceedings, and as to the firmness you exhibited towards Willie." Reading this soothing letter, Linck was approaching Canonchet when he unexpectedly met Sprague. "Why did you not obey my orders to leave this house?" Sprague shouted at him. "If you don't get out of here at once I shall find help to turn you out." This time Linck did not delay his departure and left for New York, thinking never to return.

Kate, however, was evidently determined to try to arrange some sort of discipline and supervision for Willie. His successful years in Germany undoubtedly made her hope that a German tutor might be able to control him, and in fact, Linck said that at first he found Willie "a good boy, attentive and willing to study." Kate persuaded the Professor to return and join her and the children when she arrived at Watch Hill a few days later. But once again Sprague showed up unannounced and was obviously "under the effects of drink." This time the scene was even more violent. Raising his cane, Sprague approached the tutor and shouted, "Now you damn Devil, if I find you again near my children or place, I will surely kill you; I will and take my word for it."

One would have thought that Linck would have had enough by now, but he moved to a hotel in Narragansett and a few days later once again obeyed the summons of Mrs. Sprague to come to see her, this time at Canonchet, where she was now installed. He did not even enter the house, however, as another encounter with the Governor made him feel that discretion was in order and he begged the coachman to drive off as rapidly as possible. He found shelter in a restaurant where Sprague soon followed, racing about brandishing a gun while Linck cowered in the back room. The landlady's daughter saved the day by stating that Linck had gone down into the village, whereupon Sprague "drove off at a furious rate." Linck followed the young woman's suggestion of hiring a fast conveyance and making his escape. "I jumped in and was driven home, out of harm's way," he concluded his hair-raising account.[4]

"Such is the Professor's story," commented the *Cincinnati Enquirer* "but as he fails to say anything about Conkling, it is generally believed that he is a cat's-paw to hide the scandal created by the altercation between Conkling and Sprague, which is now believed to have occurred after Sprague's return from his chase after Linck." [5] The *New York World* was more blunt. "No German Teacher Concerned," it stated. "The trouble arose not between any professor of German and ex-Gov. Sprague, but between ex-Gov. Sprague and Senator Conkling." [6] A dispatch from Washington indicated no surprise at what was becoming increasingly apparent, that it was Senator Conkling who had been the prime object of Sprague's wrath. "The news is received here as something expected, and Mr. Conkling has so few friends in Washington . . . that not many regrets are expressed on the subject." [7] *The New York Times* "funny man" wrote an editorial spoof on the affair, utterly compounding the confusion with references to "Professor Conkling" and "Senator Linck" and concluding that "the alleged Linck and the pretended Conkling are one and the same person and neither has been invented to shield the other from unpleasant notoriety . . . But then how are we to explain the testimony which asserts that the real original Senator Conkling, with his shirt front and torso, was actually seen at Narragansett Pier at the time of the tragedy." It recommends that the next time Sprague goes shooing "he will stick to some one definite kind of game, and not bang away indiscriminately at splendid Senators and modest little Germans." [8]

Reporters at once picked up the discrepancy between the original brief dispatches of the incident, which told of Senator Conkling's intercession on behalf of the unfortunate professor and Linck's story which made no mention of Conkling at all. An enterprising reporter visited the offices of the *Providence Journal,* from which the dispatch had originated, and talked with the editor who stated that Professor Linck had come to Providence at Senator Conkling's request. Conkling was a guest of Senator Anthony and the original dispatch was prepared and approved by the two senators. Mr. Danielson, the editor, stated that Mr. Conkling "very positively denied that there had been any altercation between himself and Mr. Sprague." [9]

The story as finally pieced together from a number of sources seemed to have been this. Kate was at Canonchet with her children and some house guests, a Mr. and Mrs. Martin, their daughter, and another young lady. Governor Sprague was absent in Maine and not expected back for several days when Senator Conkling arrived from Newport on Tuesday, bag and baggage. He was still at Canonchet when Governor Sprague returned unexpectedly late Thursday night. On Friday morning, Kate described later, "I was told to my surprise that Mr. Sprague had come home suddenly at 3 o'clock in the morning and had left again. I paid no attention to this, however, as his movements are always very erratic. He comes in on you like a ghost in the middle of the night and at the most unseasonable hours, and hurries away again in the same disquieting manner." She had grown accustomed to "these freaks" and went about her household affairs as usual. Conkling was reading the newspapers and Kate had just sat down to read aloud to Mr. Martin, an invalid of over seventy, when Sprague entered the room, advancing slowly toward Conkling, who rose to greet him. Sprague was overheard by people in the house loudly ordering Senator Conkling to leave, saying he would give him twenty minutes to get out of sight. Kate claimed she did not hear what words passed between the two men, "but the tone arrested my attention." Conkling went directly to her and said, "Mrs. Sprague, your husband is very much excited and I think it better for all of us that I should withdraw. If my departure puts you in any danger, do say so, and I will stay whatever the consequence." Conkling spoke calmly, Kate related, although she knew he must have been excited. She told Conkling not to mind her but that if Sprague was in a passion there was no use trying to argue with him, as "it might only lead to violence." After helping Mr. Martin to his room, Conkling went out onto the porch where young Ethel Sprague put her arm around him and begged him to stay. "I tried to be as calm as I could," Kate explained later. "When Ethel wanted Mr. Conkling to stay I said, 'No, Ethel, Mr. Conkling will go, but no one shall hurt him or us.'" Sprague, she described as standing about fifty feet off observing this. Not long after Conkling had left, on foot, Sprague followed him in the carriage. Willie told her his father had a loaded gun with him, and added, "If he shoots any one he'll kill them sure."

When Conkling arrived at the Pier, he made for Billington's café, according to witnesses, and had just reached there when Sprague drove up in a state of tremendous agitation. "You —— ——, I want you to get out of this place instantly." Further words were exchanged but no one overheard Conkling's replies. Sprague soon drove off, still in a state of great agitation. The reports indicated that Conkling did not seem at all excited and proceeded to order a lunch of milk and crackers. Twice while he was eating, a wagon from Canonchet appeared and a plump lady talked earnestly with him. Conkling seemed unhurried and it was well over an hour after the scene with Sprague that he sauntered down to the railroad station, where his luggage was already waiting for him, and boarded a train for Providence. During the time that Sprague was at the Pier in pursuit of Conkling, the house guests hurriedly left Canonchet. A little later, Kate and her three daughters also left and moved to a hotel, where they spent the night before going to Providence the next morning.[10]

The whole confused but intriguing story was just what was needed to shake people out of the summer doldrums, and papers everywhere made the most of it. "Further Information Relative to that 'Wow, Wumpus and Wiot'" were the derisive headlines in one report.[11] Everyone seemed eager to believe the worst, especially about Kate. A dispatch to the *Cincinnati Enquirer* from Washington stated that the story had created no surprise there, "the weight of expression being over the wonder that the Ex-Senator did not long ago do what he a day or two [ago] attempted to do."[12] The *Chicago Times* published a long article about the alleged affair between the Senator and Mrs. Sprague, giving all sorts of lurid details about their public antics. "Why, when I was in Washington that winter it was a matter of common report that Conkling was completely infatuated with Mrs. Sprague," a prominent official was reported as saying. "If he made a speech she was in the gallery; if he took a carriage ride she was at his side; her house was always open to him. When he made his midnight speech . . . she stayed until two o'clock in the morning. The Senators would nudge one another and remark 'Conk's audience is all here.'" Stories of Kate's "early indiscretions" in Columbus were repeated and all the old gossip found its way into print. There were tales of her "brilliant youth and her royal wealth and luxury abroad" with reports of her extravagant way of life. Conkling's past was probed for scandals as well and stories of his younger days were gathered in Utica with references made to the "slight minded yokel" about whom the initiated "wink knowingly and . . . murmur 'Roscoe.'" [13] Every possible area of fact or fiction about Kate Chase Sprague and Senator Conkling was exposed to the sneers and derision of the whole country.

Conkling was reported to be in New York. Kate was in Providence. For several days both of them maintained a discreet silence. And then they cracked. On the same day, statements appeared from both Kate and Conkling. Incredible statements. Fatal ones. Conkling, of course, with his legal background, was clever enough not to appear openly. Friends of his, however, "in view of the manifest injustice which has been done him in certain public statements . . . feel at liberty now to talk." And then these "friends" ruthlessly took the offensive and when they were done the "Sprague family troubles" were exposed for all the world to see. Sprague's financial troubles were said to have "unsettled his habits, he became intemperate and deserted his old friends for companions of low grade morals. His home became so unpleasant that Mrs. Sprague went to Europe" with her children. When she returned her relations with her husband were "friendly, but she declined to live with him unless he would change his habits of life." Sprague, nevertheless, spent some time each year with her in Washington and she spent the summer months at Canonchet. Professor Linck was described as "an impudent sort of person . . . [who] acted very indiscreetly and assumed so much authority . . .

that Sprague was indignant and ordered him away. The man was impertinent and Gov. Sprague did what all his friends approved of—kicked him out of the house." Mrs. Sprague, however, felt that Linck had not been properly treated and determined to retain him. Senator Conkling's role in the whole affair was described in glowing terms. He had come to Narragansett from Providence where he had been "engaged in settling the affairs" of the Sprague Company. "All gossip to the effect that Senator Conkling's intimacy with Mrs. Sprague had alienated her husband is false." The families have been friends for several years. "Sprague engaged Conkling as attorney in settling up his affairs and . . . Conkling has performed a great deal of legal labor in that direction, without compensation, as a friendly act." Conkling has many times tried, according to a friend, "to persuade Sprague to recover himself and break off drinking."

Conkling's actions on the day of the incident were described by his "friends" in equally high-minded and altruistic terms. Sprague "seemed to think that his wife and friends were all in a conspiracy to defend the German against him," and Conkling was drawn into the affair through his efforts to quiet Sprague. "Mrs. Sprague said after the language addressed to her by her husband she could not remain in his house, and the guests decided to go at once to a hotel." After seeing the other guests safely away, Conkling himself left the house on foot. In the later altercation in the street with Sprague, Conkling was "reproaching him for his outrageous treatment of his wife and friends . . . Among other things he told Sprague he was acting like an insane man. Sprague is very sensitive over some efforts of his friends to get him into an inebriate asylum, and took great offense at Conkling's remark, replying in a very loud tone and furious manner that he was not going to be called crazy or interfered with by any man." After a quiet lunch Conkling left for Providence where, when it was found that "false and exaggerated statements were published abroad about the affair, a simple paragraph reciting the facts was written and furnished the Associated Press." [14]

Everything in this statement points to the fact that it could only have come from Conkling. But he was extremely careful to make sure that it contained the words that he "has continually declined to make any statement himself or authorized any person to make one for him." Kate was not so clever, nor so devious. There was no effort on her part to hide behind anonymous "friends." Even the newspapers responding to the "insatiable appetite" for any detail of news about the affair showed certain qualms about publishing Kate's letter and prefaced it with an introductory remark: "It scarcely need be said here that we deeply regret that any exigency should have arisen which seems to any person to demand or warrant the publication of a statement of such a painful nature." [15]

"As you must have heard surmised," the letter began, "Governor Sprague's dissolute life and dissipated habits long ago interrupted our marital relations, though I have striven hard through untold humiliation and pain to hide from the world, for my children's sake, the true conditions of a blighted, miserable domestic life. About a year ago even this poor semblance abruptly culminated after a disgraceful orgie and arrest at Nantasket Beach, with the circumstances of which many people in Rhode Island are not unfamiliar." After that, she went on, she sought with her little girls the shelter of her father's former home, where she felt more secure and less unprotected. She went into a lengthy explanation of her financial difficulties, how the money for her support had been cut down and during the past six months had stopped altogether; about her husband's refusal to pay bills which he owed, including one for a carriage for his mother's use while she had been visiting Kate the previous year. He suggested "that I must look to my powerful Washington friends for aid," Kate said. The brutality of recent events, repetitions of similar scenes in former years "has finally driven us from the door and filled the public press of the country with a scandal too cruel to be endured without redress."

The letter goes on to relate that Sprague's "ceaseless and shameful persecution of the children's teacher is literally true" and defines the real reason for Sprague's animus toward Linck as being his "unwillingness to be subjected to the restraint at the table and in the household observances of the constant presence of a gentleman." She describes Sprague's difficulties with the trustee of his business, that he had taken some of the firm's books and refused to return them, with the result that Mr. Chafee refused to permit him to draw any money, or have anything to do with the firm until he returned the books. She had come back to Rhode Island in an effort to help solve some of the problems and to insure some financial security for the four children, the expenses for whose care and education she was bearing alone. It was in this regard that she had asked Mr. Conkling to see Sprague and to advise him. Sprague had sought legal advice from Conkling before and even close personal favors so that "Mr. Conkling was, of course, as unconscious as I that Governor Sprague sought occasion to enact the tragic role of the injured husband." As to whether "any hostile words were exchanged between Mr. Conkling and Governor Sprague at Canonchet, they alone knew what they were for no one else heard them." She knew nothing about what transpired in the village beyond the "sensational accounts given in the newspapers." [16]

Kate's letter made headlines coast to coast and one can almost hear the indrawn breath of delighted horror with which readers greeted its revelations. Although the statement by Conkling's "friends" was equally sensational in content, it received almost no notice or circulation at all, going scarcely beyond Conkling's hometown Utica newspaper. A wife's disclosures of her unhappy relationship with her husband was far more exciting and unusual.

Why would Kate present such a document for publication, exposing to full public view so much of the sordid picture of her family troubles? Kate had always been extremely reticent about her personal life and although she undoubtedly had enjoyed the attention that her social position and influence had brought her, she had never wanted or permitted anything more than a superficial view of externals. There is no question but that she acted upon the advice of friends and lawyers, including that of Conkling. The publication of the letter was not a hasty, unthought-out act, done in a fit of temper or emotional excitement. The simultaneous release of Kate's letter and the statement of Conkling's "friends," shows that this was a calculated move, a plan to discredit Sprague in the eyes of the public and show Kate as a long-suffering wife. Most of all, however, the effect was intended to present Conkling as a good Samaritan who became innocently entangled in the unfortunate affair only through motives of high-minded generosity.

It was incredibly shortsighted to imagine that these disclosures would win sympathy away from Sprague. It succeeded in doing just the opposite. Although admitting that Sprague had a quick temper, "under the circumstances and the persistent provocation, we think he was justified in doing as he is reported to have done; and the sympathy of the great mass of the public is with him," was the opinion of the *Narragansett Times*.[17] *The New York Times* reported that although the publication of the letter was supposed to excite sympathy, it did just the reverse.[18]

Sprague, in contrast, made no statements, although it had been rumored that he would. A friend who had been seen with him stated that Sprague had replied to his question about Senator Conkling: "He has tried to do here for my home what he did in Washington," and when pressed for a further explanation added, "Have you not read the Washington papers?" A reporter who claimed to have known Sprague personally asked whether he had commanded Conkling to leave his house. Sprague replied, "I did, and I ought to have done so before." He also denied having been under the influence of liquor, saying that had he been he "would not have given Conkling five minutes to leave the premises." [19]

Kate returned to Narragansett the day her letter appeared in the press and went to the home of the railroad conductor Hale and his wife who had often befriended her. There she had a stormy interview with Sprague who accused her of falsehood in the representations she had made in her published letter, and demanded to know what she had done with the $5,000 he had recently given her. He was said to be sober but laboring under great excitement. It was reported that he accused her of being unfaithful, but would not name with whom, and he declared that she poisoned the minds of the children against him and demanded that the children be surrendered to him. When he asked her if she was planning to return to Canonchet, she replied that she feared for her life if she did so. He told her he had never harmed anyone in his life. She accused him of drunkenness and brutality, of circulating base and unfounded stories about her character and of his threats to her life, including pointing a loaded pistol at her head. When Kate refused to part with her children, her lawyers were sent for, a Mr. Thomson and her cousin, Ralston Skinner, who was staying at a nearby hotel. They advised her that the father had legal rights over the children, at least in Rhode Island, and a little while later Sprague drove off to Canonchet with the three little girls, Willie having stayed on at the house all the time. Kate was greatly agitated by this and in a short time decided that she would follow her children home.[20]

Silence descended on Canonchet. No one was allowed entrance, cards were refused at the door. Although Sprague later denied it, Kate was held under a kind of house arrest. She was allowed to see her children, but no friends, nor could she communicate by letter or telegraph with anyone on the outside. A maid who was sympathetic enough to take a telegram for her was threatened with being discharged. Sprague claimed that he made these rules for his wife's peace of mind, that she had been for several days in a very excited condition. He averred that he could not "consent to her keeping up a private correspondence with the persons whose object was to destroy the peace and honor of his family." [21]

In one of his strange about-faces, however, a few days later he allowed a reporter from the *New York Sun* to enter the house. Sprague was with several of his friends and lawyers. Although the ex-Governor looked worn and strained he was agreeable and after some hesitation and delay, suddenly decided to make no objection to an interview with Mrs. Sprague.

The reporter found Kate upstairs in a sort of library. She looked extremely pale and though she manifested great self-control, her lips trembled occasionally and she showed traces of agitation. She spoke with a clarity and eloquence that were very powerful.

"I have my story to tell," she said, "and when the truth of this terrible business is known, I know I shall be justified. God knows I have no reason to fear the truth, though for thirteen years my life has been a constant burden and drag upon me." She claimed that she had borne it for the sake of her children, not for any affection that existed between her and her husband, "for there has been none for years." She categorically denied the truth of the allegation of improper relationship between herself and Conkling. "There is not a word of truth in all of these atrocious reports," she told the reporter. "Conkling never paid me any attention a wife could not favorably receive from her husband's friend, and it is false to say otherwise. Mr. Sprague was simply worked upon by his business troubles, which have been culminating for years, and by his indulgence in strong drink." Until two years earlier Sprague and Conkling had been on excellent terms, she asserted. "A petty contemptible squabble about the payment for the care of some horses sent me by Mr. Sprague . . . was the commencement of all my husband's jealousy against Conkling," she declared. Sprague had omitted sending the money for the horses and Conkling had offered to loan the money for the bill. But even after that, as late as the previous April, Sprague had asked Conkling's legal opinion about his own business affairs. Sprague was just as wild on the subject of Professor Linck. "He regarded everyone, no matter how honorable he was, a friend of mine, as an interloper and intriguer against him. His jealousy and hatred of that poor German shows the workings of his monomania. Why, he wrote a letter to Mr. Chase, a friend of mine, shortly before the affair saying that he did not care about Senator Conkling, but that he was determined to kill both him and Prof. Linck." When asked how Conkling had ventured to come under such circumstances, she explained that Conkling had come to Narragansett to use his influence to advise Sprague on a certain policy in connection with the management of his business and that she "considered that there would be no impropriety in his visiting us here for that purpose. Mr. Throop Martin, of Auburn, an old friend of Mr. Conkling and an invalid of over 70, was staying with us, together with his wife and daughter." She could see no possible harm in the presence of these guests "as my husband was constantly going and coming at intervals of a few days, and no effort was made to conceal the fact of the Senator's visit from him."

Kate then described the whole scene in detail from the time Miss Martin had met Sprague on his way into the house and had been "frightened almost out of her wits by his stopping her and telling her that 'there was going to be a tragedy in the house' " until Conkling's departure and Willie's news that his father had gone off after him in the carriage and had a loaded gun with him. "I had reason to be grateful that no one was murdered," Kate said.

She also wanted to expose another falsehood, she told the reporter, and that was that Mr. Conkling had endorsed the statement "which attributed the whole affair to my husband's hatred of Mr. Linck. I know from gentlemen who were present when that dispatch was written that Mr. Conkling disapproved of it. He has neither sought to conceal or to spread any knowledge he possesses of this wretched matter."

Kate denied that she had shown anything more than the feeling "of a warm personal friend" at the time of the Conkling-Lamar near fight on the Senate floor and claimed that she had hardly known of the affair until it was over. She also denied that she had written a note to Conkling on that occasion saying that "obviously it would be an improper and unladylike action."

"Mrs. Sprague explicitly contradicts all the stories about her undue intimacy, at Washington, with Senator Conkling, as monstrous falsehoods, and says that at the proper time and in the proper place she will show the true character and origin of the persecution." [22]

By now even the press was beginning to turn away in disgust at what was being done to Kate. *The New York Times* editorialized about the "vain Senator, who, by his undisguised, open and notorious attention to a married woman . . . had clouded the fair fame of the unfortunate lady . . . With a moral sense blunted by an abnormal egotism, it was to him delicious to know that a vain world gave him credit for dragging at the tail of his chariot a beautiful woman of historic lineage and high fame . . . Decent and conservative people have looked on with real grief. They have seen a foolish woman 'throw herself at the head' of a man who had not the self-respect nor the manliness to hold up a hand of warning and chivalrous remonstrance." [23] The *Tribune* called "for an end to this business of trying to fight the political battles of a great State over the quivering body of a woman and the heads of her defenseless children." Mr. Conkling, it stated, had little to fear from "attacks which do not take the form of accusations. But to the hapless woman in the case they are ruin . . . Bear in mind, there is absolutely no shred of proof of any criminality anywhere in the case, or even a charge of it . . . Are the good name, the happiness, the whole life of a woman to be recklessly destroyed with no greater warrant than that?" And the editorial warns the gossipmongers "that this un-American crime of slandering a woman in order to destroy a politician may lead to a reaction they little expect or wish." [24]

Nothing new came from Narragansett after that. Everything seemed quite normal and placid at Canonchet. People began to wonder if things might blow over and the papers speculated that this would not have been the first time that the stormy Sprague marriage had almost foundered and then miraculously righted itself. Fanny Sprague was reportedly in favor of a reconciliation, and that doughty old lady still wielded a strong influence in the family. She was reported as admitting that her son's habits were irregular, that he often fasted for twelve hours after which he resorted to the bottle which "helps to explain his painfully sensitive temper." He rather disliked polite society she said and "although Kate often provoked him in many ways which drove him away from the table or out of the house," the old lady admitted that he had treated Kate often "in an unbecoming manner." [25] In spite of all this, however, she still hoped that the marriage might hold together.

But the quiet at Canonchet was deceptive. Kate would never make a move without her daughters and Sprague was keeping careful watch on her for fear that she might try to escape with them. The tension increased as the hot month of August passed, and Sprague, according to Kate's later testimony, grew increasingly menacing, threatening to carry off the children to Europe and causing Kate "to fear for her personal safety and that of her children, and even her life." [26] The final explosion came one night at the end of the month. Sprague went to the nursery where Kate was with her children. Finding his way barred, he broke down the door. Seizing Kate by the arm, he dragged her to the window and tried, as he had done two years before, to push her out. The girls were terrorized, most of all undoubtedly little Kitty who saw the world not quite in focus.

The next day, however, as so many times before, everything seemed back to normal. The midday meal passed off quietly and Sprague's relative, Arthur Watson, noticed nothing out of the way. Afterward, Sprague lay down for a nap. He slept until almost dusk when he awakened suddenly. The house seemed strangely silent. He dashed outdoors and was told by one of the workmen that Mrs. Sprague and the three girls had driven off in a carriage.

Sprague thought to intercept them on the train which had just left and he managed to catch up with it at Kingston, about eight miles away, but they were not on board. Kate had managed to get away with her three daughters.

The next day, September 1, Kate's flight was front-page news and the story of Sprague's attack on her in the nursery appeared in some papers. The whole story of the Sprague-Conkling affair was brought up again and gone over in every detail. No one knew where Kate and her daughters were and speculation was high. Sprague was reported to have denied that he had shown any violence to Kate or that he had put a guard over her at any time. He expressed a "profound sadness at the loss of his daughters." All he wanted, he claimed, was "to establish a home for his children." [27] Sprague agreed in a letter to Kate's lawyers to forward to her address any articles she might need. The lawyers refused to divulge where she was staying but "offered to send any baggage to her which Mr. Sprague will permit to be removed from Canonchet." [28]

The whole battle was waged all over again in the press, and public sentiment was still divided. In Rhode Island feeling was more favorable to Sprague, especially after Kate's earlier interview and letter. On the other hand, friends of Kate were loyal to her. Opinion was unanimous, however, when it came to Senator Conkling. His role in the affair came under sharp criticism on all sides. He was blamed for having at first tried to suppress the whole story, then of having concocted the Linck fiction. He was held responsible for Kate's return to Canonchet after these first means had failed to clear up the situation, hoping thus to show that it had all been a tempest in a teapot and that there was no real marital discord nor anything for anyone to get excited about. It was even rumored that "in his purpose to prevail with Mrs. Sprague to remain in a position which could not be other than painful and loathsome, [he] even went so far as to procure from his wife a letter of condolence to Mrs. Sprague. The friends of the latter here are full of indignation over this new development, and cannot find words to express their contempt for a man who, after compromising her by his conduct, would seek to hide behind a woman's skirts, no matter what the defamation and lasting disgrace consequent to her." [29]

This is by far the most reasonable explanation of Kate's return to Canonchet after the August 8 scandal. She had been safely away with her daughters and Sprague was making no effort to get them back from her. Willie had elected to stay behind, and she knew that her fight for him was a lost cause. As Sprague had suggested to him when he was in Germany, father and son had made a sort of pact together against Kate, her plans for Willie's education, her standards of deportment and discipline. As soon as the boy returned to Canonchet he fell back into his former wild and undisciplined ways and Kate could do nothing with him. It was natural that he would elect to stay with his father at Canonchet, where he could mount his fast Indian pony and with rifle strapped to his back scour the countryside in search of adventure. The neighbors found him "an object of great annoyance," for his wild and reckless pastimes, "his ungovernable temper and vicious propensities." [30] Kate certainly did not expect this boy to choose her in any separation. As for trying to keep up any pretense that her marriage was viable, she herself had exposed its failure for everyone to see. She could not have believed that this could be undone, nor did she at any time show that she wanted it undone.

Why, then, did she return and subject herself once more to the strains and indignities which she could no longer tolerate? It is reasonable only if we consider that it might have had some importance for Conkling. His ten year undisputed tenure as boss of the Republican party in New York State had begun to crumble, and this scandal was hardly something which would bolster it up. A convention was coming in a few weeks and it would be greatly in his interest if the scandal could be hushed up or at least deflected from himself. "Everyone in Narragansett," *The New York Times* reported, believed that Kate "returned to Canonchet because she was urged to do so on behalf of Senator Conkling, whose friends in N. Y. State had been pained and shocked by the stories . . . It is difficult to find anyone here who knows anything about this matter who does not declare that when Mrs. Sprague returned to Canonchet she did so against her own wishes, and merely because she desired to comply with the request of some influential person whom she was anxious to please." [31]

If this is true, and there is considerable reason to believe it is, it would be in character for Kate. She was a fighter and, as she had proved when she was a girl in Columbus, was ready to do battle on behalf of a victim of an injustice. Regardless of what her feelings for the handsome Senator from New York actually were, he had been her friend and had tried to help her and it was through her that he had been exposed to vilification and mockery. Her letter and her statement, which were in great part a defense of Conkling, and her painful return to Canonchet could only have been prompted by a compelling reason—to come to the defense of a friend who had suffered public humiliation while a guest in her house. Kate had the kind of intense emotional nature that could head her into that kind of action.

It was understandable that it should have been widely believed that Kate and Conkling had an affair. Although Kate was in her late thirties when the gossip about them began, she was more beautiful and attractive than ever. Handsome, flamboyant Conkling was well known for his successes with the fair sex. Kate's husband was rarely in Washington. Conkling's wife almost never left Utica. That other statesmen and aspiring politicians often sought Kate out at Edgewood, and found her counsel valuable, was largely ignored in the light of the attentions to her of the flaming "Adonis of the Senate." They made a striking pair and everyone whispered about what a match they would have made. It was natural that people should have conjectured freely about those two, especially as they made no effort to hide their friendship. But that it was anything more than friendship is based only on rumor and gossip.

Kate, like her father, was sometimes fatally blind in her choice of people. Her husband, whom she had "almost worshipped" had finally destroyed her love through his intemperate, abusive, and flagrantly unfaithful conduct, and his rejection of everything that she held dear. And now Conkling, whether as friend or something more, failed her. At a time when she needed support more than ever before in her life, he was proving himself to be selfish, weak and ruthless. He had been ready to risk Kate's reputation and to enjoy it, but when the barbs turned against him, he fled. On the heels of the Narragansett scandal, Conkling removed himself from the scene as quickly as possible. After his efforts to extricate himself by exposing the secrets of Kate's unhappy marriage and himself as the disinterested mediator had failed, he simply vanished from the picture entirely, leaving Kate alone to extricate herself as best she could from a situation he had done a great deal to create. There was no more gossip about Senator Conkling and the beautiful Mrs. Sprague. There was never again anything to gossip about. As a man, the whole incident had little or no effect on Conkling at all. But a woman could not pass through such a scandal so easily. Kate had been disgraced and ridiculed and her position and reputation were severely and permanently compromised.

After her flight from Canonchet Kate and her daughters took refuge with one of her cousins, Austin Corbin, at Babylon, Long Island. No one knew where she was and the press searched high and low for her, eager for more sensational news of her escape. At Babylon she was under the protection not only of her cousin and his family but of "half a dozen men employed on the property who knew who they were, and who would have made it very unpleasant for any one who had dared to molest them," Mr. Corbin said in an interview more than a year later.[32]

Two weeks after Kate had fled Canonchet with her daughters, she left her cousin's house and arrived at Edgewood. A reporter appeared soon. He found her "looking the least bit older and fatigued." She stated her intention to make Edgewood her home and denied reports that she was planning to go abroad. "Here I can be quiet and wait for my wrongs to be righted. I have been maligned and ground down until I have felt that I was a target at which everybody could fire, and yet without means or method of redress . . . The bitterest part of my recent troubles has been that I should be thought a silly, vain woman. Why, I have been trained to look upon dignity and brains as of the highest importance, and I have a high regard for conventionalities, although I believe I have not that reputation. To be so misrepresented, so misunderstood, has given me my greatest pain. I have been charged with all sorts of misdoings, of which I am totally innocent." She claimed that although she has been credited with being at the Capitol nearly every day of the last session, she believed that since her father's death she has not been there a half dozen times in all. "Every act of mine that could be used against me has been enlarged upon by my enemies." She found the kind feelings manifested by her friends deeply touching and kindness exhibited especially in the South. "The papers there, with a chivalry that is natural, have with one accord taken my part because I was a woman and defenseless . . . Some of these days the chivalry of the North will grant me the same fairness, and I hope to show that it is not unmerited." [33]

Kate was alone with her three daughters to look out for. She had lost the protection and love of her father more than six years earlier. She had long ago lost any understanding or support from her husband and now even the semblance of a marriage was gone. The powerful Senator from New York had removed himself to a safe distance, leaving her to do what she could alone with what was left of her life.

A final farcical touch to the whole Canonchet affair occurred when Professor Linck, who it had been suggested was the only person who had really profited from the whole affair, being now the most famous German professor in the United States, sued Mrs. Sprague for $240 salary and expenses he claimed she owed him.

CHAPTER

🙠 XVII 🙡

KATE WAS NOT one to give in weakly to adversity. She had her
three daughters to bring up and educate and she knew that
the full burden of their expenses and their care would be hers
from now on.

Among the people who had defended her during the scandal
were some Washington newspaper women. Several of them had
written that there had been nothing at all unusual or uncommon
in Kate's behavior toward Senator Conkling, and one of them
commented that the way she was singled out for attack showed the
degree of "deadly malice, jealousy and hatred" of the Washington
"petticoated brigadiers." Another wrote that the slander was primarily aimed at destroying Conkling's political ambitions and that
it was not the first time that "martyred women" had been used for
this purpose.

Not long after her return to Washington, Kate gave a luncheon
for these ladies of the press. If they had expected to see a broken,
pathetic woman they were sorely disillusioned. That was not Kate's
way. Bills may have been piled high on her desk, she may have
been parting with some of her most prized possessions, and been
anxious about the future, but to show weakness would be to invite
defeat and to destroy any hope she had of bringing off some big
deal, some sale, some recouping of the Sprague position. Kate was

as impractical as her father had been. She never thought, nor had he, in terms of the weekly rent or taxes or the grocery bill. She thought in large terms of advantageous sales of property or of art objects at inflated prices. To gain success one must appear successful, and if there was one thing Kate did not want to be it was an object of pity.

Her luncheon for these powerful ladies of the press, therefore, was an extravaganza. The dining room recalled "thoughts of royal days of sunny France," wrote Olivia. A Gobelin tapestry, a priceless Persian rug, ornate screens and exquisite paintings decorated the room. Bouillon was served in bowls made from the dust of garnets from the palace of the Shah of Persia; oyster patties served on dishes decorated by a French artist which had once been in the possession of a European reigning family; sweetbreads on plates made in France, which the hostess had herself designed for the late Chief Justice. Olivia could not forget the contrast between Kate's former position and her present one and felt that the opulent display served only to emphasize the change that had come over her fortunes.[1] What Olivia did not mention, however, was that although the display was of no particular material advantage and in fact might even have aroused a certain counter-reaction, as a manifestation of Kate's spirit, of her determination not to be downed by her misfortunes, it was a gallant gesture. No bowed or cast-down look for Kate, at least in public. She would keep that charming, arrogant, upward pose of her head no matter what came.

Kate took two legal steps, the first to secure, if she could, something of her belongings from Canonchet. That place, as were all the other Sprague properties, was under the control of the trustee, Mr. Chafee. A separate trustee, Mr. Thompson, was named for Kate's property there and he was directed to proceed "immediately to take possession, by writ of replevin if necessary, of such personal property as is now in the mansion at Canonchet, and which is her separate personal estate." There was speculation, however, that "Mrs. Sprague has no personal property at Canonchet, for she packed up everything belonging to her when she left there, and took her property to Edgewood." [2]

These reports that Kate had managed to smuggle out all sorts of valuables during her last fearful weeks at Canonchet seem hardly logical. Sprague was watching her every move and would hardly have allowed trunks and boxes to be packed and shipped away. Kate tried to refute the story "going the rounds of the press that several thousand dollars worth of rich clothing etc. had been sent her from Canonchet. She says the statement is untrue, and that she has only received two deal boxes as common freight, the contents not worth a hundred dollars. Valuable mementos and all her correspondence with her late father are still withheld." [3] The proof, if proof is needed, that Kate did not make off with her possessions from Canonchet is to be found in the sales that later took place there and which contained various items which were identified as having belonged to Kate. Among the things redeemed by Sprague from a sale some years later at Canonchet was the commission of Salmon P. Chase as Chief Justice of the United States Supreme Court, signed by President Lincoln.[4] This would have been one of the first and most prized possessions that Kate would have rescued had she been able to.

Kate's efforts to establish her rights to her personal papers and belongings were unsuccessful. Not only were her claims caught up in the endless confusion and litigation that engulfed all the Sprague properties, but Sprague himself was in no mood to allow anyone's claims and he barred the door to Kate's trustee.[5] It was just one of a series of defiances of the law which Sprague managed in incredible fashion. And Willie played an important role in Sprague's maneuvers to hang on to Canonchet no matter what. One day when Mr. Thompson, the trustee for Kate's interests, was walking along the beach at Narragansett, he saw Willie and another boy standing on a hill about twenty-five feet above him. Mr. Thompson, who had known Willie since he was born, asked the boy for some directions and received a very uncivil reply. Whereupon Willie drew a pistol from his pocket and fired it directly at Mr. Thompson. Fortunately he missed. Master Willie was hauled into court but the charge was dismissed for insufficient evidence after he and his friend insisted they had been merely firing in the air, having been amusing themselves before Thompson's arrival by desultory target practice.[6]

Although Willie had stayed on with his father, Kate's relationship with her son was not wholly severed, at least during the first year after she fled from Canonchet with the girls. There is only one letter in existence, from Willie to her, but she was evidently at least able to correspond with him. His letter shows that he was as devoted as the other children to little Kitty, and he suggests to his mother that "Kitty could come here and stay with me. It is said that those with weak lungs can only be healed on the salt water. I cannot leave here so long as there is any effort on foot to interrupt things here," he adds mysteriously, and assured his mother that he can take care of Kitty and have the doctor for her "and everything else that would make Kitty comfortable. Telegraph me if any thing can be done in that way and I will see to it all. Were not your lungs in a bad way once and was it not the air at Narragansett that helpt to cure them[?]" [7]

Kate's second legal step concerned her efforts to secure a divorce and they were as long and as confused as one might imagine such a proceeding would be between Kate and William Sprague. Kate's lawyers drew up a petition that was a scorcher. In it Sprague was accused of "adultery with divers women at divers places and times" from Alexandria to Providence, naming six by name among the many others. Prostitutes were among those identified, but also on this list was Mary Eliza Viall Anderson. The charges against Eliza covered the whole period of Kate's marriage, from 1864 to 1879. The petition also charged that Sprague had been guilty of extreme cruelty: that he had assaulted her and tried to throw her from the window; that he had threatened to kill her; that he had been guilty of habitual drunkenness; that since 1879 he did not provide for her support or that of her children; that he used the vilest epithets to her; that he broke up and destroyed furniture in the house, on one occasion making a bonfire of bedding and furniture in the middle of the night; that he often said to his children that he was not their father and they were not his children; that he accused her falsely of "gross improprieties with other men, sometimes one sometimes another"; that he sought to imprison her in August 1879 at Canonchet and refused to allow her to see or communicate with her friends; that between 1865–1875 he "frequently attempted to have criminal intercourse with the female domestics and guests in the family, causing them to leave the house"; that by his violation of decency he had made the house at Canonchet "an unsuitable abode for your petitioner and her children"; that as a result in February 1877, with Sprague's consent, she left the house with her daughters, her son being then absent in Europe; that in 1879 Sprague urged her to request permission to occupy Canonchet from the trustee, Mr. Chafee, stating that it would be of "material pecuniary benefit to him in adjusting his affairs with his creditors"; that since he drove her from Canonchet he "has persistently refused to deliver to her her wearing apparel, and that of her children, and that of her servant, and he has refused to permit said property and other personal property belonging to your petitioner, including gifts from her father and friends, to be delivered to a trustee"; that since her departure he has occupied Canonchet "as a place of resort for persons of vicious reputation and bad character, consorting with them in revelry and drunkenness, and has allowed the only son of your petitioner . . . to consort and associate with persons of bad character, and to become addicted to bad habits and idleness, withholding from him all educational advantages, thereby tending to corrupt his morals and vitiate his future life." She asked for reasonable alimony, custody of the children, and the right to resume her maiden name.[8]

Sprague responded with a countersuit in which he too listed various sensational charges: that Kate had not been a domiciled resident of Rhode Island during the past year; that she had deserted his bed and board; that although he had faithfully kept and performed all his marriage covenants she "unmindful of her marriage vows and disregarding marriage covenants, hath violated the same; that she has committed the crime of adultery, and has been guilty of other gross misbehaviour, and wickedness, repugnant to and in violation of her marriage covenants" in that against his express wishes and commands and after great public scandal "kept company of, and been on terms of close and improper intimacy with other men"; that she repeatedly declared she would never live with him again; that she denied him care and duty as wife and mother; that she had "without cause turned and driven her oldest child and son out of doors"; that she squandered his property in reckless, extravagant, lavish, and foolish expenditure of money and style of living, thus further . . . embarrassing and defeating your petitioner in his effort to extricate himself and any remnant of his estate from said financial difficulties and embarrassments; "that she often travelled away from home"; that she used "slanderous and abusive language and publication of and concerning your petitioner thus rendering his life miserable." [9]

So the two parties locked horns again publicly and on the record. The actual court hearing on these petitions was held up for more than a year while friends and family attempted to intercede and bring about some sort of settlement besides a pitched public court battle. Kate's lawyers, Winterton Britton of New York, and Judge W. George Hoadly of Cincinnati felt that the Sprague side was using every possible pretext to delay the action. Judge Hoadly's account of the hearing for the divorce is illuminating. He and Mr. Britton came into court fully prepared "with depositions taken and numerous witnesses in court to support every allegation in our bill." The other side had used every pretext to postpone the trial but the court finally ruled that the hearing must proceed. Thereupon, Judge Hoadly stated, "Governor Sprague and his counsel approached us, proposing to withdraw their petition and all charges against Mrs. Sprague, if she would waive proof of adultery against him, and consent to let the case be tried on the remaining ground of cruelty and non-support. Governor Sprague then furnished Judge Hoadly with a written retraction of all charges against his wife, to be given her after the decree of divorce should be granted . . ." Upon authority from Kate to act at their discretion, Hoadly and Britton waived the more serious charges and allowed the case to rest on the less offensive ones.[10] On May 27, 1882, Kate was granted the divorce on these lesser charges and was given permission to resume her maiden name. No alimony was asked nor was it granted, although there was no "prejudice of any kind" to her right at any time in the future to move or petition for an allowance of alimony. Kate was given custody of the three girls. Willie, not being subject because of his age to the control of the

Court under the laws of Rhode Island, elected, predictably, to remain with his father.

Judge Hoadly, an eminent jurist, a former governor of the state of Ohio, was a man of unquestioned integrity. He was a long-time friend of Kate and was hardly a man who would have undertaken her cause had he had any doubts as to his ability to prove her case and to refute that of Sprague. He was also an aspirant for the Democratic nomination for the Presidency in 1884, an added reason why he would not have wanted to involve himself in unpleasant litigation in which he did not feel his case was secure. He called Sprague's bluff of countercharges and won Kate's divorce with no difficulty.

A few months after the divorce, a reporter for the *Washington Star* made his way to Edgewood and gave a vivid description of the house and its occupants. He raved about the wonderful view of the Capitol, the thickly wooded hills to the east, the complete isolation of its fifty acres. The "plain, two-story dwelling" of brick shows the "refined and elegant tastes of the presiding genius of this sumptuous abode." The furnishings in heavy, ornate Victorian style would hardly be appealing today, but then were the height of fashion. Chase's library is described as having bookshelves on three sides "surmounted by a heavy cornice and decorated in leather fringes. The topmost shelves are within hand reach, and the space between them and the ceiling, is filled by fine engravings, ideal busts, ornamental jars and vases and pieces of ancient armor, all of which are relieved against a background of figured paper of a neutral dark green tint." Family portraits, busts, and photograph albums are everywhere. Chief Justice Chase is often represented both in marble and oil, as are Nettie, Kate herself, and her four children.

If these rooms are an example of the "elegant and luxurious taste of the owner," the reporter states, it is in the children's playroom that he felt the "degree of maternal tenderness which shows that love for her offspring is the ruling passion of her heart, and that her real enjoyment is not found in the material splendor which surrounds her, and the luster of which is dimmed by the beauty of her own person and the grace of her manner and conversation." He describes how little Kitty and Portia "literally revel for several hours each day in this room which contains dolls of every conceivable size and style, many of which were purchased in France and Germany, and the room abounds with curious toys, cribs, cradles, and carriages. The floor is strewn with them, and the shelves of little cabinets are filled with these tokens of a mother's love. Little Portia and Kate are never so happy as when showing this room and its contents to occasional visitors . . . and their attentions will not cease until such guests are induced to take a swing in the grove on the lawn, and have admired their little carriage and the pair of trained goats, which they manage with the dexterity of veteran coachmen." Mrs. Sprague, he relates, has taken complete charge of her daughters' education, assisted by a capable governess, and the proficiency of the children shows her fitness for this arduous task. "It is very obvious, even to the casual observer, that in the companionship of her three daughters Mrs. Sprague finds her great consolation for the trials and disappointments of her married life . . . While her affection for her daughters is of the most devoted character, the absent son, who is in charge of his father, is not forgotten." She speaks often of him and points proudly to his portrait on the wall in the uniform of a naval cadet. "Mrs. Sprague retains much of the beauty for which she was noted in her earlier years. Time has touched her but lightly. Not a streak of grey is seen in the rich auburn hair which shades her classic brow." Although an "expression of sorrow is occasionally detected in her countenance and heard in her silvery voice . . . she is remarkable for her uniform cheerfulness. One thing is certain," he concludes, "her charm of manner and grace and elegance of her conversation are beyond the corroding touch of time, and cannot fail to render her more attractive and admired as age advances." [11]

Sprague, in the meantime, had recently been in the news on his own account. Canonchet had been sold at auction. That great and beautiful place, extending from a fifteen-hundred-foot stretch of beach over four hundred acres of land, with a farm house and farm buildings in addition to the sixty-room unfinished mansion had been sold for $62,250, 10 per cent of what the house was reputed to have cost and $30,000 less than its estimated value. It was under a sheriff's order that the property had been put up for sale to pay off some of the debts against the A. & W. Sprague Company. Sprague's hostilities and disagreements with the trustee, Mr. Chafee, had erupted two years earlier into outright violence when Chafee, emerging from a meeting, clutched Sprague by the throat and was on the point of beating him with his crutch when friends separated the two men. From then on, the enmity was total and hope for any kind of cooperation was gone. Suits and legal battles continued for years.

The day of the sale, Sprague and Willie barricaded themselves at Canonchet. A chain barred the entrance gate, planks from the bridge had been removed, and men with rifles were seen patroling the grounds. A red flag was flying defiantly from one of the towers and the master of the house was seated on the porch, a rifle across his knees. Sprague declared that Canonchet had twice before been sold and that both matters were still in court and that he was the legal tenant. The present purchaser, a Mr. Moulton of New York, was warned that he "sets foot on the property at the peril of his life." [12] It was reported that Sprague ran into Mr. Moulton at a restaurant at the Pier and accused him of having gone back on their friendship. Hearing that Mr. Chafee, his prime enemy, was on a porch overlooking the sea, Sprague, "with a half-smothered oath . . . made tracks for the piazza, threatening to thrash Mr. Chafee and dump him on the rocks below. When he got to the piazza he spoke very harshly, and was immediately interrupted by some friends of the trustee," including a Mr. Farmer. "A little cross-fire of hot language then ensued, in which Mr. Farmer, upon being told by the governor that he would thrash him, threatened to lift him up and shake him out of his boots and dump him over the piazza railing, while Mr. Chafee allowed in a confidential manner that 'he could lick a whole cow-yard of William Spragues.' The squabble ended there, but not before a great excitement had been created." [13] Sprague was on one of his rampages, as he had been three years earlier during the Linck-Conkling affair. This time, however, he found little sympathy in the press. The *Providence Journal* commented that "If this man may, with force, resist the just rights of his creditors and the mandate of the Court, any other man may follow his example, and there will remain no mode for the collection of debts." It was bad enough, the *Journal* went on, when "from fear or from sympathy" the law officer refused to serve a process "for the recovery of a woman's clothes and her children's illegally withheld from her. The connivance at that outrage naturally led to this, and the connivance at this will lead to other, if not greater ones." [14]

The house was described as being in very bad condition and the interior bare, much of the furniture having been sold. "Wanton abuse and ruin are depicted on all sides. The walls are tumbling down and everything seems to have either gone or got well started on the highway to irretrievable ruin. The want of woman's care is as apparent about the house as the lack of a kind mother's guiding hand is seen in the case of Willie Sprague." [15]

Kate must have suffered to read this about her son, but she could not have been in the least surprised. She well knew the conditions under which he was living. The next news she heard, however, came as a surprise not only to her but to everyone.

Some ten months after the divorce, Sprague, after an evening at the opera, took the train for Richmond. From there came the report that amazed even his closest friends. He had married, on March 8, 1883, Inez Weed Calvert, a beautiful divorcee whom he had met in Washington some years earlier and who had spent a season at Narragansett four years before.[16] The newlyweds left at once for Providence where curious friends were eager for a sight of the bride. A week later they moved to Canonchet where they soon settled in, Sprague still paying no attention whatsoever to the fact that the place no longer belonged to him. Other members of the bride's family soon joined them, including a younger sister, Avice.

Among the reports of the marriage was one which startled and outraged Kate. And with good reason. Sprague, in applying for the marriage license, and in his conversations with the clergyman who was to perform the ceremony, had been questioned about his previous marital status. A newspaper, *The Vindicator* in Staunton, Virginia, published his replies. "I wish to state to you the grounds on which I was divorced," he was reported as saying. "I applied for a divorce from my wife on the ground of adultery. She filed a cross bill charging me in the same offense. She, after a short while, withdrew her charges against me. I did not withdraw mine. They remained, and on that standing of the case the court in New York granted me a divorce and divided the custody of the children." The article in the Virginia newspaper, which was widely quoted by other papers, continued with the written questions and answers put to Sprague by the clergyman. "Q. Are you a divorced man or not? A. I am divorced. Q. Please state the grounds upon which the decree was granted? A. Adultery. Q. Was this charged upon your divorced wife or upon yourself? A. Upon my wife. Q. Was there any such charge preferred against you on the proceedings? A. There was not." [17]

Kate got in touch at once with her lawyers. In a letter to the editor of the *Vindicator,* Judge Hoadly and Mr. Britton laid out clearly all the facts about the divorce showing the complete lie that Sprague had perpetrated about it. After reviewing all the charges on both sides in the petitions and the decision of the court, Judge Hoadly concluded: "There has been so much misrepresentation of a defenseless woman, not only in statements of Governor Sprague referred to, but for years, that we feel called upon, as her counsel, to enter a protest, and, in view of all the facts, we have advised her to resume her maiden name." [18]

Sprague, who had successfully defied the law in refusing to allow the legal purchaser of Canonchet even to set foot on the property, was hardly bothered with a lie or two here and there, even if it blasted further the reputation of his former wife. With a whole new lease on life, he even decided to reenter politics and in an amazing show of nerve, put himself forward for and received nomination for Governor on a Reform ticket of Democrats and Independents. Even the press was shocked. Terming him a "political trickster," the *Providence Press* wrote of the "cloven hoof that is apparent to the more worldly wise . . . William Sprague, desperate from financial and social stress of weather is making a last frantic struggle to retrieve his shattered fortunes." [19] The *Norwich Bulletin* considered that "To elevate such a man as William Sprague to the honorable office of Governor of an enlightened State by the vote of the people, is to encourage robbery, cheating and repudiation among the many who are tempted to such practices." The *Boston Post* hoped to see this "political pretender so effectually whipped in the approaching election that such political harlotry will never again be attempted in the snug little State." The *Boston Advertiser* spread out the story of his bankruptcy for all to see, calling him not only a bankrupt but a "defiant bankrupt who had passed years and years in preventing his creditors from being paid." As for the Ohio papers, they practically frothed at the mouth. "Sprague is not a man of doubtful reputation," wrote the *Cleveland Leader*. "His record is beyond question shameful. It is not even certain that he is a person of sound mind, and if not legally insane, he is at least dangerously 'cranky.' . . . There is nothing in his history as a public character to inspire admiration among any but the thoughtless and vicious, and yet it is as a husband and a pretended gentleman that he has been farthest from all that right-minded people approve. William Sprague, while yet rich and powerful, scandalized society and grieved a wife of rare beauty and accomplishments almost to despair. Cruelty, drunkenness, and neglect of all the proprieties of life characterized his unhappy career as master of Canonchet . . . The saddest part of the whole wretched business is that Rhode Island knows just what Sprague is, and has known for years. He has been despised and ridiculed as he deserves." The *Cincinnati Times-Star* declared succinctly that if successful the "Great Persecuted will endeavor to wreak vengeance upon his enemies. The shot gun is to be taken from Canonchet to the State House." [20]

Many of the same papers which had attacked Kate so unmercifully nearly four years earlier now turned on Sprague, and the indulgent picture of an outraged husband defending the sanctity of his home was blotted out by the reality of his defiance of the law, his refusal at gun point to allow the legal buyer of Canonchet entrance to the property, his continuing violent behavior, and his final effrontery in seeking high public office after such a record. Many people must have had sober second thoughts about their condemnation of Kate.

A few papers did not underestimate in advance Sprague's political appeal even after all that he had done, however. The *Rhode Island Democrat* praised his "hardihood to expose corruption, to defy the power of his enemies, and to beard the very lion in his den." [21] It was a dirty campaign, not the first in Sprague's career, and he lost it hands down. It was his political swan song.

Fanny Sprague died that autumn at the age of eighty-three. She had had a long life full of great successes and many griefs. The tragic murder of her husband, the loss of three children, the ruin of the great firm which she had done so much to help build. She was universally respected and admired in Rhode Island and although her house at Cranston had come under the terms of the trust mortgage and assignment and had been sold, a life lease of the property shortly before her death was offered her at a nominal rental. This lease, however, did not carry over to Sprague, and shortly after his mother's death he was served with a writ of trespass.

On previous occasions when Sprague had bought in various items from Canonchet that had been put up for sale, rumor had it that Sprague, in spite of his bankruptcy, had managed to squirrel funds away somewhere. When the eviction notice was served for the Cranston house, a sale was arranged within a few days through a third party and the property resold to Mrs. William Sprague, the new wife. By this arrangement the property was free of any claims of the Sprague creditors.

Not long after Sprague's remarriage, Kate decided to take her daughters to Europe and to educate them there. Not only was she convinced of the great advantages of a thorough knowledge of languages, and that the cost of a first-rate education abroad was less than it would be at home, but she probably dreaded the thought of subjecting the girls to the gossip and whispers about their parents to which they would be subjected in a school in Washington. She rented a small house at Fontainbleau and put the girls in school there. Kate had dropped out completely of the social and political scene and only very rarely did her name appear in any newspapers. One reporter wrote from Paris in 1885, in a London paper, that she had "met Mrs. Kate Chase Sprague at a recent reception. She still has the same handsome face and bright intellect as in the old days when both shone so brightly in Washington society. Mrs. Chase is living here quietly, studying painting if I am not mistaken." The Paris *Morning Herald* correspondent wrote that she often saw Mrs. Sprague "who is living at Fontainbleau, where her children find education. She looks well and wears all the old gaiety and brightness which once gave such charm to Washington society of her time, which was perhaps its best." [22] Kate kept these clippings, a pale reminder of her former prominence.

Kate was always able to put up a bold front in public and this period was no exception. But her financial difficulties accumulated and her situation began to grow more desperate. She had by now quietly sold practically everything that could be sold—her jewels, her furs and laces, her valuable china and glass and silver, paintings and other furnishings, probably for a fraction of their original cost.

Although living quietly and in retirement, Kate did not lose interest in the political scene. An interesting story is told about her while Mr. Levi Morton was Minister to France. He needed certain information of a delicate but very important nature. The case was such that it was impossible for him or any of his staff to do anything about it and he was in a quandary how to proceed when a friend suggested Kate Chase. "If anyone in the world can get what you want she is the woman," Morton was assured. He thereupon invited Kate for a dinner and broached the subject to her. Kate smilingly refused, but showed such interest in the affair and asked so many questions that he felt sure she was about to change her answer. She did not, however, and Morton spent the next few days still puzzled as to how he should proceed. Suddenly a letter arrived for him, unsigned, and in it was the information that he needed, all very clearly and satisfactorily presented. Later he found out that the note had been sent to him by Kate. She had done what he asked, although wanting to appear anonymously.

Another anecdote is told of Kate that she accompanied a French woman, a friend of hers, to witness a duel. When one of the participants was wounded at the first shot, the French woman began to scream and would have revealed their presence if Kate had not clapped her hand over the woman's mouth and told her to be still. Kate, it was said, was not at all disturbed by the sight of blood and smiled and seemed to think the whole thing well worth traveling so far to see.[23]

Kate was fascinated with French history and her knowledge of it was such that several people suggested that as she was able to discourse on it so fluently and with such penetration, and to bring it all so alive, she ought to do a series of articles on it all. Napoleon was a subject of great interest to her and she considered him "the most wonderful man, as to power, gifts and resources that the world has seen." She regretted that he did not "close his career dramatically and grandly after Waterloo, by self-destruction, instead of perishing by inches of rage and humiliation at St. Helena." [24] In spite of everything, Kate evidently had much of her old fire and determination, as well as her always interested and active mind.

Kate stayed almost three years in France before she returned in the summer of 1886 with her daughter, Ethel, now a young lady of seventeen. The two younger girls were left at Fontainbleau. The occasion for Kate's return was twofold. Arrangements which had been subjected to endless delays had finally been completed for the removal of her father's body to Spring Grove Cemetery in Cincinnati. And she hoped to effect the sale of a valuable painting which she still owned and which she counted on to finance another period of education and care for her children.

Kate's arrival stirred old memories and reporters sought out the woman who had once dominated Washington society. Her remarks on social life must have disappointed them somewhat, though it could hardly have come as a surprise in view of the way society had treated her when she was slandered. "I wish to be retired and secluded," she told a reporter. "In that world of Parisian life I take no interest. Gayety in fashionable life I do not enjoy. I have my children to care for and enjoy. My wish is to bring them up to be educated and good women, an honor to themselves and American womanhood. That is a woman's sphere in life. The glitter and transient pleasures of social life are but vanishing joys. They soon pass and leave nothing."

Kate, who was reputed to have wielded greater political influence than any other woman, gave a succinct answer when asked about the activities of the women suffragettes. They had her sympathy, she said, but she had such unbounded faith in the power of women that she believed "they will do whatever they want to do; whenever they want to vote they will vote, and no power on earth will stop them." The reporter caught her fire and commented: "There is not only the old spirit of the brilliant buckeye in this assertion, but good common sense." [25]

The reinterment of her father's body was the occasion for long and formal ceremonies both in Washington and in Cincinnati. Salmon Chase's career was recalled not only in the fervent eulogies but in press reports. Governor Foraker of Ohio issued invitations to an impressive list of national dignitaries to be present at the Memorial services in Cincinnati. It is interesting to note the name of Roscoe Conkling among these, though there is no mention that he attended. The special train from Washington was met by a delegation upon its arrival in Cincinnati. Kate, whose life and career had been prominently recalled in connection with the planned ceremonies, was accompanied by her daughter Ethel. Nettie, her husband and son, Edwyn Chase Hoyt, had arrived the night before, and were at the station to greet the funeral train upon its arrival, Nettie, on the arm of Governor Foraker. First to get off the family car was the Chief Justice of the United States Supreme Court and two Associate Justices. Then came Kate with her daughter and Chase's old friend Miss Susan Walker. Kate was found to be "still majestic and handsome. Her plain black suit and pretty crepe bonnet lent a charm to her face, and brought out the marks of sorrow and trouble. She talked in hurried whispers to her daughter Ethel, a slender girl about seventeen years of age. When she caught sight of her sister Mrs. Chase smiled sweetly, but with a sadness of expression which never quite left her mobile countenance."

At the memorial service at the Music Hall every seat was filled and many stood for the memorial exercises. A stirring eulogy which reviewed Chase's career in glowing terms was delivered by Judge Hoadly; tributes were given by Governor Foraker, Mr. Butterworth, head of the Congressional delegation, and others. "Mrs. Kate Chase was the cynosure of all eyes," the *Cincinnati Enquirer* noted. She sat next to Nettie on whose right was Ethel about whom it was remarked that "she inherits but little of her mother's beauty. The only feature in which there is any resemblance between mother and daughter is the nose. Both noses are slightly retroussé." [26]

The organ pealed out at the end of the ceremony and the cortege formed outside. Chase was finally laid to rest in the cemetery which contained the graves of his three wives and the infant children who had been buried with them.

Although seven years had passed since the Conkling scandal, not everyone had forgotten it and even on this occasion of solemn tribute to her father, the cold hand of bigotry reached out and touched Kate. Lucy Hayes, when her husband had been President, had allowed no liquor, not even wine, to be served at the White House. Few could resist this soft, iron-willed woman, not even resolute General Sherman. "In her gentle hands the general who opposed professional moralists and religious reformers was very pliable. The First Lady soon had Sherman singing hymns regularly in the choruses that she organized among official guests; more marvelous than that, she got him to issue an order to the army to drink less because she wished it." [27] When Julia Foraker, wife of Ohio's Governor and life-long friend of the Chase family, planned to entertain Kate on the occasion of this tribute to her father, Mrs. Hayes thought differently. Approaching Mrs. Foraker shortly before Kate was to arrive, she took her aside and in a soft voice said: "My dear, I hear you are about to entertain Mrs. X. Why should it be you? We must not judge her . . . Let the Lord do that. But I think . . . in your position . . . to countenance even the appearance of evil is a mistake."

"She spaced her words a little. That was all," Julia Foraker remarked. "She drifted away with a faint rustle of black silk, a faint fragrance of tea rose. We did not speak of it again." [28]

Kate did have loyal friends and relatives in Ohio, however, and invitations poured in on her from all sides, but she could not accept them and returned the same night to Washington with the rest of the funeral party. She had urgent needs to meet and no time then to spend in visits.

Kate had once again been brought into the limelight in connection with these final memorials for her father, and people throughout the country recalled her past triumphs, her charm and beauty. Among these, perhaps not too surprisingly in view of his mercurial temperament, was none other than William Sprague. Unfortunately for him, he allowed his expansive mood to lead him into a public statement about the virtues of his former wife. "Mrs. Katherine Chase is a woman of rare attainments," he was quoted as saying. "She has a brilliant mind and many accomplishments, she is a woman of ardent affections, and nature has been munificent in bestowing upon her rare charms of person and manner. She will bring up her daughters well, and they will make fine women." And then, like a self-appointed guardian, Sprague went to her defense in a fantastic illustration of the whims and changes that could take place in his attitudes. "The world has been very inconsiderate in its treatment of her," he remarked smugly. "She is devoting herself to her children, to bring them up to be good and noble women, in honor to their blood and parentage, and she should be permitted to follow these instincts of maternity without intrusion of public comment or scandal. Every word uttered she may endure, but can the children live it down? Mrs. Chase was always a high-spirited woman accustomed to exercising her own will, and she will always do that." He goes on to say complacently that he believes that she is well off having inherited some property from her mother and also her father. He himself gave her $50,000 at one time. "Judging from her usual conservatism in money matters and her business tact, she must have sufficient to make her comfortable if used with discretion. That she will do. I learn that her style of living near Paris is very plain, but respectable and comfortable." [29]

This amazing statement was published in a Philadelphia paper and promptly copied in several others, including the *Providence Journal*. Needless to say Inez Sprague was thrown into a state of fury at Sprague's tender and protective mood of the moment toward his first wife. Poor Sprague must really have paid for his indiscretion. He tried later to say that his letter had been "butchered," but the newspapers gave no credence to this for "no newspaper considers it necessary to change a signed article." [30] The second Mrs. Sprague's reaction was so violent that she herself felt called upon to retort. Her statement is a charming indication of her feelings toward her predecessor, a tissue of lies cemented together with jealousy, hate, and vitriol. In an open letter to the *Narragansett Herald* she declared: "Since Katherine Chace [sic] has been agitating the removal of her father's body, she has beguiled the interim by entertaining reporters with reminiscences, and shadowing forth her charms, assuring the public she married Governor Sprague to further her father's political interests, thus martyring herself on the altar of Mammon. A recent article in the *Philadelphia Times* has been extensively quoted, purporting to have been an interview with Mr. Sprague, but which emanating from the same source as the rest, has demanded in justice to truth and decency a denial in detail.

"By her own confession, purity, refinement, and all the other instincts of womanhood were warped and blighted when she sold herself to Governor Sprague. Treachery and deceit were the parents of disloyalty and disunion, from which naturally issues treason and continued spite. I have ever felt kindly towards her—for her actions have given me the love of the noblest and grandest of men, and would only ask her to hesitate ere she bring into connection with her a name that belongs wholly and entirely to another.

"I do not object to her regaling her friends by expatiating on her personal attractions (if she permits her fondness for the antique to carry her to such length) neither do I object to her reveling in past conquests, if she can find listeners, but I demand that she does not refer to my husband in any form whatever. We extend to her our united pity, which she ever and always will command." [31]

This letter deserves to be set beside the vituperative volume published by Mary Eliza Viall Anderson. In spite of all she had suffered from him, Kate still seemed to be able to arouse Sprague's ladies to frenzies of jealousy. The violence of this outburst of fabrications makes one wonder whether he might not still have cherished some feelings for Kate. A reaction of this sort toward Kate on the part of his second wife should certainly have been based on something more than his rather surprising but actually harmless statement.

Inez had tried to eliminate all traces of Kate from her life with Sprague, something that was not easy to do. Not only was there Kate's son, but there was Canonchet, that magnificent house which, even though unfinished and run down, was filled with memories and the imprint of Kate's taste. Sprague had managed successfully to refuse to turn over the property to the buyer, Mr. Moulton, and finally, upon her husband's death, Mrs. Moulton quit-claimed the property and transferred title, not to William Sprague, but once again to Mrs. William Sprague. Sprague had arranged a mortgage for the $62,500, the price of Moulton's original payment, thus, in effect, buying it back in his wife's name.

Inez promptly set about restoring and changing the mansion and, if Kate's extravagances seemed large, the new Mrs. Sprague was not far behind her. She completed the grand, unfinished ball room, transforming it into a music room where she enjoyed entertaining her friends with her singing, described by one of her guests: "She shrieked like a peacock, but she thought she could sing." [32] All traces of Kate were eliminated in the master bedrooms where Inez decorated the walls with romantic panel paintings interspersed with little Cupids. The ceiling was adorned with paintings of Love Asleep and Love Awake. The bathroom presented a scene of an ocean sunset with mermaids disporting themselves in the water. A central figure was Love riding a dolphin. A long hall on the second floor leading from the grand staircase was constructed, and a sixty-foot canvas depicted a river scene complete with swans floating on the surface and a ten-foot artificial waterfall which, "with its rocks and plants and running stream of water was realistic." [33] But with the best will in the world, all traces of Kate could not be obliterated from the house she had created. Perhaps it was Sprague who insisted on keeping Chase's old room as it always had been, and various guest rooms where the famous had visited just as Kate had planned them.

Kate probably heard something about the changes at Canonchet. She had always aroused great loyalty among the people who worked for her and she had good friends at Narragansett who must have kept her informed. It was not Canonchet which interested her, however. It was her son, and the growing tragedy of his situation. There are no existing letters to show whether Kate was able to maintain contact with Willie during her years abroad. It is clear, however, that it was to his mother that he turned, and in desperation, in the autumn of 1886.

CHAPTER

XVIII

SHORTLY AFTER her marriage, the second Mrs. Sprague brought some of her family to live at Canonchet, including a younger sister, Avice. The two sisters caused quite a stir at the beach where Inez furnished much material for letters of seaside correspondents with her "striking bathing costume." During the season of 1884, a visitor to the Pier named Garrett Wheaton was introduced to Inez and her sister and seemed to be on friendly terms with Sprague also. Mr. Wheaton paid marked attention to Avice, but, to everyone's surprise, he was cut out by a younger man. People had been talking about how Willie Sprague had abandoned "his mustang and rifle, and was no longer seen making his wild dashes over the hedge and ditch or shooting yellow-legs in the salt marshes. He became the cavalier of his aunt by marriage, and it is said even read poetry to her on the rocks, where the roar of the surf furnished the accompaniment." [1] It was noted that the young man had been allowed to grow up almost without attention since his parents' divorce. For several summers after he left his mother's care he had "roamed about the village, roughly clad in winter and barefooted and coatless in summer. He was once seen with newsboys selling the daily newspapers, and his shooting escapade of three or four years ago will be remembered." [2]

This flurry of interest in Willie Sprague was occasioned by the announcement that he and Avice Weed had married on July 25, 1885. The marriage reportedly had taken place in New York and the young couple had gone back to Canonchet to live with his father and stepmother who were her sister and brother-in-law. "The preparations for the marriage were kept very quiet. The young couple, both of whom are under 21 years of age, returned here this morning and announced themselves as man and wife. The Governor and Mrs. Sprague are reported as content over the match, and the entire family is now at Canonchet." [3]

For a few months everything was reported to be going smoothly, but soon Willie and his bride were seen less and less in each other's company and gossips at the Pier said that finally they scarcely ever met at all. "Tongues of scandal" began to wag with the name of Avice and Mr. Wheaton. "For a time young Sprague did not seem to have paid much attention to the apparent intimacy, but at length he showed signs of uneasiness and grew nervous and discontented." [4] Soon it was rumored that he had gone to New York where, it was said, Mr. Wheaton had found him a job. He was seen once or twice after that at Narragansett but almost never in the company of his wife.

Willie's departure for New York, scarcely a year after his surprise marriage, coincided with Kate's return to America in the summer of 1886. In great inner distress, the boy turned to his mother and they met again after their long separation. It must have been a harrowing experience for Kate to see the boy for whom she had had such hopes in the condition of confusion and distress in which she found him.

Willie was working at Long Island City in a machine shop for the Long Island Railroad. He was trying to make a go of his job and to rehabilitate himself, but it was not easy. He was eager to see as much as possible of his mother and sister although he begged off from accompanying them to any "public place of amusement . . . I hope you will not take it amiss," he wrote his mother, "when I say that I feel very reluctant to attend with yourself and sister. I look so very shaky and generally dilapidated." [5]

Slender and dark-haired like his father, Willie had also inherited all of Sprague's tendencies to self-doubt and dissipation, increased by the neglect during his formative years and the difficulties and sorrows of his own life. His letters to his mother must have raised the specter of distant ghosts of the long-gone past. "I am heartily ashamed of myself for not having written before and explaining why I have not put in an appearance," he wrote Kate. "I cannot plead an excuse except my usual lack of promptness and energy. Sunday before last I expected to get a night off, but there being no one to fire the engine, I was compelled to go on. Last Sunday I could have come, but not having heard from you, I was in doubt whether I would find you at home, and having the whole week before me I thought the better plan would be to write and await your reply."

The occasion for Willie's hesitancy in visiting his mother at that moment was not at all because of his work or of any question about finding her in, but was due to something that had happened which troubled him deeply and made him fear that the renewed relationship with his mother might be interrupted. Some three weeks earlier, on November 3, 1886, Avice had given birth to a baby girl, whom she named Inez. Willie had been unable to bring himself to tell his mother of this in advance of the event, although on his brief visits to Narragansett he must himself have known of it. "I do so hope," he continued his letter to Kate, "that nothing has, or will occur to mar the happiness I have derived, from seeing yourself and sister after such a long separation. Must our relations so pleasantly begun, be brought to a speedy end on account of the birth of the child. Of course my duty is plain, and for me there is but one course to pursue, but I feel, and am so utterly alone, and at times feel so discouraged, that I cannot bear to think that you will act differently towards me; yet no one realizes more keenly than I, your position.

"If I have spoken as you may think, without sufficient judgement and unnaturally you must attribute it to a too vivid imagination if it leads me to err.

"I shall anxiously await your reply, although I do not deserve it; do make some excuse for me." [6]

Insecure as he was, and with the bitter experiences he had been through, Willie was ready to doubt even his mother's devotion.

But Kate did not waver in her loyalty to him. She was outraged by everything that had been done to him and he must have poured out his heart to her not only about his marriage but many other things besides. Eager to use whatever influence or connections she had, Kate did everything she could to help Willie toward some kind of career and future. To her old friend, Whitelaw Reid, she wrote with all her old fire that she "grieved to darken the hour we had together today by a tale so revolting and sinister as the history of the inhumanity practised upon my poor boy. It passes belief, it is monstrous. But the boy must be saved. He inherits the blood of a great and good man who, even while Willie was a baby, indulged in plans and hopes for his future career as a good and eminent man; how his grandfather's great heart would ache could he know of this sad and blighted young life.

"With your connections and knowledge of the Pacific Coast and the industries, can not some opening be found for my boy there? He would not be discouraged by beginning very modestly and I should have faith in his succeeding." [7]

Kate did succeed in getting Willie a better position in New York where he went to work as a photoengraver with the World Publishing office. "I am very much pleased," Willie wrote Kate. "How I am to thank you for this I do not know, but how deeply and truly gratefull I am, I hope in time I will be able to prove." He felt that he had a chance for advancement once he learned how to etch the plates and was already starting at work as an assistant to the man who had charge of the department. "I will not attempt to write more at present," he ended in a mood again reminiscent of his father, "for fear that I will become disgusted with my letter and consign it to the waste basket as I have done about 40 times since receiving your first." [8]

Kate also helped her son to take legal steps to end his unfortunate marriage and the following spring he and Avice were divorced. It was reported that the ground for the petition was that "Willie was led into the marriage, and that in contracting it he was not a free agent." [9]

Once again, Inez Sprague commented for the press, although on this occasion she was more wary than before. In an interview she stated that both the young people wanted the divorce. When asked whether she knew "on what grounds he asks for his divorce," she answered, "No. I told you. I can't see any grounds."

"It is reported that he says he was drawn into it against his will."

A shrug of the shoulders was the only answer.

"Have you heard of any other grounds?" she asked.

"There is talk of a gentleman who——"

"Oh, it must be Mr. Wheaton. He's just a friend of ours, and is staying with us so as to be nearer his business."

After a few more questions as to Willie's whereabouts the reporter felt that Inez Sprague "thought the interview had gone far enough." He had at least found out that neither she, nor the Governor, nor her sister would have any objections to the divorce. When asked whether Willie's had been a happy marriage she replied, "Don't ask me too many questions. I'm afraid of reporters." [10]

Soon after the divorce, Avice married Mr. Wheaton, who possessed a considerable fortune, and they settled in happily at Canonchet.

Kate was having her own troubles aside from those connected with her son. Her finances were in desperate condition. Her hope had been to try to sell a portrait of the great physician, William Harvey, done by a contemporary Italian painter. She believed that it should fetch a high price, but such sales were not so easily or quickly arranged as she had hoped. With her funds depleted, and eager to return to her two younger daughters who were still in Europe, Kate was almost frantic with worry. She took a step finally which could not have been easy for her—she literally begged a friend for a loan on the picture to tide her over. "If I could borrow a small sum upon it *now*," she wrote to Whitelaw Reid, "say one or two thousand dollars, it would enable me to go at once to Europe, provide for my children for three months ahead, and come back and begin serious work upon my father's biography."

Through most of the remaining years of her life the plan of a biography of her father, or of reminiscences of her own life, were to be dangled before Kate from various sources. But nothing ever materialized. Long years before she had confessed to her father that she hated writing, even writing letters, and he had scolded her gently saying that she certainly was not gifted in this regard but that if she gained proficiency she would learn not to resent it. It was not so much a distaste for the technical aspects or the work that deterred Kate, however. She had always had a diffidence toward revealing personal or intimate details of her family life, with the one fatal exception of the Conkling scandal when she had opened the floodgates. When R. B. Warden was working on her father's biography, he felt that she put every obstruction in his way. She was willing for her father's official life to be written about but more than reluctant for details of his personal life to be exposed. So, although there would have been a good deal of ready cash for Kate had she consented to capitalize on her father's life and her own, she could never bring herself to do it.

There was always Edgewood which could be sold, but her advisors did not think the moment wise for such a sale, as prices were depressed. The expenses of the children's education were far less in Europe, she explained to Mr. Reid, but she needed a thousand dollars to carry out her plan. She did not want to play on the sympathies of her friends by telling the "denial and self-sacrifice" she had practiced during these latter years. "I shrink from making such a demand upon even the sympathies of my friends—fancy then the extremity which drives me to ask them to help me with money." [11]

The hoped-for loan was not forthcoming, however, and Kate had to postpone her plans. She did finally manage to go abroad and to bring Portia and Kitty back to Edgewood, which was to be home from now on. But something had to be done to improve her financial position.

Kate remembered her early years on the farm outside Cincinnati and the country holidays in New England during her school years. Why not try to turn Edgewood into a paying proposition? Long years ago, it had been a farm and a successful one. So she set to and determined to make a go of it somehow. One of the reporters who always found a good story in Kate Chase when things were slow in other directions visited her at this period. Washington society saw little of her these days, he noted, but he saw in her "the saving adaptability of all people of sense. She is interested in her gardening and in her daughters' education. She rides and drives and fills up a life that would seem singularly empty. She makes no apology or explanation for her altered style of living. Probably she inherits her father's incapacity for moneyed affairs," he observed. "Whatever might have been said of her, the invincible courage she has shown in misfortune commands respect. The old house is full of relics of splendor . . . Everywhere shabbiness and splendor go hand in hand, but the shabbiness is not vulgar, nor is the splendor obtrusive. It would be brave to rashness for someone to pity Mrs. Chase for her surroundings, or for anything else about her. She makes a certain fitness and seemliness for herself out of it all." [12]

Kate at no time received any financial help from Sprague toward the care and education of their children. A few weeks after her eighteenth birthday, Ethel announced that she proposed to go on the stage. Although she had none of her mother's beauty, her face lit up with animation that made one forget her rather large and heavy features. She stated that her mother made no objection to her ambitions, although she had advised her to wait until she was at least eighteen before going on the stage. Ethel had been fortunate in having met many of the theatrical greats including Modjeska, Henry Irving, and others. They had all been very encouraging to her and told her that she had a real talent which one day would bring her public recognition if she persevered. Ethel was clearly enthusiastic about her future career. "This has been the dream of my life," she stated. "I realize all the consequences of the step, I think, and I am prepared to accept the burden of the work that will fall upon me." [13] Ethel did actually join Richard Mansfield's company a few years later and toured with it for several seasons before her marriage to a young physician, Frank Donaldson.

Willie's star did not rise. He lost his position in New York and moved to Edgewood where for a time he worked in a government department, but that too did not last. Nor did a job he had for a time in Pittsburgh. In the late autumn of 1889, Kate's health was extremely poor and she took a short trip abroad. Ethel had been studying in Philadelphia and the two younger girls were left in the care of a former governess at the Fifth Avenue Hotel, under the special care of Mrs. Morello, the proprietress. Ethel saw her mother off and wrote her brother, who was staying at Edgewood, "We have just come back after seeing Mother off for Europe . . . After seeing what condition she was in I realized that it was the best thing she could do especially as she has some letters to write that will pay her." So Kate perhaps did finally earn a little with her pen, probably comments on the European scene. "Really I was worried about her," Ethel continued. "She seemed so ill and so nervous. I have never seen her quite so bad before that. I persuaded her to take Miss Brooks and go without further ado and leave the children here with me. She will rest better and be back sooner in that way. My course in Philadelphia is nearly over and I shall come here and be with them very soon . . . The trip will no doubt do Mother lots of good and she needed it badly. We are all awfully broken up about the parting . . ." Ethel enclosed fifty dollars for Willie's current expenses and cautioned him to be very careful with it as it was all they would get until hearing again from their mother, "but I know you will do that, we are used to it you and I." She hopes he will take good care of himself, the place and the dogs, but adds, "I am so upset that I don't know what I am writing and hope it's clear . . . I feel so awfully about Mother. She seemed so ill that I really feel it unsafe for her to travel alone." [14]

Kate did manage the trip successfully and returned home perhaps with renewed courage and strength to face her many problems. She had not entirely given up hope of getting back some of her own and her father's personal papers from Canonchet, especially as Willie was once more in occasional contact with his father even if on very guarded terms. He was evidently extremely bitter toward his stepmother and her sister, his ex-wife. In a letter to Kate he wrote that he had wanted some books that his father had once given him and wrote "the Governor" asking for them. Sprague replied that "the woman," as Willie termed her, would be in Washington as General Butler's guest in January and would leave the volumes there, but evidently did not. Willie, however, was interested in more than the books. The Sprague Company suits were still not settled and he hoped that something might be salvaged there. He wanted especially to protect his interests against those of his stepmother. "I have been turning this matter (the trust deed, which virtually means the Quidnick property) over in my mind and conclude that it will not do to remain passive and see everything gobbled up by this rapacious unprincipled female. So in my reply I told father I intended to see him during the year if I could possibly arrange it. I want to learn more about this matter, there may be a ghost of a chance, and it is also possible that some changes have taken place in the domestic affairs. At any rate I have determined to look the matter up a bit. It now occurs to me that as I have in a measure paved the way for a visit, it would be a good plan for me to run down and see the Gov. without coming in contact with these detestable parasites—and that I can arrange through a friend of mine at the Pier. I think it is the only feasible plan that offers any prospect of success.

"I would bring up the subject of the papers incidentally and possibly could induce him to go over to Gov. Sissons with me and secure all the papers that still exist. The Gov. used to live at a place called Seaconnett about 15 miles across the Bay, but I am under the impression that he sold out some time ago—he's a regular Col. Sellers chock full of schemes. At any rate this is worth considering. I am very anxious to help you if I can." [15]

Willie did visit Narragansett and see his father briefly, but he had no success in securing for himself or his mother and sisters any share of property. He had no money. He had no job. He had no prospects. His one hope became, as with so many others, to find a new life and fortune in the West. Kate did all she could to help and finally, after considerable difficulty and delay, the prospect of a job on a newspaper in Seattle presented itself, although it was a rather tenuous one. And so Willie started West in the summer of 1890. Reaching Chicago, he decided to stay there until the situation in regard to the Seattle job was clear. "I have secured a very fine position," he wrote his mother happily from Chicago, and he thanked her for her "kind donation" of money which was given him through a friend. [16]

Kate was relieved to hear from him as the reports of the "terrible heats in Chicago" had distressed her, knowing as she did how he felt intense heat. "We are all well," she assured him. "Mr. Compton has taken Kitty in hand for chest development, and the child seems to take new courage and animation with the deep breathing, and I hope for great results. Portia's voice grows apace and their enthusiasm for their music reconciles them to the quiet and monotonous life we lead." [17]

Willie was in a state of euphoria about his new position in Chicago. He was tired after work "but it is such a glorious tired," he told his mother. "I cannot describe to you how glad I am to be at work again even though at present it is not a very remunerative work." His job was with the Westinghouse Electric Co. and he felt he had a chance to display his electrical bent. "We are going to fit out a shop in the top of the Buildg. and then I expect to be in my glory." He tells her he has already started on an electric alarm clock which, although nothing particularly new, is new in its arrangement. He is working in the fixture department at the moment and feels that if he has any good in him at all, it will show itself here. The job he was waiting for, in Seattle, may prove to be bona fide and if so he will, after this work, "have my mind *stored* with usefull knowledge which possibly I may be able to apply to better advantage there than here." He finds his surroundings delightful and has met a great many nice fellows "who don't drink." [18]

After two months in Chicago, Willie decided to go on to Seattle where he was given a position in the engraving department on the *Seattle Daily Journal*. But Willie's moods, so like his father's, fluctuated wildly from high to low, from a euphoria such as he had felt in Chicago to the utter despair which overtook him in Seattle some two weeks after his arrival there. In a moment of final tragedy, Willie Sprague took his own life.

Kate received the news from a reporter while she was at lunch and he found her grief very affecting. At first she absolutely refused to believe it and was convinced that her son's death had been accidental. "I can't conceive that he killed himself," she was reported as saying. "I received a cheerful letter from him from

Chicago only a few days before he left that city. There was nothing to indicate that he was not feeling well and happy." [19]

Sprague learned of his son's death from a terse telegram from Seattle, and a reporter who visited him the next day was the first to furnish him with any of the details. He found Sprague stooped and looking far from well although "not much past his prime . . . Though calm, it was evident that the news was a shock to the governor and that he felt it more than he was willing to show." He had not heard much from Willie, he told the reporter, and nothing since a post card the previous month. "Will was always more with his mother than with me," Sprague told the reporter, "and never confided in me his plans, save through an occasional letter. I had the impression that all was well . . . He was always a restless, roving lad and impatient of disappointment. He very likely made an end to himself in a fit of despondency at having gone out there so far to no purpose. That is the only explanation I am able to give." [20]

One wonders what Sprague's reaction was when he read the letter addressed to "Dear Father," that was found in Willie's room.

"This time I will not plead poverty as an excuse for inflicting this pencil-written affair upon you. I have merely neglected to provide myself with ink . . . I sent you a postal upon the eve of my departure as an item of news, as I imagine that news is pretty scarce down there—not that you [don't] have your little diversions and slight sensations in the matrimonial line, for instance, but then one always likes to hear from former friends and acqaintances. Not that you have given me any encouragement to spring my bright scintillations of wit and humor upon you. Oh, no—quite the contrary."

The letter goes on to relate about his job in Chicago which paid him nine dollars a week. After paying room and board and laundry, that left him with three dollars to invest or not as he saw fit but "for some reason I cannot explain in practice the $3 never appeared.

"Your letter was one of those cold and chilling communications that pass between men when one gets a bill of goods charged for more than is shown in the invoice. Talk to me about the howling blizzard of the North Pole, the awful absence of heat when a friend won't lend you a V! Lord, Massey! these take seats away back in the rear, and hide their faces in very shame in the face of that letter! With my sensitive and highly considerate nature, I cannot conceive how a man can so ruthlessly knock a man down, gouge his eye and otherwise figuratively abuse him, with so little, or, in fact, no cause. But it really matters little, except to my feelings, and they are practically of no use, except to myself."

He went on to say that he left Chicago with great reluctance. Holmes, a friend of his there, has the faculty of "making me see life in anything but a dark and gloomy aspect . . . He has been what a dear and beloved wife would have been to another man. To be sure, he neither sewed on my buttons, nor called me 'sweety' nor 'tooty-wootsy,' but the moral effect was there.

"Out here I am thrown among strangers again, cast upon a desert isle as far as soul communication is concerned. I cannot tell how I long for love and affection, that I have never experienced, and cannot describe, yet long for. Ah me, I fear my dream will never be realized. But this sentimental 'biz' will never do. I had a lot of it stowed up and had to work it off. I have a boozy recollection of having written you a letter containing an outline of a proposition made me by these people, and there . . ." [21] The unfinished letter ended abruptly. Evidently begun on his way to Seattle, it was one of the many letters that young Will wrote and never sent.

This tragic and revealing letter was published for the whole world to read and Kate must have cringed to see her son's deepest feelings become a subject of public sensationalism. She well knew how bitterly Willie had reacted toward what he felt was his father's rejection of him and how, in spite of everything, he still longed for his affection and approval. She blamed Sprague for the years of neglect when Willie had run wild without discipline or direction, and for the travesty and betrayal of his marriage. If there was anyone in the world who should have understood Willie it was the father whom he so resembled. On the day that she received the news of her son's death she wrote Sprague:

Governor Sprague.

This terrible blow ends our poor boy's sad life of struggle and disappointment. If God forgives you, He will be merciful indeed, for at your door lies this unnatural crime.

A home I have sacrificed everything in life to maintain, the heritage of the man who loved us all and died so full of confidence and hope—A mother's heart full of devotion, patience and hope, all were powerless to save this poor boy from what he called his "heritage of woe"—A letter from him the day he left Chicago for Seattle dated Sept. 19 was cheerful and hopeful.

What bitter disappointment and desolation of spirit must he have endured to have induced self-murder. I have telegraphed to friends in Seattle to do all that can be done to properly bestow the poor body. Will you meet me in New York within a few days to determine upon arrange[ments] for its final interment.

    A broken hearted
        Mother

In this sad rite I cannot but believe that you will wish to act with me.[22]

Willie had been born at Narragansett in June in the first fresh flush of summer. His life and future seemed singularly blessed with golden circumstances and opportunities. Twenty-five years later his body was returned to the place of his birth on a sere and cold October day, with the wind from the ocean whipping dying leaves from their branches and scattering sand in aimless, lost patterns like the forgotten hopes and dreams of childhood.

Kate could not mourn her son in a private ceremony. The funeral was held at St. Peter's-by-the-Sea and as she was entering the church, accompanied by Ethel and Portia, and a young man who was reported engaged to Ethel, Governor Sprague, with Inez, Avice, and her new husband Col. Wheaton, and the child, were just alighting from their carriage. Kate with her daughters sat on the left side of the church; Sprague and his group on the right. Between them was the casket almost completely covered with a floral arrangement in the form of an anchor with the word "Hereafter" traced in purple immortelles. On a small card were the words, "With his mother's unfaltering devotion." The only other floral tribute was a square of white roses with "Papa" in letters of

purple in the center. It is doubtful whether Kate noticed it, or the
assembled Weed-Sprague contingent on the other side of the aisle,
or even the fact that Mrs. Byron and Mrs. Amasa Sprague chose to
sit near her.

After the service was ended at St. Peter's-by-the-Sea, the casket
was taken by train to Providence. Governor Sprague did not accompany his son's body to its last resting place at the Sprague
family mausoleum at Swan Point Cemetery but was "represented"
by two friends. Kate and her daughters did make the last journey.
A crowd of over a thousand morbid sightseers was waiting for the
train when it arrived at Providence and it was difficult for the
funeral cortege even to pass through. Another crowd was waiting
at Swan Point. Kate was visibly affected throughout. At St. Peter's
she had broken down at the end of the service and wept on the
shoulder of one of her former servants from Canonchet. At Swan
Point she broke down again "weeping and trembling under her
sorrow." [23]

Kate's grief and the tragic direction her life had taken aroused
great feelings of compassion for her. In spite of her eleven-year
absence, people at Narragansett had not forgotten her nor changed
in their devotion. After Willie's death, Kate received a remarkable confirmation of this devotion in a letter from the superin-
tendent of Canonchet:

"I have made up my mind to write to you ever since I saw your
lovely face once more but have put it off until now. For I have
felt so bad for you ever since poor Willie's Funeral that it seemed
as if I could not write when I attempted to do so. For it is hard
work for me now to control my feelings every time I think of the
near and dear boy who is layed away from our view and in particular yours. For well do I know that you loved him with all of your
heart and we all did unless it was his Father and he most every one
here thinks that he did not care any thing for his only son and
there is lots here of people, Mrs. Chase, that would liked to have
mobbed him after it was over to think that he would not even go
to the train to see his boys remains put on the train much more
not go to Swan Point. Oh it was Terrible and he gets it now on
all sides for he has no Friends at Narragansett but on the other

side Dear Mrs. Chase Every Body is a friend to you now that talks about it and of course I hear a great deal about it and I am here all the time and I myself I can truly say I never felt any worse when I lost my dear mother." He could not believe the news of Willie's death at first and knew that it would "set you out of your mind to hear it. Oh I always loved Willie as I was with him so much and at times had the care of him that he was very near and dear to me and I think of him often and I allways shall." Willie had promised to send him a photograph of himself when he had been at the Pier the previous February and he begs Mrs. Chase to send him one, and also of the young ladies if that is possible. And then he added a bit of news about Canonchet which, "they say is to be sold to a rich party in New York and the money is all ready to be payed over when the Ex. Gov. will sign the deed which they say he will not do unless his wife will give him one half which it is said she will not do." [24] Canonchet was not sold, however, until many years later when it was bought by Avice, then married to her third husband.

Kate grieved for her son and his lost dreams and the tragedy of his death. So many years before, on the occasion of Willie's first birthday, Sprague had written of the mission that little sons have to bring their parents close: "One in aims, one in plans, one in pleasures and one in pains. One in affliction and disappointment . . . What a holy mission has our little Willie to perform. I know he will perform it." [25] But there was no one, Sprague least of all, to whom she could turn for comfort now. At one point she even sought help from a medium and noted down in her elegant handwriting the message she wanted to transmit: "Is my son William Sprague present and does he know how I mourn him and can he advise me what it is best to do for his sisters' benefit." [26] It would be nice to believe that she found at least some solace with these messages, whatever the answers may have been.

CHAPTER
XIX

AFTER Willie's death, Kate was ever more pressed by her troubles in trying to make ends meet and was anxious about the future for her girls, especially little Kitty. Nothing, however, could make a sound, conservative financier out of Kate, and one can almost imagine her grandmother, Jeanette Chase, bemoaning the fact that Kate had inherited her father's lack of money sense instead of her own thrifty, practical nature. Kate had been trying to augment her woefully inadequate income by supplying hotels in the city with eggs and butter and vegetables. But as many an "amateur farmer" learned to his regret, farming is not the easiest way to earn a living. Kate was forced to borrow money and soon had a mortgage of over $36,000 on the Edgewood property. The improvements she tried to make to develop it as a farm were costly and unproductive in the end and succeeded only in plunging her ever deeper into the abyss of financial ruin. She had always believed that she could sell Edgewood for a large sum, enough to pay off all her debts and assure the future. She seemed finally to have come to the realization that she could not continue as she was doing and, miraculously as it seemed, she succeeded in finding a buyer, a Mr. Hamlin, who would pay her $115,000 for the place. He was an elderly gentleman from Ohio, a former member of Congress and an old friend of Salmon Chase. It really looked at last as though Kate's fortunes had turned for the better. One day, however, when Mr. Hamlin was walking around the property wanting a last look before the final settlement of the sale, he was set upon by a young thief. Mr. Hamlin at first did not seem to be seriously injured, but the shock proved too much and within a few days he was dead.

Edgewood was then put up at auction in the summer of 1895, and bought in for the sum of the mortgage by the trust company that held it. Although financial institutions are not noted for softness of heart or sentimentality, Kate Chase had proved her exceptionality before this. The trust company decided that they would give her special consideration, as the daughter of a most distinguished American, and she was given an option on the property for a period of six months during which time she could buy it back for a sum representing her indebtedness and interest on the debt.

Kate went first to Ohio, where she found a welcome and a response but not much money forthcoming. Thereupon she decided to go to the hub of the financial world, New York.

It had been many years since Kate had made use of the charm and influence which had made her legendary. The passage of time had not been gentle with Kate these last years since the death of her son. She had often done hard physical work in her farming efforts, and had sometimes delivered vegetables and eggs and butter herself, driving around to the delivery entrances of hotels in the ballrooms of which she had once reigned as queen. Her health too had suffered. Liver and kidneys were not functioning as they should. Her face had become puffy and eyelids reddened. Kate Chase, nevertheless, was not going to visit her former friends of Wall Street like a broken-down suppliant. She put a blond wig over her once marvelous auburn hair, now faded and gray; the proud head was still carried at the same confident tilt. But nothing could hide the ravages that time, ill health, and grief had made. Henry Villard wrote his wife that not having seen Kate in over thirty years "it gave me quite a shock at first to be received by an aged woman with hardly any traces of her former beauty." Although Kate had lost her beauty, she had not, however, forgotten how to charm and create illusion, for Villard went on, "But she is still very intelligent, vivacious and determined as of old and very ladylike withal." [1]

Mrs. Villard was glad to invite Kate to visit them. As a young girl when she had first visited Washington, she had admired Kate and felt there was no one like her. At her first large ball she remembered the elegant women, the colorful diplomatic corps, and dignified senators. "The center of attraction, the belle of the ball, was the fascinating Kate Chase . . . [She] was the most bewitching of queens in the garden of roses . . . a regal figure, around which diplomats and military men were drawn all seeking a smile or a dance." [2] Kate had been kind to the young woman then and Mrs. Villard had not forgotten it. What a change she noted now. "Mrs. Kate Chase looks like a wreck of her former self," she commented later. "False blond hair, powder and paint and weary, half-closed eyes make a sad impression on one." [3]

But Kate got the money she needed through the assistance of Villard and others who made up a fund to take up the mortgage. High-spirited Kate at first did not agree to any restriction in her management of the estate, but the gentlemen who were investing in it were reported, justifiably, to feel that Kate was not a person who could manage any future disposal of the property in the most businesslike manner.[4] In the end, Kate agreed to the conditions and for the first time in many years felt a modicum of security that she at least would have a roof over her head.

She continued to try to earn money by farming and wrote exquisite little notes to her favored customers in the elegant handwriting that had not altered an iota since her girlhood.

> I was sorry not to be able to send you the asparagus and rhubarb for your dinner today.
>
> Kindly give your order at night for the next day and we will be glad to fill it if we have what you wish . . . What we have is good and I am pleased to send it to one so appreciative as you always are. We have now milk—2 fresh cows and a good deal of milk and cream. Are there any of your neighbors who would care to have our milk and cream?
>
> My work this year is largely field work. My men go to work

early and are constantly busy until six p.m. and we run no wagon so can only serve after working hours.[5]

Kate still sometimes dreamed that she would try to restore Edgewood to its former splendor, but she had neither the money nor the energy to undertake such a task. Much of the furniture had been sold when the place had been auctioned and many of the rooms were bare and comfortless. One of the things Kate had clung to was the marble bust of her father which stood in his old library, now empty except for a few dusty chairs and tables piled by the windows. Disorder, decay and silence permeated everything, one observer noted. "Not a sound is heard about the house, and over the whole place hangs an air of solitude, of desolation that makes the dingy mansion seem a black cloud in a bright landscape." [6]

The children were grown up now. Ethel was married and came only occasionally for brief visits with her little son, Chase Donaldson, Kate's only grandchild. The little boy stayed once for several months with his grandmother. He delighted her and Kate pronounced him "all Chase." Portia, a few months before Kate's death, moved back to Narragansett. She had met her father for the first time in many years at a Washington hotel and had not even recognized the broken man until he was pointed out to her.

Kate was left almost entirely alone with fragile little Kitty, although a few months before her death one of her faithful cousins from Ohio visited her and they talked over old times, summoning up vividly for Kate the long-buried past.

Edgewood was a place of memories and dreams long gone—the nearby hill where Kate had so often visited the First Rhode Island Regiment and its youthful commander; the library where Chase's white marble bust presided eerily at night while ghosts from the past crowded Kate's memory—Lincoln, Garfield, Grant, Sumner, Johnson, Sherman, and a host of others, all gone now. Fiery Conkling too was dead, victim of his own inflexible will in the blizzard of 1888. He had started walking from his office on Wall Street right into the teeth of the storm. After three miles and three hours he reached his club on Twenty-fifth Street, stomped into the lobby and went down, full length, like a great felled oak tree.

Sprague was not so fortunate. He would outlive Kate by some fifteen years and would see his beloved Canonchet burned to the ground. His last years would be spent in Paris far removed in time and space from those proud days on which his mind increasingly dwelt when he had been the youthful War Governor.

Kate never complained those last, hard, bitter years, nor did she make excuses for her surroundings to the few people who ever visited her at Edgewood. Even her severest critics admired her fortitude in distress. In recognition perhaps of her illustrious former days, a position was finally offered her in one of the government departments, and she hoped to be able to keep herself and Kitty on what it would pay her. But the offer came too late. Poverty and hard work had taken an increasing toll and at last Kate's health broke completely. But she managed to keep going until nearly the end.

After Kate's death her daughters closed the house; the furniture was sent away to be auctioned. Little Kitty clung to Portia who would care for her during the few brief years remaining to that fragile child. The dogs were taken to their new homes several miles away. Edgewood was dark and deserted, left to its ghosts. Everything was gone, the triumph and the tragedy, all gone. Only the dogs remembered and made their way back across the whole city and up the overgrown road to the familiar, weather-beaten porch. Perhaps they had come back to the long-gone sound of a bugle call from the nearby encampment on a summer's night so many years before, or the echo of gay laughter when a dashing young officer on a magnificent white horse, the yellow plume in his hat catching the wind, galloped over the hills, an enchanted young girl at his side.

NOTES

NOTES

CHAPTER I

1. Mary Merwin Phelps: *Kate Chase: Dominant Daughter*, (New York: Thomas Y. Crowell Co., 1935), p. 12.
2. Carl Schurz: *The Autobiography of Carl Schurz*. (New York: Charles Scribner's Sons, 1961), pp. 154, 118.
3. Robert Bruce Warden: *An Account of the Private Life and Public Services of Salmon Portland Chase*. (Cincinnati: Wilstach, Baldwin & Co., 1874). p. 208.
4. *Ibid.*, p. 27.
5. *Ibid.*, p. 63.
6. *Ibid.*, p. 55.
7. *Ibid.*, p. 65.
8. *Ibid.*, p. 70.
9. *Ibid.*, p. 85.
10. *Ibid.*, p. 84.
11. *Ibid.*, p. 90.
12. *Ibid.*, p. 110.
13. *Ibid.*, p. 118.
14. *Ibid.*, p. 121.
15. *Ibid.*, p. 124.
16. *Ibid.*, p. 164.
17. *Ibid.*, p. 175.
18. *Ibid.*, p. 193.
19. *Ibid.*, p. 242.
20. *Ibid.*, p. 267.
21. Warden: *op. cit.*, p. 286.
22. *Ibid.*, p. 287.
23. *Ibid.*, pp. 290–91.

CHAPTER II

1. Warden: *op. cit.,* p. 293.
2. J. W. Schuckers: *The Life and Public Services of Salmon Portland Chase.* New York: D. Appleton & Co., 1874. p. 78.
3. *Ibid.,* p. 79.
4. Warden: *op. cit.,* p. 307.
5. Phelps: *op. cit.,* p. 26.
6. *Ibid.,* p. 32.
7. Warden: *op. cit.,* p. 331.
8. Although it has usually been accepted that Kate Chase was sent to Miss Haines's School at the age of seven, she herself wrote that "when I was eight Grandpa taught me to print my letters and the first correspondence after I went away from home to school, at nine years of age, that I held with my father, was in printed characters . . ." Kate Chase Sprague to William Sprague, Jr., January 13, 1877. Special Collections, Brown University Library (Hereafter cited: BUL, Sp. Coll.).
9. Julia Newberry: *Julia Newberry's Diary.* (New York: W. W. Norton & Co., 1933), p. 36.
10. The Historical Society of Pennsylvania, Chase Collection. Belle Chase to Kate Chase, December 11, 1850. (Hereafter cited: HSP, Chase Coll.)
11. Ishbel Ross: *Proud Kate.* New York: Harper & Brothers, 1953. p. 26.
12. Phelps: *op. cit.,* p. 66.
13. *Ibid.,* p. 49.
14. HSP, Chase Coll., S. P. Chase to Kate Chase, December 5, 1851.
15. *Ibid.,* S. P. Chase to Kate Chase, July 8, 1852.
16. *Ibid.,* S. P. Chase to Kate Chase, March 4, 1852.
17. *Ibid.,* S. P. Chase to Kate Chase, June 30, 1852.
18. *Ibid.,* S. P. Chase to Kate Chase, January 23, 1853.
19. *Ibid.,* S. P. Chase to Kate Chase, May 21, 1852.
20. *Ibid.,* S. P. Chase to Kate Chase, August 10, 1852.
21. *Ibid.,* S. P. Chase to Kate Chase, December 21, 1852.
22. *Ibid.,* S. P. Chase to Kate Chase, January 23, 1853.
23. *Ibid.,* S. P. Chase to Kate Chase, September 15, 1854.
24. *Ibid.,* S. P. Chase to Kate Chase, December 20, 1853.
25. *Ibid.,* S. P. Chase to Kate Chase, September 15, 1854.
26. *Ibid.,* S. P. Chase to Kate Chase, April 13, 1855.
27. BUL. Sp. Coll.
28. HSP, Chase Coll., S. P. Chase to Kate Chase, May 27, 1855.
29. *Ibid.,* S. P. Chase to Kate Chase, June 21, 1855.
30. BUL, Sp. Coll., Kate Chase Sprague *Diary,* November 4, 1868.

CHAPTER III

1. Bill Arter: *Columbus Vignette. Columbus Dispatch,* September 28, 1969.
2. Phelps: *Op. cit.,* p. 87.
3. HSP, Chase Coll., S. P. Chase to Kate Chase, July 25, 1856.

4. Virginia Tatnall Peacock: *Famous American Belles of the 19th Century.* (Philadelphia: J. B. Lippincott, 1901), p. 207.
5. *Ibid.,* p. 214.
6. *Cincinnati Enquirer,* August 13, 1879.
7. HSP, Chase Coll., S. P. Chase to Kate Chase, September 15, 1858.
8. *Ibid.,* S. P. Chase to Kate Chase, April 30, 1859.
9. Schurz: *Op. cit.,* p. 154.
10. *Ibid.,* p. 154.
11. *Ibid.,* pp. 155–56.
12. *Ibid.,* p. 155.
13. Schurz: *Op. cit.,* p. 161.
14. Warden: *Op. cit.,* p. 366.
15. Ross: *Op. cit.,* p. 54.
16. Warden: *Op. cit.,* p. 369.

CHAPTER IV

1. Henry Adams: *The Education of Henry Adams.* (Boston: Houghton, Mifflin Co., 1918), p. 99.
2. William Howard Russell: *My Diary North and South.* (New York: Harper & Brothers, 1954), pp. 18, 19.
3. *Ibid.,* p. 32.
4. *Harper's Weekly:* March 23, 1861.
5. Russell: *Op. cit.,* p. 27.
6. *Cincinnati Enquirer:* August 1, 1899.
7. Thomas Graham Belden and Marva Robins Belden: *So Fell The Angels.* (Boston: Little, Brown & Co., 1956), p. 30.
8. *Harper's Weekly:* April 27, 1861.
9. Carl Sandburg: *Abraham Lincoln: The War Years.* (New York: Harcourt, Brace & Co., 1939), vol. I, p. 230.
10. *Ibid.,* p. 231.
11. Margaret Leech: *Reveille in Washington.* (New York: Harper & Brothers, 1941), p. 65.
12. *Harper's Weekly:* May 18, 1861.
13. Phelps: *op. cit.,* p. 124.
14. BUL, Sp. Coll., Kate Chase Sprague: *Diary,* November 11, 1868.
15. Elizabeth Keckley: *Behind the Scenes.* (New York: Arno Press and *The New York Times,* 1968), pp. 124–25.
16. Russell: *op. cit.,* p. 215.
17. *Ibid.,* p. 223.
18. Leech: *op. cit.,* p. 101.

CHAPTER V

1. HSP, Chase Coll., Janette Chase to Kate Chase, September 29, 1861.
2. Charles Carroll: *Rhode Island: Three Centuries of Democracy.* (New York: Lewis Historical Publishing Co., 1932), vol. II, pp. 754–60.

3. BUL, Sp. Coll., William Sprague to Kate Chase Sprague, May 27, 1866.
4. *Ibid.*, William Sprague to Kate Chase, June 8, 1863.
5. *Ibid.*, Kate Chase Sprague: *Diary,* November 11, 1868.
6. All accounts by William Sprague of the Battle of Bull Run from: *Congressional Globe:* April 8, 1969, pp. 618–19 and *Providence Evening Bulletin:* May 25, 1887.
7. Russell: *op. cit.,* pp. 224–25.
8. BUL, Sp. Coll., William Sprague to Kate Chase Sprague, May 27, 1866.
9. HSP, Chase Coll., S. P. Chase to Kate Chase, September 2, 1861.
10. *Ibid.,* S. P. Chase to Kate Chase, no date.
11. *Ibid.,* Janette Chase to Kate Chase, January 28, 1862.
12. *Cincinnati Enquirer:* August 13, 1879; BUL, Sp. Coll., William Sprague to Kate Chase Sprague, May 21, 1866.
13. Mary Eliza Viall Anderson: *The Merchant's Wife.* (Boston: for the Author, 1876), pp. 42–43.
14. *Ibid.,* p. 24.
15. *Ibid.,* pp. 20–21.
16. *Ibid.,* pp. 21–22.
17. HSP, Chase Coll., S. P. Chase to Kate Chase, June 25, 1862.
18. *Ibid.,* S. P. Chase to Kate Chase, June 29, 1862.
19. *Ibid.,* S. P. Chase to Kate Chase, July 2, 1862.
20. *Ibid.,* S. P. Chase to Kate Chase, July 11, 1862.
21. *Ibid.,* S. P. Chase to Kate Chase, July 6, 1862.
22. *Ibid.*
23. *Ibid.,* Janette Chase to Kate Chase, January 24, 1862.
24. *Ibid.,* S. P. Chase to Kate Chase, June 20, 1862.
25. Emily Edson Briggs: *The Olivia Letters.* (New York: The Neale Publishing Co., 1906), April 23, 1868, p. 70.
26. BUL, Sp. Coll., Janette Chase to Kate Chase.
27. *Cincinnati Enquirer:* August 13, 1879.
28. BUL, Sp. Coll., William Sprague to Kate Chase Sprague, May 27, 1866.
29. *Ibid.,* William Sprague to Kate Chase, June 8, 1863.
30. *Cincinnati Daily Times:* August 15, 1879.
31. BUL, Sp. Coll., William Sprague to Kate Chase Sprague, May 9, 1863.
32. HSP, Chase Coll., S. P. Chase to Kate Chase, no date.

CHAPTER VI

1. BUL, Sp. Coll., William Sprague to Kate Chase, June 7, 1863.
2. HSP, Chase Coll., Salmon P. Chase to William Sprague, June 6, 1863.
3. BUL, Sp. Coll., William Sprague to Kate Chase, June 9, 1863.
4. *Ibid.,* June 9, 1863.
5. *Ibid.,* June 15, 1863.
6. LC, Chase Coll., William Sprague to S. P. Chase, June 24, 1863.
7. BUL, Sp. Coll., William Sprague to Kate Chase, July 16, 1863.
8. *Ibid.,* July 19, 1863.
9. *Ibid.,* July 2, 1863.
10. *Ibid.,* August 4, 1863.

11. *Ibid.,* July 22, 1863.
12. *Ibid.,* September 20, 1863.
13. *Ibid.,* September 19, 1863.
14. *Ibid.,* September 19, 1863.
15. *Ibid.,* September 22, 23, 1863.
16. Phelps: *Op. cit.,* p. 136.
17. BUL, Sp. Coll., William Sprague to Kate Chase, June 7, 1863.
18. *Ibid.,* October 22, 1863.
19. *Ibid.,* September 22, 1863.
20. *Ibid.,* October 27, 1863.
21. *Ibid.,* October 31, 1863.
22. *Ibid.,* October 20, 1863.
23. *Ibid.,* September 23, 1863.
24. *Ibid.,* November 4, 1863.
25. LC, Chase Coll., William Sprague to S. P. Chase, November 4, 1863.
26. BUL, Sp. Coll., William Sprague to Kate Chase, October 27, 1863.
27. *Ibid.,* November 4, 1863.
28. *Ibid.,* September 22, 1863.
29. *Ibid.,* October 22, 1863.
30. *Ibid.,* November 2, 1863.
31. *Ibid.,* October 23, 1863.
32. *Ibid.,* Kate Chase Sprague: *Diary,* March 29, 1868.

CHAPTER VII

1. Descriptions of wedding from *New York Times,* November 15, 1863.
2. Peacock: *Op. cit.,* p. 208.
3. BUL, Sp. Coll., Kate Chase Sprague: *Diary,* November 11, 1868.
4. LC, Chase Coll., William Sprague to S. P. Chase, November 21, 1863.
5. *Ibid.,* William Sprague to S. P. Chase, December 2, 1863.
6. William Roscoe Thayer: *The Life of John Hay.* (Boston and New York: Houghton, Mifflin & Co., 1916), pp. 201–02; Sandburg: *Op. cit.,* vol. III, pp. 639–40.
7. BUL, Sp. Coll., William Sprague to Kate Chase Sprague, October 14, 1863.
8. *Ibid.,* Kate Chase Sprague to William Sprague, December 11, 1863.
9. *Ibid.*
10. *Ibid.,* Kate Chase Sprague to William Sprague, December 12, 1863.
11. *The Crisis* (Columbus, Ohio) December 9, 1863, reprinted from the *Brooklyn Eagle.*
12. BUL, Sp. Coll., William Sprague to Kate Chase Sprague, December 12, 1863.
13. *Ibid.,* Kate Chase Sprague to William Sprague, December 24, 1863.
14. *Ibid.,* December 29, 1863.
15. *Ibid.,* William Sprague to Kate Chase, June 9, 1863.
16. *Ibid.,* William Sprague to Kate Chase Sprague, December 31, 1863.
17. *Ibid.,* Fanny Sprague to Kate Chase Sprague, January 1, 1864.
18. Ross: *Op. cit.,* p. 129.

19. Schuckers: *Op. cit.,* pp. 499–500.
20. *Ibid.,* pp. 500–01.
21. *Ibid.,* pp. 501–02.
22. Albert Bushnell Hart: *Salmon Portland Chase.* (Boston and New York: Houghton, Mifflin & Co., 1899), p. 435.
23. Ross: *Op. cit.,* p. 152.
24. Warden: *Op. cit.,* p. 581.
25. BUL, Sp. Coll., Kate Chase Sprague to William Sprague, March 4, 1864.
26. *Ibid.,* Kate Chase Sprague: *Diary,* November 4, 1868.
27. *Ibid.*
28. *Ibid.,* William Sprague to Kate Chase Sprague, no date.
29. Warden: *Op. cit.,* p. 260.
30. *Ibid.,* p. 585.
31. *Ibid.,* p. 584.
32. Schuckers: *Op. cit.,* 509.
33. HSP, Chase Coll., S. P. Chase to Kate Chase Sprague, July 11, 1864.
34. Schuckers: *Op. cit.,* p. 511.
35. Sandburg, *Op. cit.,* Volume III, p. 585.
36. Schuckers: *Op. cit.,* p. 513.
37. Warden: *Op. cit.,* p. 630.
38. Nicolay and Hay: *Abraham Lincoln, A History.* (New York: *Century,* 1890), vol. IX, p. 395.
39. Sandburg: *Op. cit.,* vol. III, p. 597; Schuckers: *Op. cit.,* p. 488.

Chapter VIII

1. Schuckers: *Op. cit.,* p. 512.
2. HSP, Chase Coll., S. P. Chase to Kate Chase Sprague, August 26, 1864.
3. BUL, Sp. Coll., William Sprague to Kate Chase Sprague, November 24, 1864.
4. LC, Chase Coll., Kate Chase Sprague to S. P. Chase, August 29, 1871.
5. BUL, Sp. Coll., Kate Chase Sprague: *Diary,* November 11, 1868.
6. BUL, Sp. Coll., William Sprague to Kate Chase Sprague, December 25, 1864.
7. Warden, *Op. cit.,* p. 639; Schuckers: *op. cit.,* p. 518.
8. HSP, Chase Coll., S. P. Chase to Kate Chase Sprague, March 28, 1865.
9. *Ibid.,* June 19, 1865.
10. BUL, Sp. Coll., Kate Chase Sprague: *Diary,* November 4, 1868.
11. LC, Chase Coll., S. P. Chase to Kate Chase Sprague, June 24, 1865.
12. *Ibid.,* William Sprague to S. P. Chase, August 21, 1865.
13. HSP, Chase Coll., S. P. Chase to Kate Chase Sprague, August 17, 1865.
14. LC, Chase Coll., William Sprague to S. P. Chase, August 28, 1865.
15. HSP, Chase Coll., S. P. Chase to Kate Chase Sprague, September 4, 1865.
16. C. G. Bowers: *The Tragic Era.* (Houghton, Mifflin & Co., 1929), p. 253.
17. Phelps: *Op. cit.,* p. 177.
18. Elizabeth Fries Ellet: *Court Circles of the Republic.* (Hartford: Hartford Publishing Co., 1869), p. 550.
19. *Ibid.,* p. 554.

20. Katherine Chase Sprague vs. William Sprague, divorce petition.
21. BUL, Sp. Coll., Kate Chase Sprague: *Diary,* November 4, 1868.

CHAPTER IX

1. BUL, Sp. Coll., William Sprague to Kate Chase Sprague, April 14, 1866.
2. *Ibid.,* April 30, 1866.
3. *Ibid.,* May 8, 1866.
4. *Ibid.*
5. *Ibid.,* May 9–12, 1866.
6. *Ibid.,* May 22, 1866.
7. *Ibid.,* May 18, 1866.
8. *Ibid.,* May 27, 1866.
9. *Ibid.,* 2nd letter May 27, 1866.
10. *Ibid.,* June 11, 1866.
11. *Ibid.,* June 8, 1866.
12. *Ibid.*
13. *Ibid.,* June 11, 1866.
14. *Ibid.,* June 26, 1866.
15. *Ibid.,* June 28, 1866.
16. *Ibid.,* June 11, 1866.
17. *Ibid.,* July 8, 1866.
18. *Ibid.,* June 28, 1866.
19. *Ibid.,* June 29, 1866.
20. *Ibid.,* July 6, 1866.
21. *Ibid.,* July 19, 1866.
22. HSP, Chase Coll., S. P. Chase to William Sprague, July 25, 1866.
23. BUL, Sp. Coll., William Sprague to Kate Chase Sprague, July 12, 1866.
24. *Ibid.,* June 8, 1866.
25. *Ibid.,* August 8, 1866.
26. Phelps: *Op. cit.,* p. 186.
27. LC, Chase Coll., S. P. Chase to Kate Chase Sprague, September 10, 1866.
28. BUL, Sp. Coll., William Sprague to Kate Chase Sprague, August 27, 1866.
29. *Ibid.,* September 2, 1866.
30. *Ibid.*
31. *Ibid.,* September 17, 1866.
32. Phelps: *Op. cit.,* p. 188; *New York World,* September 14, 1866.
33. *Ibid.,* p. 189.

CHAPTER X

1. HSP, Chase Coll., S. P. Chase to Kate Chase Sprague, January 4, 1867.
2. LC, Chase Coll., S. P. C. to Janette Chase, March 23, 1867.
3. *New York World:* February 20, 1870.
4. *Cincinnati Enquirer:* August 1, 1899.
5. Bowers: *op. cit.,* p. 255.
6. Briggs: *op. cit.,* p. 51.

7. *New York Times:* May 13, 1868.
8. Warden: *op. cit.,* p. 696.
9. *Ibid.,* p. 684.
10. *Ibid.,* p. 683.
11. *Ibid.,* p. 685.
12. *Ibid.,* p. 695.
13. LC, Chase Coll., S. P. Chase to Kate Chase Sprague, May 10, 1868.
14. BUL, Sp. Coll., Kate Chase Sprague: *Diary,* March 29, 1868.
15. Warden: *op. cit.,* p. 693.
16. *Ibid.,* p. 700.
17. *Ibid.,* pp. 701–2.
18. Charles Hubert Coleman: *The Election of 1868.* (New York: Columbia University Press, 1933), p. 125.
19. *New York Times,* July 10, 1868.
20. HSP, Chase Coll., Kate Sprague to S. P. Chase, July 5, 1868.
21. Warden: *Op. cit.,* pp. 704–75.
22. HSP, Chase Coll., S. P. Chase to Kate Chase Sprague, July 7, 1868.
23. *Ibid.*
24. *Ibid.,* S. P. Chase to Kate Chase Sprague, July 10, 1868.
25. *Ibid.,* Kate Chase Sprague to S. P. Chase, July 7, 1868.
26. *Ibid.,* Kate Chase Sprague to S. P. Chase, July 10, 1868.
27. *Ibid.,* Kate Chase Sprague to S. P. Chase, July 5, 1868.
28. *New York Times:* July 10, 1868.
29. LC, Chase Coll., Kate Chase Sprague to S. P. Chase, July 10, 1868.
30. *New York Times:* July 8, 1868.
31. Coleman: *Op. cit.,* pp. 231–32.
32. *Ibid.,* p. 232.
33. Warden: *Op. cit.,* pp. 705–06.
34. HSP, Chase Coll., Kate Chase Sprague to S. P. Chase, July 7, 1868.

Chapter XI

1. Phelps: *Op. cit.,* pp. 142–43.
2. BUL, Sp. Coll., Kate Chase Sprague: *Diary,* November 4, 1868.
3. HSP, Chase Coll., S. P. Chase to Kate Chase Sprague, August 9, 1868.
4. LC, Chase Coll., S. P. Chase to Kate Chase Sprague, September 29, 1868.
5. *Ibid.,* Kate Chase Sprague to S. P. Chase, October 5, 1868.
6. Anderson: *Op. cit.,* p. 29.
7. BUL, Sp. Coll., Kate Chase Sprague: *Diary,* November 11, 1868.
8. *Ibid.,* December 27, 1868.

Chapter XII

1. *Congressional Globe:* 41st Congress, 1st Session: March 15, 1869, pp. 64–66.
2. *Ibid.,* March 19, pp. 156–8.
3. *Ibid.,* p. 159.
4. *Ibid.,* March 24, pp. 243–5.

5. *N. Y. Times,* March 26, 1869.
6. *Congressional Globe,* April 3, 1869, p. 475.
7. *Ibid.,* April 8, 1869, p. 614.
8. *Ibid.,* April 8, 1869, pp. 615–17.
9. *Ibid.,* April 8, 1869, pp. 618–20.
10. *Ibid.,* April 24, 1869, p. 244.
11. *N. Y. Herald,* April 16, 1869.
12. Herbert Agar: *The Price of Union.* Boston: Houghton, Mifflin Co., 1950, p. 485.
13. Adams: *op. cit.,* p. 272.
14. Anderson: *op. cit.,* p. 42.
15. *Ibid.,* pp. 41–42.
16. HSP, Chase Coll., S. P. Chase to Kate Chase Sprague, April 15, 1869.
17. *Ibid.,* S. P. Chase to Kate Chase Sprague, April 17, 1869.
18. *Ibid.,* S. P. Chase to Kate Chase Sprague, April 26, 1869.
19. *Ibid.*
20. *Ibid.,* S. P. Chase to Kate Chase Sprague, April 29, 1869.
21. *Ibid.*
22. LC, Chase Coll., S. P. Chase to William Sprague, May 2, 1869.
23. *Ibid.,* S. P. Chase to Kate Chase Sprague, May 4, 1869.
24. *Ibid.*
25. HSP, Chase Coll., S. P. Chase to Kate Chase Sprague, May 14, 1869.
26. *Ibid.,* S. P. Chase to Kate Chase Sprague, September 15, 1869.
27. *Ibid.*
28. *Ibid.,* October 1, 1869.
29. *Ibid.*
30. *Ibid.,* September 23, 1869.

Chapter XIII

1. Briggs: *op. cit.,* April 23, 1868, p. 195.
2. *Ibid.,* February 15, 1870, p. 70.
3. LC, Chase Coll., S. P. Chase to Kate Chase Sprague, November 7, 1869.
4. Warden: *Op. cit.,* p. 722.
5. *Ibid.,* p. 723.
6. Schuckers: *Op. cit.,* p. 620.
7. Warden: *Op. cit.,* p. 721; S. P. Chase to Janette Chase, October 15, 1870.
8. *Providence Journal:* October 31, 1870.
9. *New York Times:* January 5, 1871.
10. *Ibid.*
11. *Providence Press:* November 3, 1870.
12. *Ibid.*
13. *Providence Journal,* November 8, 1870; Belden, *op. cit.,* p. 256.
14. *New York Times:* February 28, 1871.
15. HSP, Chase Coll., S. P. Chase to William Sprague, July 25, 1866.
16. LC, Chase Coll., R. C. Parsons, to S. P. Chase, February 16, 1871.
17. BUL, Sp. Coll., Kate Chase Sprague: *Diary,* November 4, 1868.
18. LC, Chase Coll., Kate Chase Sprague to S. P. Chase, August 29, 1871.

19. *Ibid.*
20. Warden: *Op. cit.,* p. 727.
21. *Ibid.,* p. 728.
22. Schurz: *Op. cit.,* p. 162.
23. LC, Chase Coll., Mrs. C. S. Eastman to S. P. Chase, July 19, 1863.
24. Schurz: *Op. cit.,* pp. 161–62.
25. Warden: *Op. cit.,* p. 705.

CHAPTER XIV

1. This birth date for Portia Sprague is given on her Certificate of Death, issued by the Office of the Town Clerk at Narragansett, thus showing that she was the youngest of the four Sprague children and not the third, as has been usually stated.
2. BUL, Sp. Coll., Clarkson Potter to Kate Chase Sprague, September 14, 1874.
3. *Providence Journal:* October 9, 1890.
4. BUL, Sp. Coll., Janette Chase Hoyt to Kate Chase Sprague, October 13, 1874. Kate Chase Sprague to Janette Chase Hoyt, October 13, 1874.
5. *Ibid.,* William Sprague to Clarkson Potter, October 24, 1874.
6. *Ibid.,* Clarkson Potter to William Sprague, October 26, 1874.
7. *Ibid.,* William Sprague to Clarkson Potter, October 28, 1874.
8. *Ibid.,* Kate Chase Sprague to Janette Chase Hoyt, Paris, November 22, 1875.
9. *Ibid.,* William Sprague to Clarkson Potter, letter received December 13, 1875.
10. *Ibid.,* Kate Chase Sprague to Clarkson Potter, Paris, November 22, 1875.
11. Phelps: *Op. cit.,* pp. 242–3.
12. BUL, Sp. Coll., Kate Chase Sprague to General W. T. Sherman, Wiesbaden, January 22, 1875.
13. *Ibid.,* Kate Chase Sprague to Amasa Sprague, Homburg, May 26, 1875.
14. *Ibid.,* Kate Chase Sprague to William Sprague, Paris, December 2, 1875.
15. *Ibid.,* Kate Chase Sprague to William Hoyt, Paris, December 2, 1875.
16. *Ibid.,* Kate Chase Sprague to William Sprague, Paris, December 2, 1875.
17. *New York Times:* May 2, 1881.

CHAPTER XV

1. BUL, Sp. Coll., Kate Chase Sprague to William Sprague Jr., November 19, 1876.
2. *Ibid.,* January 1, 1877.
3. *Ibid.,* January 10, 1877.
4. *Ibid.,* January 13, 1877.
5. *Ibid.*
6. *Ibid.,* February 10, 1877.
7. Katherine Chase Sprague vs. William Sprague, divorce petition.
8. BUL, Sp. Coll., Kate Chase Sprague to William Sprague, Jr., May 9, 1877.

9. *Ibid.,* April 1, 1877.
10. *Ibid.,* May 9, 1877.
11. *Ibid.,* June 8, 1877.
12. *Ibid.*
13. *Ibid.,* William Sprague to William Sprague, Jr., November 17, 1876.
14. *Ibid.,* November 15, 1877.
15. *Ibid.,* Kate Chase Sprague to William Sprague, Jr., February 8, 1878.
16. *Ibid.,* March 26, 1878.
17. *Ibid.,* June 26, 1878.
18. *Ibid.,* July 18, 1878.
19. Anderson: *Op. cit.,* pp. 3, 4.
20. *Ibid.,* p. 24.
21. *Providence Journal:* August 14, 1879.
22. BUL, Sp. Coll., Kate Chase Sprague to William Sprague, Jr., April 20, 1879.
23. *Ibid.,* April 30, 1879.
24. *Ibid.,* March 11, 1879.
25. *Ibid.,* April 20, 1879.
26. Donald Barr Chidsey: *The Gentleman from New York: A Life of Roscoe Conkling.* (New Haven: Yale University Press, 1935), p. 91.
27. *Cincinnati Enquirer:* August 12, 1879.
28. Chidsey: *Op. cit.,* p. 226.
29. *New York Times:* March 2, 1877.
30. Chidsey: *Op. cit.,* pp. 233–4.
31. *New York Times:* January 25, 1877.
32. Donald Barr Chidsey, in his biography of Roscoe Conkling, found "no proof" that Kate and Conkling were lovers (pp. 118–19). In a letter to the author he writes: "I never had any faith in the story of an affair between those two. I would have liked evidence of something of the sort . . . and if I had possessed any such evidence I would certainly have used it." (January 12, 1970)

Chapter XVI

1. *The Providence Press:* August 11, 1879.
2. *New York Times:* August 13, 1879.
3. *Ibid.,* August 10, 11, 1879.
4. *Providence Journal:* August 11, 1879; *Cincinnati Enquirer:* August 12, 1879.
5. *Cincinnati Enquirer:* August 12, 1879.
6. *New York World:* August 11, 1879.
7. *The Providence Press:* August 12, 1879.
8. *New York Times:* August 13, 1879.
9. *Ibid.*
10. *Providence Journal:* August 11–19, 1879; *New York Times:* August 11–19; *Cincinnati Enquirer:* August 13–16; *Narragansett Times:* August 15, 1879.
11. *Providence Journal:* August 12, 1879.
12. *Cincinnati Enquirer:* August 12, 1879.

13. *Ibid.*
14. *Utica Daily Observer:* August 15, 1879; copied from *New York Graphic,* August 14, 1879.
15. *Providence Journal:* August 14, 1879; *New York Times:* August 15, 1879.
16. *Cincinnati Enquirer:* August 15, 1879; *New York Times:* August 15, 1879; *Providence Journal,* August 14, 1879.
17. *Narragansett Times:* August 15, 1879.
18. *New York Times:* August 16, 1879.
19. *Cincinnati Enquirer:* August 14, 1879.
20. *Ibid:* August 15, 1879.
21. *Providence Journal:* August 19, 1879.
22. *Providence Journal:* August 19, 1879; *New York Sun:* August 17, 1879.
23. *New York Times:* August 19, 1879.
24. *New York Tribune:* August 20, 1879.
25. *New York Times:* August 19, 1879.
26. Katherine Chase Sprague vs. William Sprague, divorce petition.
27. *New York Times:* September 2, 1879.
28. *Ibid.,* September 3, 1879.
29. *Ibid.,* September 1, 1879.
30. *Providence Journal:* October 9, 1890.
31. *New York Times:* September 3, 1879.
32. *Providence Journal:* December 21, 1880.
33. *Ibid.,* September 22, 1879.

Chapter XVII

1. Briggs: *Op. cit.,* pp. 405–08, April 15, 1880.
2. *New York Times:* October 20, 1880.
3. *Providence Journal:* May 29, 1880.
4. *Ibid.,* October 12, 1880.
5. *Ibid.,* September 30, 1880.
6. *Ibid.,* November 15, 1880.
7. BUL, Sp. Coll., William Sprague, Jr. to Kate Chase Sprague, September 7, 1880.
8. Katherine Chase Sprague vs. William Sprague, divorce petition.
9. *New York Times:* June 28, 1881.
10. *Ibid.,* April 18, 1883.
11. *Washington Star,* October 7, 1882.
12. *Providence Journal,* August 28, 1882.
13. *The Providence Press:* August 16, 1882.
14. *Providence Journal:* August 28, 1882.
15. *Ibid.,* August 27, 1882.
16. *New York Times:* March 10, 1883.
17. *Ibid.,* April 18, 1882.
18. *Ibid.*
19. *The Providence Press:* March 31, 1883.
20. All quoted from *Providence Journal:* March 30, 1883.
21. *Ibid.*

22. BUL, Sp. Coll., newspaper clippings among papers of Kate Chase Sprague.
23. *Cincinnati Enquirer:* August 1, 1899.
24. *Boston Herald:* August 16, 1886.
25. *Narragansett Times:* August 6, 1886.
26. All accounts of ceremony from *Cincinnati Enquirer:* October 13–15, 1886.
27. Lloyd Lewis: *Sherman: Fighting Prophet.* (New York: Harcourt, Brace & Co., 1958), p. 623.
28. Julia B. Foraker: *I Would Live It Again.* (New York: Harper & Bros., 1932), p. 76.
29. *Providence Evening Telegram:* October 12, 1886.
30. *Rhode Island Democrat:* October 29, 1886.
31. *Ibid.*
32. Phelps: *Op. cit.,* p. 272.
33. *Providence Journal:* October 12, 1909.

<h3 style="text-align:center">CHAPTER XVIII</h3>

1. *The Providence Press:* May 1887.
2. *Boston Herald:* July 26, 1885.
3. *Ibid.*
4. *The Providence Press:* October 9, 1890.
5. BUL, Sp. Coll., William Sprague, Jr. to Kate Chase, November 4, 1886.
6. *Ibid.,* November 22, 1886.
7. LC, Chase Coll., Kate Chase to Whitelaw Reid, November 29, 1886.
8. BUL, Sp. Coll., William Sprague, Jr. to Kate Chase, February 16, 1886.
9. *The Providence Press:* May, 1887.
10. *Providence Evening Telegram:* May 14, 1887.
11. LC, Chase Coll., Kate Chase to Whitelaw Reid, November 29, 1886.
12. *Narragansett Times:* June 3, 1887.
13. *Providence Evening Telegram:* October 27, 1887.
14. BUL, Sp. Coll., Ethel Chase Sprague to William Sprague, Jr., October 5, 1889.
15. *Ibid-.* William Sprague, Jr. to Kate Chase, January 20, 1890.
16. *Ibid.,* June 30, 1890.
17. *Ibid.,* Kate Chase to William Sprague, Jr., July 11, 1890.
18. *Ibid.,* William Sprague, Jr. to Kate Chase, July 19, 1890.
19. *The Telegram* (Providence): October 9, 1890.
20. *Ibid.*
21. *Providence Journal:* October 15, 1890.
22. BUL, Sp. Coll., Kate Chase to William Sprague, October 8, 1890.
23. *Narragansett Times:* October 24, 1890; *Providence Journal,* October 22, 1890.
24. BUL, Sp. Coll., Perry Greenman to Kate Chase, December 1, 1890.
25. *Ibid.,* William Sprague to Kate Chase Sprague, July 8, 1866.
26. *Ibid.,* note in handwriting of Kate Chase.

NOTES

Chapter XIX

1. Ross: *Op. cit.,* p. 280.
2. Phelps: *Op. cit.,* p. 279.
3. Ross: *Op. cit.,* p. 281.
4. *Washington Star:* July 22, 1895.
5. University of Michigan Library, Mary Merwin Phelps Collection: Kate Chase to Mrs. Bancroft, May 7, 1897.
6. *Washington Post:* July 28, 1895.

INDEX

INDEX